THE RULE OF LAW IN THE EUROPEAN UNION

This is a book about the internal dimension of the rule of law in the European Union (EU). The EU is a community based on law which adheres to and promotes a set of common values between the Member States. The preservation of these values (such as legality, legal certainty, prohibition of arbitrariness, respect for fundamental rights) is pivotal to the success of European integration and the well-being of the individuals within it. Yet, the EU rule of law suffers from an imposter syndrome and has been the subject of criticism: ie that it is only part of the EU agenda in order to legitimise sweeping new powers and policies, and that it plays little or no role in promoting a culture of compliance for either deviant EU Institutions or for Member States.

This book will examine whether the EU rule of law deserves those criticisms. It will offer an analytical guide to the EU rule of law by conceptualising it and locating it within the sources of EU law. It will then ask whether the EU is based on the rule of law—a question which is answered in the affirmative, but one which has to be considered in the context of compliance and the overall effectiveness of the EU enforcement acquis. It is argued that, while the EU means well in its aim to preserve unity in an increasingly diversified Europe, the extent to which it can pave the way to a better world (based on a transnational rule of law concept akin to good governance and improvement of citizens' lives) is dependent on the commitment of all European integration stakeholders to the EU project.

Volume 78 in the Series Modern Studies in European Law

Modern Studies in European Law
Recent titles in this series:

The Legitimacy of Family Rights in Strasbourg Case Law:
Living Instrument or Extinguished Sovereignty?
Carmen Draghici

Strengthening the Rule of Law in Europe:
From a Common Concept to Mechanisms of Implementation
Edited by Werner Schroeder

The Pluralist Character of the European Economic Constitution
Clemens Kaupa

Exceptions from EU Free Movement Law
Edited by Panos Koutrakos, Niamh Nic Shuibhne and Phil Syrpis

Reconceptualising European Equality Law: A Comparative Institutional Analysis
Johanna Croon-Gestefeld

Marketing and Advertising Law in a Process of Harmonization
Edited by Ulf Bernitz and Caroline Heide-Jörgensen

The Fundamental Right to Data Protection:
Normative Value in the Context of Counter-Terrorism Surveillance
Maria Tzanou

Republican Europe
Anna Kocharov

Family Reunification in the EU
Chiara Berneri

EU Liability and International Economic Law
Armin Steinbach

The EU and Nanotechnologies: A Critical Analysis
Tanja Ehnert

Human Rights Between Law and Politics:
The Margin of Appreciation in Post-National Contexts
Edited by Petr Agha

The European Union and Social Security Law
Jaan Paju

The Rule of Law in the European Union: The Internal Dimension
Theodore Konstadinides

**For the complete list of titles in this series, see
'Modern Studies in European Law' link at
www.bloomsburyprofessional.com/uk/series/modern-studies-in-european-law**

The Rule of Law in the European Union

The Internal Dimension

Theodore Konstadinides

·HART·
PUBLISHING
OXFORD AND PORTLAND, OREGON
2017

Hart Publishing
An imprint of Bloomsbury Publishing Plc

Hart Publishing Ltd
Kemp House
Chawley Park
Cumnor Hill
Oxford OX2 9PH
UK

Bloomsbury Publishing Plc
50 Bedford Square
London
WC1B 3DP
UK

www.hartpub.co.uk
www.bloomsbury.com

Published in North America (US and Canada) by
Hart Publishing
c/o International Specialized Book Services
920 NE 58th Avenue, Suite 300
Portland, OR 97213-3786
USA

www.isbs.com

HART PUBLISHING, the Hart/Stag logo, BLOOMSBURY and the
Diana logo are trademarks of Bloomsbury Publishing Plc

First published 2017

British Library Cataloguing-in-Publication Data
A catalogue record for this book is available from the British Library.

ISBN: HB: 978-1-84946-470-3
        ePDF: 978-1-50991-655-9
        ePub: 978-1-50991-654-2

Library of Congress Cataloging-in-Publication Data

Names: Konstadinides, Theodore, author.

Title: The rule of law in the European Union : the internal dimension / Theodore Konstadinides.

Description: Portland, Oregon : Hart Publishing, 2017. | Series: Modern studies in European law ;
volume 78 | Includes bibliographical references and index.

Identifiers: LCCN 2017018590 (print) | LCCN 2017022467 (ebook) | ISBN 9781509916542 (Epub) |
ISBN 9781849464703 (hardback : alk. paper)

Subjects: LCSH: Rule of law—European Union countries.

Classification: LCC KJE5037 (ebook) | LCC KJE5037 .K67 2017 (print) | DDC 341.242/2011—dc23

LC record available at https://lccn.loc.gov/2017018590

Typeset by Compuscript Ltd, Shannon
Printed and bound in Great Britain by TJ International Ltd, Padstow, Cornwall

To find out more about our authors and books visit www.hartpublishing.co.uk. Here you will find extracts,
author information, details of forthcoming events and the option to sign up for our newsletters.

Foreword

Born as the ideological child of the Enlightenment, the rule of law forms the cornerstone of liberal democracies, a principle so fundamental that without it 'no man could endure to live in this country' as the Lord Chief Justice was invited, and came to accept, in *Entick v Carrington*. In the European Union, adherence to the rule of law ensures ideological continuity, fosters a sense of belonging among the Member States, and is a *sine qua non* for its legitimacy. The EU endorses a substantive and not merely a procedural notion of the rule of law, Article 2 TEU proclaims that the Union is founded on the values of respect for human dignity, freedom, democracy, equality, the rule of law and respect for human rights, including the rights of persons belonging to minorities. Article 2 also states, echoing Strasbourg jurisprudence, that these values are common to the Member States in a society in which pluralism, non-discrimination, tolerance, justice, solidarity and equality between women and men prevail.

This original monograph is the first comprehensive examination of the way the EU and its institutions understand the rule of law in the EU polity. It traces its evolution as it has morphed through the European integration journey, identifies tensions, and highlights inconsistencies. The book explores the conceptual and normative foundations of the rule of law in the EU, its standards and the mechanisms for its enforcement. Theodore Konstadinides engages with some profound questions and does justice to a topic whose importance can hardly be overstated. What are the standards of the EU rule of law and how do they differ from those of the national constitutions? Are those standards applied in the same way to the EU institutions and the Member States or is there a federal bias in favour of the former? Does the EU legal system provide the necessary mechanisms to ensure that both its institutions and the Member States are held to account? To what extent is it correct to say that Member States are treated equally? How can rule of law standards be articulated at EU level where Member States appear to challenge the core values of Article 6 by interfering, for example, with the independence of the judiciary? And how can the rule of law be upheld in the light of the multiple existentialist crises that have beset the EU?

Since the ECJ declared in its seminal judgment in *les Verts* that the European Community is a community bound by the rule of law, the integration project has undergone defining changes. On the one hand, EU law has undergone a process of formalisation. This is evidenced by the express enshrinement of rights in constitutional texts, culminating in granting the Charter binding force, the adoption of comprehensive legislation in areas such as equality and data protection, the articulation of human rights policies in the external field, and a more forceful articulation of a rule of law agenda by the Commission. On the other hand, EU law has become, in many respects, less coherent, more uncertain and even less formal. This has resulted from the rise of soft law, the proliferation of international treaties standing alongside the EU framework which pursue EU related objectives and share the EU institutional framework, and numerous developments in the case law which have led to silent constitutional amendments as important and far reaching as those brought by express treaty revisions. Such contradictions pose important challenges when the political institutions of the EU and its judiciary seek to articulate a rule of law narrative.

One of the themes that emerges from this book is the role of the ECJ in articulating rule of law standards. By continuing to refer, even in the post-Charter era, to general principles of law as a source of law alongside its written constitution, the ECJ signals that normativity is not exhausted in constitutional text. Reliance on general principles illustrates that the Court follows a substantive, Antigonean, perception of the rule of law. Recent years have also witnessed increasing judicial reliance on the principle of autonomy of EU law. The principle exerts important influence but its meaning remains elusive. It can best be understood as a defence mechanism. Founded on primacy, it seeks to safeguard the Court's own jurisdiction and its defining role in the development of EU law. The rise of autonomy can be seen as a sign of maturity of EU law and increasing confidence on the part of the Court. It has however a Janus-like face: whilst in *Kadi* it was used to enhance fundamental rights, in Opinion 2/13 it was used to lessen their protection. It is essentially a principle that defines the EU's judicial universe according to a set of priorities established by the ECJ. The more the case law relies on the principle of autonomy, the more the articulation of rule of laws standards becomes self-referential at the risk of divergence from the jurisprudence of the national constitutional courts and of Strasbourg.

The publication of a monograph on the rule of law in the EU is certainly timely. Although in its sixty years history the European integration project has not been a stranger to challenges, perhaps in no other time has it been confronted with such a constellation of major predicaments: terrorism, the Eurozone crisis, the migration challenge and Brexit have all, each in their own way, tested the EU's conception of the rule of law leading to some constitutional convulsions. Some of them have been contained better than others.

The handling of the Eurozone and the migration crises has revealed a yawning gap between political aspirations and legal reality; and recent developments in Poland and Hungary suggest a value gap which is liable to challenge the underpinnings of the integration paradigm. The EU faces here a delicate balancing exercise. The more aggressively it pursues a rule of law agenda, the more it risks the criticism that it seeks to patronise the Member States and meddle in their internal affairs. If, on the other hand, it assumes the rule of a deferential observer, it risks the criticism that it does not take the rule of law seriously: it becomes an empty rhetoric that serves as a veneer of legitimacy.

This book provides an original critique of the most important constitutional principle and its application in contemporary EU law. Its publication comes at a particularly opportune moment. It makes a very valuable contribution to EU law discourse and will leave the reader wiser.

Takis Tridimas
London 25 June 2017

Preface

This is a book about the rule of law in the European Union (EU) as a principle upon which the EU is founded. It focuses upon the internal dimension of the rule of law in the EU—that is the rule of law as it applies to the EU institutions, the Member States' authorities and EU citizens. Our starting point is that the EU is a community based on law which adheres to and promotes a set of values which are in their majority common between the Member States. The preservation of these values (including, for instance, the prohibition of arbitrariness and respect for fundamental rights) is pivotal to the success of European integration and the well-being of the individuals within it. Hence, the ability of the EU to enforce respect to the rule of law by all actors that partake to European integration is a condition *sine qua non* of its existence. Our focus on enforcement will not neglect 'design'. Instead, this book will dedicate equal space to both components of the rule of law. It will commence in Part I by providing an analytical guide to the meaning, legal geography and protection of the rule of law in the EU and will proceed by providing an account in Part II of the EU standards in place to ensure its respect, at both the EU and domestic level. It will also consider whether these standards are appropriate for the EU to protect the principle upon which it is founded.

The book inevitably records the transformation of the EU rule of law from a political programmatic principle as initially intended by the Treaty drafters to a legal justiciable one by the CJEU during the emergence and development of EU constitutionalism to, more recently, a political monitoring principle that places emphasis on the EU political institutions' assessment of Member States' adherence to the rule of law. It discusses the dynamics of compliance generated by each transformation and argues that, despite certain weaknesses in its conceptualisation and enforcement, the rule of law in the EU is generally complied with. As such, it does not have to become a different proposition. Yet, the book contends that EU institutions need to explore structure and metre in the application and enforcement of the rule of law both as a legal and as a political principle. At the same time, it acknowledges that—to paraphrase from the European Council Bratislava Declaration in 2016—although 'the EU is not perfect ... it is the best instrument we have for addressing the new challenges we are facing',[1] including those against the rule of law in the continent.

The idea for this book came around 2012, when the role of the rule of law in the EU had attracted limited scholarship. This has recently changed. There are numerous 'on the ground' pieces about rule-of-law problems in various Member

---

[1] European Council, Bratislava Declaration and Roadmap, 16.09.2016, available from www.consilium.europa.eu/en/press/press-releases/2016/09/16-bratislava-declaration-and-roadmap/.

States, but also on a variety of other subjects relevant to rule-of-law compliance at the national level. Yet, an overview approach, while valuable to the rule-of-law meaning, content and compliance levels at both the EU and its Member States, is in short supply and it often seems to have been overtaken by events. The purpose of this book is therefore to provide an overarching guide to the rule of law in the EU—an overview and a critique by reflecting both on the rule of law's meaning and content as well as emerging questions pertinent to its enforcement at the EU level.

   Some of the individual criticisms made in this book—for instance, those related to EU competence creep and *locus standi* in judicial review of EU legislation (areas which are crucial to the often overlooked question of the EU's own compliance with the rule of law)—have been made before albeit in a different context and form. This is perhaps because despite its constitutional advancements, the EU's endemic complications remain essentially the same. Still, a critic may remark that bringing them together under the heading of the rule of law does not by itself tell a new story. Their omission, however, from this book could have been perceived as an indication that neither a structured delimitation of competences nor effective judicial protection are important in the current discussion about the rule of law in the EU. Of course, there are also 'new stories' to be told in this monograph in relation to the rule of law at the EU side. These concern, for instance, the possibility of EU institutions acting in breach of EU values in the realm of migration or in relation to the Euro-crisis. We will also look into the utility of the Article 7 TEU 'rule-of-law mechanism' in light of recent systemic problems arising in some Member States. The Polish derogatory attitude to the EU during 2016 has been particularly relevant in this context. While even in those areas academic literature and current affairs blog commentary is proliferating, I will try to tell the story through my own experience, thoughts and reflections.

Acknowledgements

A number of people have assisted in completing this book, to whom I am ever so grateful for their guidance, tips and direct and indirect encouragement. I wish to thank my family, including my in-laws, former and current colleagues and friends for their direct and indirect contribution. Acknowledgments are also given to Rudy Baker, Sionaidh Douglas-Scott, Ioannis Glinavos, Filippo Fontanelli, Alexandros Kargopoulos, Sabine Michalowski, Julien Sterck and Panos Koutrakos for kindly listening to some of the ideas expressed in this book and for offering their advice. I would especially wish to acknowledge the kindness of Anastasia Karatzia, Maria Ioannidou, Tobias Lock and Noreen O'Meara who went out of their way to read and comment on early sketches and drafts from this book. Thanks also goes to Di Donnelly who kindly offered to spiral-bind my early drafts so that I could take my eyes off the screen. I would further like to express my appreciation to Valsamis Mitsilegas for offering me a visiting fellowship at the Queen Mary Law School in order to complete this book. I also wish to thank Penny Green for her warm welcome and Paul Gragl and Violetta Moreno-Lax for taking the trouble to organise a Keynote event at the Queen Mary Centre for European and International Legal Affairs where I first presented on the topic of the book. Last but not least, I wish to thank Takis Tridimas for being such a great mentor and friend. It is an honour and privilege that he accepted to write the foreword for this monograph.

I dedicate this book to Natasha and Nicholas who waited along my way and kept me in good humour. I would like to express my particular gratitude to Richard Hart who believed in this project. I also wish to thank Rachel Turner, Sinead Moloney and the Hart team for their patience and the editorial direction I received along the journey of writing and publishing this book. This work reflects the law as it stood on 1 February 2017. Any errors or omissions are entirely my responsibility.

Theodore Konstadinides
London
7 March 2017

Contents

Introduction

> Zeitgeist comes from the outside, but works on the inside.
> It affects everyone, but not everyone is affected in the same way.[1]

IN RECENT YEARS, the concept of the rule of law has become an international term or trend—an empty vessel or a legal zeitgeist, depending upon one's view.[2] Everyone is up for it: from countries like China promoting a 'socialist' rule of law model to international organisations like the World Trade Organization (WTO) using the rule of law as a means to facilitate trade between states.[3] Perhaps to a greater extent than other international organisations, the rule of law is epitomised by the EU legal system. Instead of establishing its own rule of law conception, the EU aspires to uphold and improve the rule of law as it is commonly understood in the Member States and charges them with its promotion. It advances a system where laws are applied and enforced. Such a system is based on shared fundamental principles, often termed by the Court of Justice of the European Union (CJEU) 'general principles of EU law', which are rooted on the values enshrined in the legal systems of the Member States. As a system where laws are applied and enforced, the EU offers a dynamic way of extending the rule of law principles beyond the strict bounds of the nation state.

Historically, the rule of law has been influenced by a process of cross-fertilisation and spill over that has taken place over time amongst the various EU Member States' legal orders. Textually, it is part of the EU common values listed in Article 2 of the Treaty on European Union (TEU) which also include human dignity, freedom, democracy, equality and respect for human rights. These values, favoured by the rule of law, reinforce trust between the Member States and when transfused into EU legislation they supply the EU legal order with legitimacy and integrity. They also grant the EU citizen a host of enforceable rights as a part of their natural

---

[1] K Knausgaard, *Boyhood Island* (London, Vintage Books, 2014) 4.

[2] Paul Craig explains that 'A "health warning" is in order for anyone venturing into this area: a cursory glance at the index of legal periodicals revealed 16,810 citations to books and articles concerned with the rule of law, and that is certainly an underestimation, since many articles discuss the concept in ways that might not necessarily be picked up by the search engine and the number only covers legal material.' Select Committee on Constitution, 6th Report, App 5, 11 July 2007. See also P Craig, 'Formal and Substantive Conception of the Rule of Law: An Analytical Framework' [1997] *Public Law* 467, available from www.publications.parliament.uk/pa/ld200607/ldselect/ldconst/151/15115.htm.

[3] For instance, as Sandhu comments, 'the WTO dispute settlement system relies on active engagement by all members in order to create a judicial system which ultimately provides "a level playing field" for litigants based on the rule of law'. N Sandhu, 'Member Participation in the WTO Dispute Settlement System: Can Developing Countries Afford not to Participate?' 5 (1) (206) *UCL Journal of Law and Jurisprudence* 146, 147.

birth-right—rights which every so often we take for granted.[4] Yet, there are still numerous open questions about the rule of law's practical application. As often noted, 'its uniform rhetorical acceptance has often veiled the concrete realities of living under it.'[5]

Since the rule of law encompasses broad and often abstract commitments, it would be useful to provide an example of cross-border situations where it is in short supply or under threat. In EU law, the rule of law can, therefore, be undermined in cases where a Member State aggressively interferes with EU citizens' free movement rights[6] to situations when restrictions are placed upon their ability to vote in European Parliament elections.[7] It follows that the repeated abuse of EU substantive rights by Member States risks a descent into uncertainty and arbitrariness and may generate an EU pathology that would place at risk both the course of European integration and the legal position of the individual who enjoys rights and freedoms under EU law.[8] In this context, understanding the rule of law's substantive requirements and ensuring EU law's capacity to be enforced is crucial. Accordingly, it may be argued that the rule of law may be thrown into sharp relief in case of failure of the EU to identify relevant breaches consistently and systematically and resort to prompt and robust sanctions in order to punish defiant Member States. Still the rule of law is hard to pin down. In most cases it forms an ideal which has to be read in the light of objective rules laid down within EU constitutional law. As such, the EU political institutions would not purport to enforce the rule of law in an abstract sense. They would rather seek to identify a 'wrong' in a Member State's administrative practice which requires their intervention and (similar to Lord Carnwath's account on judicial review in the UK) 'look for a legal hook to hang it on. And, if there is none suitable, one may need to adapt one.'[9] Likewise, in the relevant litigation, EU judges would seldom proclaim that 'we are now adjudicating on a rule of law question' as such. Equally, their competence to sanction Member State 'wrongs' is restrained by the limited scope of EU law.

The above reflections aside, the role of the EU as a rule-of-law disciplinarian seems to have extended in recent years beyond classic cross border areas covered

---

[4] See for example the debate pertinent in the months after the UK–EU referendum on leaving the EU about whether UK nationals could get associate EU citizenship post-Brexit: 'EU Citizenship Proposal could Guarantee Rights in Europe after Brexit' *The Guardian* 9 November 2016, available from www.theguardian.com/world/2016/nov/09/eu-citizenship-proposal-could-guarantee-rights-in-europe-after-brexit.

[5] BL Burger et al, 'Introduction: Does Law Matter? The New Colonial Legal History' in H Foster et al (eds), *The Grand Experiment: Law and Legal Culture in British Settler Societies* (Vancouver–Toronto, UBC Press, 2008) 2.

[6] See *R (Lumsdon and others) v The Legal Services Board* [2015] UKSC 41, para 37.

[7] Case C-650/13 *Delvigne* [2015] ECLI:EU:C:2015:648.

[8] This is concerning since 'legal certainty—not legal indeterminacy—is a guiding principle of European legal systems.' See JR Maxeiner, 'Legal Certainty: A European Alternative to American Legal Indeterminacy?' (2007) 15 *Tulane Journal of International & Comparative Law* 541, 543.

[9] Lord R Carnwath, 'From judicial outrage to sliding scales—where next for Wednesbury?', ALBA Annual Lecture, 12 November 2013, 19, available at https://www.supremecourt.uk/docs/speech-131112-lord-carnwath.pdf.

by 'textbook' EU law. The EU has taken interest in enforcing the values enshrined in Article 2 TEU, inclusive of the rule of law. Especially during the last five years, the EU has expressed concerns at the situation in certain Member States in relation to the exercise of democracy, the rule of law and their domestic system of checks and balances[10]—otherwise areas that do not squarely fall within the scope of EU law. While the EU's involvement in the affairs of Member States that demonstrate a slide into authoritarianism raises questions of competence of the EU institutions' mandate to intervene in domestic internal situations, it seems to have been enabled by the broad drafting of Article 7 TEU which relates to the values referred to in Article 2 TEU and the establishment of a political satellite framework set up by the EU Institutions.[11] Both provide a legal and political early warning system in case of a risk of breaches of EU core values, and a sanctions mechanism in the event of a serious and persistent breach by a Member State. Hence, to use an example, the reintroduction of the death penalty by a Member State would be contrary to the EU's fundamental values and would presumably lead to the application of the relevant framework for rule-of-law enforcement.[12]

No doubt, the newly-usurped rule-of-law guardian role of the EU fuels criticism. A number of academic works have already addressed the EU's rule-of-law's enforcement shortcomings.[13] Most of them have not addressed in detail the red herring issue of EU competence to intervene in domestic affairs but have rather focused on the operability of Article 7 TEU. Some commentators explain this trend due to the fact that it is firmly accepted now that EU membership not only implies compliance with Treaty rights but also with EU values as enshrined in Article 2 TEU.[14] But such acceptance begs the question of how far can reliance on EU values

---

[10] See for an early reference: European Parliament Resolution of 16 February 2012 on the recent political developments in Hungary 2013/C 249 E/08, para 1.

[11] See especially: Commission Communication 'A new EU Framework to Strengthen the Rule of Law' 1 COM (2014) 158 final.

[12] See Commission Staff Working Document on the Application of the EU Charter of Fundamental Rights 2015, COM (2016) 265 final. This is discussed in the document with reference to a press interview of 28 April 2015 of Hungarian Prime Minister Orbán viz a debate on the reintroduction of the death penalty. 'The Commission noted that Hungary had in the meantime clarified that it had no intention to introduce the death penalty. Accordingly, no legal action was required by the Commission at this stage.'

[13] See indicatively: LFM Besselink, 'The Bite, the Bark and the Howl: Article 7 TEU and the Rule of Law Initiatives' in A Jakab and D Kochenov (eds), *The Enforcement of EU Law and Values: Ensuring Member States' Compliance* (Oxford, Oxford University Press, 2016); D Kochenov and L Pech, 'Upholding the Rule of Law in the EU: On the Commission's Pre-Article 7 Procedure as a Timid Step in the Right Direction', Robert Schuman Foundation, EU Working Paper RSCAS 2015/24; C Hillion, 'Overseeing the Rule of Law in the EU' in C Closa and D Kochenov (eds), *Reinforcing the Rule of Law Oversight in the European Union* (Cambridge, Cambridge University Press, 2016); JHH Weiler, 'Reinforcing the Rule of Law Oversight in the European Union', Robert Schuman Foundation, EU Working Paper RSCAS 2014/25.

[14] Hillion, in particular, submits that EU primary law 'provides a solid constitutional basis for an active EU *engagement* to ensure compliance with the values of Article 2 TEU in general, and the rule of law in particular.' C Hillion, 'Overseeing the Rule of Law in the European Union Legal Mandate and Means', Swedish Institute for European Policy Studies (SIEPS), European Policy Analysis, Issue 2016:1, 3.

be stretched and become a *carte blanche* to EU involvement in national affairs. The focus of academic debate on 'bettering' the Article 7 TEU procedure may also be justified given the numerous flaws that characterise not just this particular provision but more broadly the idea of rule-of-law enforcement in the EU. To mention but only a few of its shortcomings, Article 7 TEU has selective application, it requires very high thresholds in the Council to trigger the relevant sanction mechanism, and so far both the Commission and Member States have lacked the political commitment to make serious use of it. Even worse, Jean-Claude Juncker, President of the Commission, noted that the refusal of some Member States to make use of Article 7 TEU cancels it de facto.[15] Thus, despite its good will to enforce virtuous practice across the Member States by first extending EU law compliance outside cross-border situations and beyond mere breaches of substantive provisions, the EU has entered uncharted territory. Such a development may in turn expose the EU's power limits as well as democratic and rule of law flaws, both internally viz the restrictive interpretation for the entire system of the judicial review of EU law and externally viz the EU's international responsibility for wrongful acts with regard to, for instance, the implementation of various 'anti-crises' measures.[16]

To offer an example, the EU can be challenged by the governments it targets through the early warning mechanism of Article 7 TEU for using an abstract conception of the rule of law as the perfect excuse to legitimise the penetration of EU law into national affairs without express Treaty authorisation. For instance, threatening the Commission with an annulment action may be in order in circumstances that EU rule-of-law interference may pose a threat to other values such as subsidiarity and national identity also protected by the Treaty.[17] Rule of law confrontation can also fuel negative government propaganda about the role of the EU more widely as a 'smash and grab' entity. The ground is already prepared with the current wave of anti-establishment populism in Europe. Trust may also be in short supply in certain Member States, in that not only have they witnessed that even within the bounds of its competence EU decisions often threaten to destabilise the workings of the welfare state[18] or the individual's legal position,[19]

---

[15] See comment in: L Pech, 'Systemic Threat to the Rule of Law in Poland: What should the Commission do next?', *VerfBlog*, 31 October 2016, available from http://verfassungsblog.de/systemic-threat-to-the-rule-of-law-in-poland-what-should-the-commission-do-next/.

[16] F Casolari, 'The EU's Hotspot Approach to Managing the Migration Crisis: A Blind Spot for International Responsibility?' (2015) 25 *The Italian Yearbook of International Law* 109.

[17] See Ministry of Foreign Affairs Statement on Polish Government's Response to Commission Recommendation of 27.07.2016, available from www.msz.gov.pl/en/p/msz_en/news/mfa_statement_on_the_polish_government_s_response_to_commission_recommendation_of_27_07_2016.

[18] For instance, in Case C-127/08 *Metock* EU:C:2008:449 the CJEU held that a third country national unlawfully present in the EU would be able to rectify his irregular migration status through marriage to an EU migrant.

[19] For example, in the Cypriot bailout cases Advocate Generals Wathelet and Wahl opined that the annulment and damages actions brought by bailed-in (commonly referred to as 'haircutted') depositors against EU institutions (particularly the Commission and the ECB) for the restructuring of the Cypriot banking sector should be dismissed as inadmissible. See CJEU Press Release No 44/16, 21.04.2016, available at http://curia.europa.eu/jcms/upload/docs/application/pdf/2016-04/cp160044en.pdf.

but also that such decisions are often hard to challenge. Indeed, the CJEU has imposed limits on the extent to which such challenges may be brought and on the powers of national courts in such cases.

Taking the above situations into account, this book will offer a critical analysis of the *internal* dimension of the rule of law in the EU as opposed to the rule of law in the context of EU external relations viz the dissemination of 'European' values.[20] It explores, in particular, the conceptual framework underpinning the EU's rule-of-law mandate in the backdrop of multiple crises in Europe, the rising vigilance amongst the EU institutions (especially the Commission and the Council) to measure and sanction rule-of-law infringements in the Member States, and rekindled debates about the operation and monitoring of the rule of law at the EU level. Since any reference to an EU rule-of-law conception has to prescribe the specific context of such referral, the book adopts a definition of the rule of law as a concept pertaining to the EU constitutional and justice system—a 'behaviour yardstick' for both the EU and its Member States.[21] It focuses primarily on the rule of law's doctrinal and normative significance and explores the factors influencing the ability of the relevant EU mechanisms to hold the EU and the Member States to it. While it spends time discussing the culture of compliance within the EU, focusing inevitably on rule-of-law 'enforcement', it does not pretend that 'design' is not an issue—meaning the way in which historical, socio-economic, institutional and domestic realities and idiosyncrasies serve to shape and even distort the meaning of the rule of law in the EU.[22]

Accordingly, the book asks the following question: is the EU based on the rule of law in the sense that neither its institutions nor the Member States can avoid review of their acts in conformity with the constitutional charter of the Union— the Treaty? We answer in the affirmative. The rule of law has traditionally been effectively guaranteed by the legality of the measures taken by the EU institutions and the wide jurisdiction conferred on the CJEU to annul any measures where the EU legislature exceeded or misused its powers, or infringed essential rules. It is also secured by the enforcement actions lodged before the CJEU by the Commission against the Member States for infringing the Treaty or EU secondary legislation. Last, the rule of law is providing the individual with possible means of redress against the EU institutions and the Member States. Indeed, as former Advocate General Jacobs has pointed out, in its seminal Le Verts judgment[23] the CJEU combined 'three powerful notions: a Constitution, a Community based on the rule of law, and a complete system of remedies.'[24]

---

[20] See in this respect: L Pech, 'Rule of Law as a Guiding Principle of the European Union's External Action' (2012) 3 CLEER Working Papers.

[21] As it will be established, the rule-of-law definition provided by the CJEU is specific contrasted with the absence of any definition by the Treaty in Art 2 TEU and the procedure laid down in Art 7 TEU.

[22] D Kochenov, 'EU Law without the Rule of Law' (2015) *Yearbook of European Law* 1, 7.

[23] Case 294/83 *Les Verts v Parliament* [1986] ECR 1339.

[24] F Jacobs, *The Sovereignty of Law: The European Way* (Cambridge, Cambridge University Press, 2006) 145. *Les Verts v Parliament*, ibid.

In all the above-mentioned instances, the EU is applying an integrative conception of the rule of law which relies on a recognisable ethos born out of common
experience as to how the concept operates in the Member States and some basic
tenets of the EU's longstanding 'Constitution'. Such a transnational conception
of the rule of law requires engagement and commitment to the EU project by
all actors involved. For instance, Floris De Witte has made reference to solidarity
as a redistributive commitment that in its absence 'all ambitious conceptions of
justice will collapse.'[25] Member States shall therefore effectively act jointly by sharing their powers while EU citizens shall build their confidence in the EU institutions' capacity for fostering social solidarity. However, both the Member States'
and citizens' commitment to the EU project has been somewhat shaken in recent
years by, inter alia, the modalities of the system of EU law enforcement. For how
can one commit to a 'club' when there is a general perception between its members that its rules and procedures intended to ensure disciplinary action are biased
towards them but favourable towards the 'Executive Committee'? Likewise, how
can one commit to a 'club' when offending members either receive no sanction by
the 'Executive Committee' for their misconduct or are, at best, arbitrarily singled
out and embarrassed for their misbehaviour? While we shall acknowledge the fact
that there is no equivalent in international law to the EU law *enforcement acquis*,
there appears to be an overlying perception of double standards in its application.
Let us briefly consider them.

First, the main expression of disapproval against the system of EU law enforcement is predicated on the fact that despite EU excessive regulation, the EU institutions' acts tend to be less prone to review compared to those of the Member States.
This appears to be the case even when national standards aim at achieving a better
threshold of individual protection compared to EU legislation. On the one hand
this arrangement occurs due to the EU institutions' propensity to reach for coherence and integrity in the overall legal order. On the other hand, it brings to the fore
issues of constitutional identity such as those raised (directly) in the preliminary
references in *Melloni* and (rather indirectly) in *Jeremy F* over the right to effective
judicial protection and remedy.[26] Both cases are illustrative of the different ways in

---

[25] F De Witte, *The Emergence of Transnational Solidarity* (Oxford, Oxford University Press, 2015)
5. De Witte's conception is akin to the internal market, economic and social cohesion, and industrial
relations. This notion is fundamental in the development of the concept of 'social Europe'. Mutual
solidarity also appears in Art 67 (2) TFEU (framing a common policy on asylum, immigration and
external border control), Art 122 TFEU (financial assistance in cases of severe difficulties caused by
natural disasters or exceptional occurrences), and Art 194 TFEU (Union policy on energy). In the area
of security and defence, solidarity has acquired a new legal dimension, viz Art 42 (7) TEU (mutual aid
and assistance clause) and Art 222 TFEU (solidarity clause).

[26] Case C-399/11 *Melloni* [2013] ECLI:EU:C:2013:107. The CJEU held that the surrender of a person to the judicial authorities of another Member State pursuant to a European Arrest Warrant (EAW)
cannot be made subject to the possibility of judicial review of the conviction handed down in absentia.;
Case C-168/13 PPU *Jeremy F* [2013] ECLI:EU:C:2013:358. Contrary to *Melloni*, the CJEU held that EU
law does not prevent Member States from providing for an appeal suspending execution of a decision
extending the effects of a European Arrest Warrant.

which a national court can describe national identity and how the CJEU balances
conflicting interests in light of the unity and effectiveness of EU law. Sterck argues
that the different outcomes of these cases (Spain 'lost' in *Melloni* while France
'won' in *Jeremy F*) have taught us that the way national judges describe identity to
their European counterparts in the CJEU has certain resonance to whether or not
Member States will ultimately extract from the CJEU a judgment which is favourable to their constitutional specificities. While, for instance, the description of
Spanish national identity (pointing to the prevalence of the right to defence under
the Spanish Constitution over the execution of the European Arrest Warrant)
in *Melloni* as raised by the Tribunal constitucional would have undermined EU
law primacy, such a possibility was redundant in *Jeremy F* since from the outset
the Conseil constitutionnel gave precedence to the issue of compatibility with EU
law obligations over that of principles of constitutional rank in France, intimate
to national identity.

What is more, depending on the manner in which a national court is formulat-
ing the 'identity question' it may afford a better margin of discretion for the Member State whose 'identity' is in question—of course always within the limits posed
by EU law.[27] For instance, the somewhat unilateralist tone used by the BVerfG in
Gauweiler did not invite the CJEU to enter into a dialectic discussion over EU law's
impact upon German constitutional identity and its intricacies. This is because,
according to the BVerfG, it is not the task of the CJEU to determine the limits
of national constitutional identity.[28] In the end, however, the BVerfG yielded to
the CJEU's interpretation that the Outright Monetary Transactions (OMT) programme for the purchase of government bonds on secondary markets was compatible with EU law (no reflection on identity was made by the CJEU).[29] But why
is the CJEU indifferent to identity concerns and how does its lack of engagement
in this regard affect the rule of law and the vertical separation of powers in the
EU? Like Craig commented about the outcome of *Melloni*—the CJEU decided not
to pay heed to the very high threshold of Spanish constitutional standards with
regard to the rights of the accused not out of self-interest but more out of concern for potential constitutional problems that a decision in line with the Spanish
Constitution would have created for the EU-27 Member States' protection threshold expressed through EU law.[30]

Yet, it can be argued that while the EU institutions generally mean well, the
extent to which they carry out their good intentions can pave the way to a better
world (arguably a transnational rule of law which is based on the ideals of good

---

[27] J Sterck, 'Easier Done than Said: The Efficiency of Constitutional Identities in EU Law'
(December 2016, with the author).

[28] Federal Constitutional Court, Press release no 9/2014 of 7 February 2014, available at www.bun-
desverfassungsgericht.de/en/press/bvg14-009en.html.

[29] Case C-62/14 *Peter Gauweiler and Others* [2015] ECLI:EU:C:2015:400.

[30] P Craig, 'UK, EU and Global Administrative Law: Foundations and Challenges', Hamlyn Seminar,
IALS, 28 October 2015, 17:00-19:00. An adverse decision favouring the Spanish threshold of protection for the defendant would have questioned the primacy and unity (not just uniformity) of EU law.

governance and improvement of citizens' lives) or a bad place, as the adage goes. EU intentions are often not communicated well enough to the public and often create a sense of 'us' (the state and its elected government) against 'them' (a European bureaucracy which lacks structures of democratic will-formation). This tension has been evident in the Brexit debate and can, inter alia, be attributed to Douglas Scott's criticism that 'engagement and dialogue has not been greatly evident in the twenty-first-century European Union'.[31] As a result, certain Member States feel less inclined to accept the basic tenets of the EU's Constitution and by extension its rule-of-law vision. Their decision to abstain from the EU's integrationist logic is often influenced by the inflated claim that there is too much integration and too much freedom of movement which creates 'injustice' at the domestic level.[32]

Second, although the EU is based on law, its means of forcing Member States to explicitly comply with the concept can be characterised as a rather arduous journey. The EU has recently appeared ready to intervene in order to defend the rule of law by using the Article 7 TEU 'nuclear option'.[33] Poland is the first test case where a rule-of-law orientation debate was launched in 2016 followed by an 'opinion' and 'recommendation'.[34] It is an important test of EU constitutionalism both on the EU and on the Member State level. Still, however, it is a test that has been strongly resisted by newer Member States, such as Poland and Hungary, who view the rule-of-law mechanism as a set of double standards aimed at them (as opposed to their older counterparts). The question of double standards is manifest even in the manner the EU has launched its recent rule-of-law early warnings against backsliding newer Member States. For instance, but for two Article 258 Treaty on the Functioning of the European Union (TFEU) cases on the early retirement of judges and the removal of the data protection of the ombudsman, Hungary was left unscathed by the early warning mechanism of Article 7 TEU.[35] It therefore escaped any other action against it following an allegation (which never quite developed into a rule-of-law dialogue between the EU and the Hungarian national authorities) about systemic threats to the rule of law. Furthermore, the EU institutions' recent proposals for an EU-wide rule-of-law dialogue are noble means to raise awareness about the broader political state of Europe but they presuppose a two-way symmetric communication if they are to produce any tangible result in helping some Member States to become more European-minded.

---

[31] S Douglas-Scott, *The Law After Modernity* (Oxford, Hart Publishing, 2013) 339.

[32] This is particularly crucial since the EU is yet to emerge from its relationship with its Member States with a clear-cut division of competences. One should be reminded the UK's position in relation to 'an ever closer union' prior to the negative referendum on EU membership. See part 3 of David Cameron's letter to Donald Tusk titled 'A new settlement for the UK in a reformed EU'.www.gov.uk/government/uploads/system/uploads/attachment_data/file/475679/Donald_Tusk_letter.pdf.

[33] C Closa, 'Reinforcing EU Monitoring of the Rule of Law: Normative Arguments, Institutional Proposals and the Procedural Limitations' in Closa and Kochenov (n 13) 28.

[34] See: Commission Opinion of 1 June 2016 regarding the Rule of Law in Poland; Commission Recommendation of 27.07.2016 regarding the rule of law in Poland, C (2016) 5703 final.

[35] See R Uitz, 'Poland, Hungary and Europe: Pre-Article 7 Hopes and Concerns', *VerfBlog*, 14 March 2016, http://verfassungsblog.de/poland-hungary-and-europe-pre-article-7-hopes-and-concerns/.

Once again, the EU institutions mean well to establish such communication but the extent to which they carry out their good intentions is subject to political dynamics and commitment by the EU institutions and the Member States to protect and promote the rule of law—and a coherent action plan is somewhat lacking at the time of writing this book.

The book adopts an up-to-date review of the application and enforcement of the Lisbon Treaty provisions relevant to the rule of law. It also observes the role of the relevant EU institutions' commitment to the rule of law. For instance, it draws upon the relevant case law of the CJEU in order to observe the way in which the Luxembourg judges have contributed to the maintenance of the rule of law by providing judicial oversight over the exercise of EU public powers and their compatibility with fundamental rights. We will also look into the mandate of the Commission to hold the Member States to the rule of law as well as the jurisdiction of national courts to review EU legislation for compatibility with their domestic constitutions and thus hold the EU institutions to the rule of law. We shall demonstrate that the role of the rule of law in the EU is to articulate that while power should be effectively exercised in the EU, the possibility of its arbitrary exercise shall be securely limited.

The reader may use this book as a guide to discover her connection with the EU rule of law. She will be provided with information about the relevant textual references, judicial pronouncements and political attempts that provide us with fragments of the EU rule-of-law puzzle, founded at different moments in time during European integration and following distinctive historical trajectories. I have tried to use examples where appropriate in order to better illustrate some points. I also acknowledge that the UK features in this book more than any other Member State. My 'bias' is purely related to the fact that I am an adoptive Londoner and to me the UK represents 'the domestic'. Of course the UK has always been unique in its relationship with the EU and, as we know, it recently decided to part ways from it. For the purpose of this book, however, and since the UK has not formally departed from the EU (at the time of writing Her Majesty's Government has not yet served the EU Institutions with an Article 50 TEU notice),[36] it is treated as a Member State. Beyond such semantics, the morphology; legal geography; the degree of respect; and the outcomes of the EU rule of law will be the main threads which will bring the different chapters of the book together comparing past experiences to current transitional moments.

The book will deal with questions that are as much relevant to the practical lawyer, as they are to the jurist and the policy maker. It also aims to enhance the law student's textbook knowledge about the concept of the rule of law and the nature and scope of EU law. It is argued that, on the one hand, the rule of law is relevant to countering systemic threats posed by certain Member States which challenge the way the EU pursues its objectives. For instance, in the context of the recent migration

---

[36] See *R (Miller) v Secretary of State for Exiting the EU* [2017] UKSC 5.

crisis, some commentators have criticised the situation in a number of Member States. They have warned that the necessity and proportionality of any further expansion of border checks outside the Schengen Borders Code (Article 25) by the Member States has to be subject to EU rule of law scrutiny.[37] On the other hand, it is submitted that the rule of law is a means of tempering the exercise of EU power, especially with regard to EU and national emergency measures following the Eurozone and migration crises that have raised considerable suspicion about the EU defaulting in its own rule-of-law terms. Certain scholars, for instance, have lamented 'the decline in social rights, broadly defined, in a number of Eurozone Member States intensely affected by the [Eurozone] crisis.'[38] Likewise, non-governmental organisations (NGOs) such as Amnesty International have criticised the EU for lack of balancing of solidarity and responsibility in managing asylum and migration policy.[39] It is hoped that this book will contribute to and advance the debates regarding the effectiveness of EU rule-of-law controls.

The objective of the book is, therefore, to map out the features of the EU legal order that correspond to the rule of law and the outcomes the rule of law is perceived to facilitate in the EU by also focusing on its enforcement. Our inquiry takes stock of past academic research on the rule of law which has focused on the rule-of-law generating capacity of the EU legal institutions. For instance, former Advocate General Jacobs' seminal Hamlyn Lecture looked at the focal role of the CJEU in ensuring that the rule of law is observed amongst the Member States.[40] Others have engaged with rule of law promotion as advanced by the EU political institutions in particular concrete cases—for instance, in the field of EU enlargement and external relations.[41] More recent studies of the rule of law in the EU tend to focus on the rule-of-law intervention capacity of the EU political institutions in order to temper lawless and capricious exercises of power in the Member States.[42]

Current literature is understandably focused on criticising the limited means at the EU's disposal to tackle challenges against its fundamental principles in an open and democratic society. A less discussed area which impacts on the quality of the rule of law at the supranational level concerns the EU's adherence to the rule of law including the issue of Member States' authorities questioning the extent of their obedience to EU law. This is an occurrence often observed in the relevant literature in terms of constitutional pluralism—a theory that advocates that in the EU no single institution, whether national or supranational, shall claim ultimate

---

[37] S Carrera, S Blockmans, D Gros and E Guild, 'The EU's Response to the Refugee Crisis: Taking Stock and Setting Policy Priorities' CEPS Essay No 20, 16 December 2015.
[38] C Kilpatrick and B De Witte, 'A Comparative Framing of Fundamental Rights Challenges to Social Crisis Measures in the Eurozone', SIEPS European Policy Analysis 2014:7, available from www.sieps.se/sites/default/files/2014_7epa_eng_A4_0.pdf.
[39] See Amnesty International Public Statement, 27 June 2016, available from www.amnesty.eu/content/assets/public_statements/EUR0343192016ENGLISH.pdf.
[40] Jacobs (n 24).
[41] EO Wennerström, *The Rule of Law and the European Union* (Uppsala, Iustus Förlag, 2007).
[42] C Closa and D Kochenov (n 13); W Schroeder, *Strengthening the Rule of Law in Europe: From a Common Concept to Mechanisms of Implementation* (Oxford, Hart Publishing, 2016).

authority.[43] As it will be discussed, in order to keep any EU expansionist claims of authority at bay, some Member States have placed particular emphasis on the EU institutions' obligation to respect their constitutional identities as protected both by virtue of the Treaty and national constitutions. Specifically, some national courts have perceived certain constitutional idiosyncrasies to act as safeguards against any intrusive action from the part of the EU institutions. The *Gauweiler* case, mentioned earlier, is indicative of how in a purely unilateral fashion, German Constitutional Court judges have chosen to keep open the opportunity to forestall the application of EU law in their country. On the other hand, the CJEU has considered 'national identity' as a programmatic notion giving it a light assessment in its case law.[44] As such, it is rather unclear whether constitutional pluralism expressed in this manner is normatively inviting as a discourse or if adherence to it as a model of governance is capable of advancing more 'justice' in the EU.[45]

I. CONTENTS OF THE BOOK

The book contains six chapters and is virtually divided into two parts: i) *Design* (conceptualisation/location/interpretation); ii) *Enforcement* (disciplinary function of the EU rule of law). The first part on *Design* presents the constitutional protection of the rule of law in the EU legal order. Chapter 1 ('Foundations') provides some background viz the book's conception of the rule of law and the two subsequent chapters provide insight into the substance of the EU rule of law. In particular, Chapter 2 ('Conceptualising the EU Rule of Law') sets up the origins and definitional contours of the EU rule of law, whilst Chapter 3 ('Locating the EU Rule of Law') focuses on the legal geography and express commitment undertaken by all Member States to safeguard the rule of law. It analyses the relevant provisions of the Treaty of Lisbon and the EU Charter of Fundamental Rights that refer to the rule of law in a declaratory fashion and cherry picks certain justiciable principles that underpin it as a restraint against abuses of power. It also analyses the rule of law as a juridical construction looking, in particular,

---

[43] Viola explains: 'Hence legal pluralism designates a normative situation in which different legal orders concur and compete in the regulation of a course of action or sets of actions concerning social relations of the same kind. The respective competences are in principles not exclusive and give rise to normative overlaps without distinguishable hierarchies of the sources of law.' F Viola, 'The Rule of Law in Legal Pluralism' in T Gizbert–Studnicki and J Stelmach (eds), *Law and Legal Cultures in the 21st Century: Diversity and Unity* (Warszawa, Wolters Kluwer Polska, 2007) 109.
[44] See for instance: Case C-208/09 *Sayn-Wittgenstein* [2010] ECR I-13693; Case C-213/07 *Michaniki* [2008] ECR I-9999.
[45] G Davies, 'Constitutional Disagreement in Europe and the Search for Pluralism' in J Komárek and M Avbelj (eds), *Constitutional Pluralism in Europe and Beyond* (Oxford, Hart Publishing, 2012); see on constitutional pluralism AS Sweet, 'The Structure of Constitutional Pluralism' (2013) Yale Law School, Faculty Scholarship Series. Paper 4624. http://digitalcommons.law.yale.edu/fss_papers/4624J; See on criticism: Baquero Cruz, 'The Legacy of the Maastricht Urteil and the Pluralist Movement' (2008) 14 *European Law Journal* 389.

at the way the CJEU has championed in its case law the concept of a Union based on the rule of law. In particular, it examines the degree to which the EU institutions and Member States alike are held to the law and are thereby subject to the jurisdiction of the CJEU.

The second part of the book on *Enforcement* focuses on the EU rule of law in action. It is divided into two chapters. Chapter 4 ('Holding EU Institutions to the Rule of Law') looks into rule of law enforcement against the EU institutions viz substantive due process. On a similar note, Chapter 5 ('Holding Member States to the Rule of Law') discusses the ability of the EU as a community based on the rule of law to exercise democratic oversight over its Member States and sanction them via the public enforcement 'infringement' procedure pursuant to Articles 258–260 TFEU which is designed to compartmentalise and remedy EU law breaches. It also looks into the broad political sanction mechanism of Article 7 TEU. While the former procedure is aimed at addressing any breach of EU law, the latter is a nuclear option, aimed to tackle serious and continuing breaches of the values enshrined in Article 2 TEU, the rule of law inclusive. The conclusive chapter brings the book's findings together and entertains the idea of the EU rule of law expanding beyond the reach of the EU—the notion of a wider 'global' rule of law underpinning international constitutionalism and global governance—one based on commitment and solidarity from all actors that partake in European integration.

All in all, the book seeks to explore the notion of the rule of law in the EU as a constitutional controlling factor, assess the contribution of the CJEU and the EU political institutions in its enforcement, discuss its salient features and criticise current trends of rule-of-law regression from both the EU and national perspective. The aim is not to merely reflect upon the EU rule of law as a prima facie example of transnational legal process. Through the analysis undertaken, the reader will be guided through the institutional interaction and the processes that render the rule of law a distinctive feature of the EU legal order but not too different to the concept as understood in national constitutional traditions. In this respect, the EU rule of law is mindful of its domestic heritage and has also been enriched with new properties which have in turn been internalised by the Member States. National legal systems have benefited from such cross-fertilisation of principles such as proportionality, which entails—as Jacobs stresses—a 'two-way-process', since these general principles of EU law often derive from domestic sources.[46] The development of the EU rule of law has, therefore, a profound impact upon the formulation of the Member States' own notion of the rule of law and the evolution and scope of the EU constitutional project. As ever, protecting common values is a matter of paramount importance for the process of European integration.

---

[46] Jacobs (n 24) 17. See also on a thorough explanation of general principles of EU law: Opinion of Advocate General Trstenjak in Case C-282/10 *Dominguez* [2011] ECLI:EU:C:2011:559, paras 91–98. See also *GCHQ* [1985] AC 374, Lord Diplock (para 410).

Part I

Design

1

Foundations of the EU Rule of Law

I. THE EU AS A SYSTEM WHERE LAWS ARE APPLIED AND ENFORCED

A. Institutional Understandings of the EU Rule of Law

THE EU IS based on the rule of law. All EU legislative measures must be authorised by the Treaties and share the voluntary and democratic approval of all Member States. EU law may be technical but it is also traceable to the individual whose life is affected by it. Almost every aspect of EU legislative activity and judgment is captured, circulated and criticised online.[1] For the purpose of this book we shall refer to the rule of law in the context of the EU constitutional framework as the 'EU rule of law'. This reference does not imply the creation of a new concept of the rule of law but rather a system where laws are applied and enforced as opposed to a system characterised by arbitrary rule.[2] While appreciating that there are alternative views on the topic, the book will focus on the EU rule of law as a concept which is based on commonly accepted standards while, like in every other legal system, it maintains its own unique properties.

We will, in particular, reflect on what is and what ought to be the EU rule of law and discuss its transition from a political declaratory and programmatic principle to a concrete legal and justiciable one that warrants legal responsibility, accountability and liability. The rule of law is crucial to the practice of the EU institutions. Not only do they claim to both preserve and protect it but they also help to define it since the rule of law lacks a definition in the Treaty on European Union (TEU). There is sufficient evidence in the Court of Justice of the European Union (CJEU)'s case law, the Advocate Generals' Opinions[3] and the recent rule-of-law

---

[1] In case this does not happen, EU institutions can be compelled to do so. See for instance: Case T-331/11 *Besselink v Council* [2013] ECLI:EU:T:2013:419 regarding the publication of the Draft Council Decision authorising the Commission to negotiate the EU-ECHR Accession Agreement; See also Reg 1049/2001 (concerning public access to EU documents) in the light of Laurent Pech's (satisfied) request to the Commission to make public its opinion of 1 June 2016 on the rule of law in Poland.

[2] See Case C-362/14 *Schrems* 6.10.2015, ECLI:EU:C:2015:650, para 60; AG Bot Opinion in Cases C-404/15 and C-659/15 PPU *Aranyosi and Căldăraru*, 03.03.2016, ECLI:EU:C:2016:140, para 11; See European Commission, Press Release: 'European Commission presents a framework to safeguard the rule of law in the European Union', Annex 2: The rule of law in the Union legal system, 11 March 2014, available from http://europa.eu/rapid/press-release_IP-14-237_en.htm.

[3] See Case C-362/14 *Schrems* 6.10.2015, ECLI:EU:C:2015:650, para 60; AG Bot Opinion in Cases C-404/15 and C-659/15 PPU *Aranyosi and Căldăraru*, 03.03.2016, ECLI:EU:C:2016:140, para 11.

deliberations of the Commisssion on a 'rule of law framework' that the rule of law in the EU essentially means a system where laws are applied and enforced.[4]

i. The European Judges' Understanding of the Rule of Law

Perhaps the most dominant institutional understanding of the rule of law as a legal principle that applies *internally* (as opposed to that applying in the context of EU external relations)[5] is that expressed by European judges. Taking as a starting point the Treaty's commitment to respect the rule of law as a foundational and common value, the CJEU and the General Court have given the concept a central place in the EU administrative system. According to the CJEU, in particular, the rule of law encompasses a complete and coherent system of procedural routes to obtain review of the acts of the EU and national administration.[6] After all, the right to effective judicial protection, a general principle of EU law—also enshrined in Article 47 of the EU Charter of Fundamental Rights—is an essential element of the EU rule of law. In this respect, the EU rule of law represents a set of legal limits—what Raz has called a virtue by which a legal system is to be judged.[7] Moreover, as it is well recorded, European judges often apply an integrative conception of the rule of law by interpreting EU law's formality in light of its rational ends, ie promoting European integration. National judges too apply EU legal norms consistently with a European vision in mind. National courts, therefore, have become EU courts in their own right in numerous areas involving the rule of law (broadly construed).

In 2007, the *Common Market Law Review* featured an editorial comment titled 'The Rule of Law as the Backbone of the EU'. Suffice to mention one statement which, as it will be discussed, enframes the CJEU's understanding of the rule of law at the EU level: 'Judicial protection and the rule of law go hand in hand: you can't have one without the other.'[8] This understanding of the EU rule of law resembles Lord Hope's remark in *Jackson* that 'the rule of law enforced by the courts is the ultimate controlling factor on which our constitution is based'.[9] The above connections

---

[4] See European Commission (n 2).
[5] One of the key clauses in EU external relations are those inserted in EU international agreements which stipulate that democracy and the rule of law and respect for human rights and fundamental freedoms are essential elements. See for instance: Commission Communication on the inclusion of respect for democratic principles and human rights in agreements between the Community and third countries, 23 May 1995, COM (95) 216 final. Also see more recently Case C-263/14 *Parliament v Council* [2016] ECLI:EU:C:2016:435 where the CJEU stressed that the EU-Tanzania Agreement's aim, 'to which its content corresponds, is to promote the rule of law and respect for human rights ...' (para 36); Case C-330/15 P *Tomana v Council* [2016] EU:C:2016:601 is also interesting in the context of respect for human rights and the rule of law in the external domain.
[6] '[T]he review by the Court of the validity of any Community measure in the light of fundamental rights must be considered to be the expression, in a community based on the rule of law, of a constitutional guarantee stemming from the EC Treaty as an autonomous legal system which is not to be prejudiced by an international agreement.'
[7] J Raz, 'The Rule of Law and its Virtue' (1977) 93 *Law Quarterly Review* 195.
[8] 'Editorial Comments' (2007) 44 *Common Market Law Review* 875. See also Case 294/83, *Les Verts* [1986] ECR 1339, para 23.
[9] *R (Jackson) v Attorney General* [2005] UKHL 56, para 108.

of the rule of law with judicial protection find expression in Article 19 (1) Treaty on European Union (TEU) which provides the CJEU with the following mission statement: that it shall ensure that in the interpretation and application of the Treaties the law is observed. Indeed, such reference to 'the law' goes beyond the Treaties—the EU's primary law. It can freely be interpreted as referring to the rule of law.

We can accordingly take a narrow view of the EU rule of law as the basis of EU administrative law and focus on how the CJEU is tempering the power of national and European public bodies by holding them accountable for the legality of their actions. We may draw the relevant evidence from enforcement proceedings against Member States in breach of their Treaty obligations and in judicial review actions against EU acts.[10] Judicial review, of EU secondary legislation, in particular, is central to the CJEU's interpretation of the EU rule of law. It has also been crucial in promoting the idea that since mutual trust among Member States and their respective legal systems is the foundation of the EU, there are certain minimum standards for the rule of law which are shared between Member States.

The CJEU has been instrumental in spelling out that the EU rule of law shares both formal and substantive dimensions, discussed in more detail in Chapter 2.[11] As we will see, the substantive formulation of the rule of law in the EU adds a more 'tangible' layer of protection to the declaratory commitment of the EU to the rule of law as expressly mentioned in the Treaty. In this respect, the rule of law forms more than part of a bundle of overlying principles together with democracy and human rights in that it places the individual at the forefront of EU integration. Specifically, the CJEU has interpreted the Treaty broadly in order to overcome its procedural limitations and enforce compliance with the rule of law by providing a litigation platform to individuals and ensuring effective judicial review viz fundamental rights protection. In this direction, the CJEU has historically demonstrated readiness to unearth certain general principles from Treaty provisions and, as Craig notes, 'treat them as truly general in their application across the Community legal order.'[12] Sometimes, it has been criticised for over-stepping its mandate

---

[10] See Case 294/83 *Les Verts* [1986] ECR 1339; Case C-402/05 P and C-415/05 P *Kadi* [2008] ECR I-6351, para 4, 81, 281. See also A Rosas, 'Counter-Terrorism and the Rule of Law: Issues of Judicial Control' in M Salinas de Frías et al (eds), *Counter-Terrorism, International Law and Practice* (Oxford, Oxford University Press, 2012).

[11] See P Craig, 'Formal and Substantive Conceptions of the Rule of Law: an Analytical Framework' [1997] *Public Law* 467–87; F Jacobs, *The Sovereignty of Law: The European Way* (Cambridge, Cambridge University Press, 2007) 7; F Jacobs, 'The Lisbon Treaty, the Court of Justice and the Rule of Law' in N Nic Shuibhne and L Gormley, *From Single Market to Economic Union: Essays in Memory of John A Usher* (Oxford, Oxford University Press, 2012) Ch 19; P Craig, 'Theory and Values in Public Law: A Response' in C Harlow, P Craig and R Rawlings (eds), *Law and Administration in Europe: Essays in honour of Carol Harlow* (Oxford, Oxford University Press, 2003) 30, 31.

[12] P Craig, *UK, EU and Global Administrative Law* (Cambridge, Cambridge University Press, 2015) 333. Craig points out that the CJEU's decisions in the 1970s were particularly influential: Case 11/70 *Internationale* [1970] ECR 1161 and Cases 117/76 and 16/77 *Ruckdeschel* [1977] ECR 1753. Since then, both the CJEU's jurisprudence and the Member States have given prominence to respect to fundamental rights in EU law.

taking a more active role than a mere internal market referee.[13] Nonetheless, the CJEU's interpretation of the Treaty has been pivotal in the recognition of the EU as a community governed by the rule of law. As put by Advocate General Cosmas in *Deutsche Telekom*:

> [R]egardless of whether th[e] economic objective truly reflected the intentions of the historical Community legislature, it no longer corresponds to present-day thinking. In a community governed by the rule of law, which respects and safeguards human rights, the requirement of equal pay for men and women is founded mainly on the principles of human dignity and equality between men and women and on the precept of improving working conditions, not on objectives which are economic in the narrow sense ...[14]

The acceptance of substantive attributes of the EU rule of law by European courts is of course not sufficient in itself to generate a unitary conception of the rule of law or give the principle a 'meta' quality. Having said that, we can provisionally accept that the CJEU's case law has led to some conceptual convergence of rule of law elements which has been bred further in the domestic setting by the fact that EU law rules directly over the activities of the Member States.[15] In this respect, it is worth noting that not only have European Courts relied on the authority of EU law to ensure domestic compliance with the EU *acquis* but they have also used it to force good practice in the Member States outside the strict application of EU law and promote global standards. For instance, in *Balázs-Árpád Izsák*, the General Court established that infringement of international commitments, such as the protection of minorities, by a Member State may amount to an infringement of the values laid down in Article 2 TEU, falling under the procedure of Article 7 TEU and thus capable of leading the Council to suspend certain rights flowing from the Treaties.[16] In this respect, one could argue that the EU contributes to a more global conception of the rule of law.

ii. The EU Political Institutions' Understanding of the Rule of Law

In addition to the CJEU's interpretation of the rule of law, the EU political institutions have for some time been applying the concept of the rule of law as a political

---

[13] See, for instance, the recent Danish Supreme Court's reaction to the *Mangold* judgment in Case no 15/2014—a follow up to the CJEU's decision in Case C-441/14 *Ajos* [2016] ECLI:EU:C:2016:278. In line with *Mangold* the CJEU held that Council Dir 2000/78/EC on equal treatment in employment and occupation, must be interpreted as precluding in private disputes national legislation which deprives an employee of entitlement to a severance allowance where he is entitled to claim an old-age pension from the employer under a pension scheme which the employee joined before reaching the age of 50, regardless of whether the employee chooses to remain on the employment market or take his retirement. See summary of the Danish case at: www.supremecourt.dk/supremecourt/nyheder/pressemeddelelser/Pages/TherelationshipbetweenEUlawandDanishlawinacaseconcerningasalaried employee.aspx.

[14] Case C-50/96 and Joined Cases C-234/96 and C-235/96 *Deutsche Telekom* [2000] ECR I-00743, para 80.

[15] See N Barber, *The Constitutional State* (Oxford, Oxford University Press, 2012).

[16] Case T-529/13 *Balázs-Árpád Izsák* [2016] ECLI:EU:T:2016:282, para 8.

process all across EU policies.[17] Their understanding includes adherence to certain written and unwritten principles (such as legality, legal certainty and equality before the law). Not only have these points been identified by the EU institutions as 'common' between the Member States but, as we will observe, they are also manifest in the CJEU's relevant jurisprudence. The EU institutions have been guided by the Treaty's wording which provides that the rule of law applies in three separate contexts: first, as a common value in EU internal policies as appears in the Preamble to the TEU and Article 2 TEU. Second, the rule of law manifests itself in Article 21 (1) TEU as an exported norm—a 'missionary principle'.[18] Likewise, it consists of a condition for EU membership in Article 49 TEU—a 'yardstick'. Third, following accession, Member States need to observe and promote the EU values and, as mentioned, Article 7 TEU establishes a procedure to sanction, inter alia, rule of law breaches—'a stick'. It should be stressed that although Article 49 TEU and Article 7 TEU imply similar obligations, when used as a 'yardstick' and as a 'stick', the EU rule of law acquires a tailored and broader scope of application which differs from our understanding of the rule of law at the national and even at the international level.

What is more, the application of the rule of law by the EU institutions has created a division between internal and external manifestations of the rule of law and thus a case to argue that although the concept of the EU rule of law is the same in essence (ie pointing to a system where laws are applied and enforced), there is a multiplicity of rule-of-law versions or 'conceptions' which differ in the arrangements of their components.[19] Likewise, the engagement of the EU political institutions is likely to differ between the internal and external conduct of the EU regarding the rule of law. But even within the internal sphere of EU law, the role of institutions and their involvement in enforcing discipline is likely to be different depending on the provision that is used. For instance, it is the Commission that enforces internal discipline against deviant Member States—it traditionally determines under Articles 258–260 of the Treaty on the Functioning of the European Union (TFEU) the existence of Member States' deviations from the EU *acquis* and penalises them accordingly. With reference to the rule of law, however, in accordance with Article 7 TEU, the Commission works closely with the European Parliament and the Council in order to guarantee its respect as a fundamental value of the EU and to ensure that EU law, values and principles are respected. Still, the Commission has a key role in using the rule of law as a 'stick', because under

---

[17] This is especially in the context of EU external relationships where the rule of law is a benchmark and a guiding principle. See L Pech, 'Rule of Law as a Guiding Principle of the European Union's External Action' CLEER Working Paper 2012/3.

[18] The rule of law as a value applies also to external EU policies (see Art 3(5) TEU). Art 2 also makes it clear that these values are shared by and among the Member States.

[19] EO Wennerström, *The Rule of Law and the European Union* (Uppsala, Iustus Förlag, 2007) 50 onwards.

Article 7 TEU it is responsible for identifying serious and persistent breaches against the EU's democratic fabric.[20]

The above leads us to consider what the EU political institutions would regard as rule-of-law breaches. So far, empirical evidence suggests that breaches may include: systemic rule of law backsliding affecting the proper functioning of a Member State's institutions and mechanisms. They also pertain to other violations which may put into sharp relief the EU's capacity to guarantee that all Member States act in full compliance with the common values enshrined in the Treaty. The above situations may include (not exclusively) the rights of minority groups,[21] the protection of asylum seekers[22] and media pluralism[23]—to mention but a few problem areas.[24] Yet, as Frans Timmermans (the Commission Vice-President in charge of rule-of-law issues) commented, 'there are situations which do not fall under the scope of EU law, and cannot be said to meet the threshold of Article 7, but which do raise concern regarding the respect of the rule of law in a particular Member State.'[25] As already mentioned previously, this is a rather delicate matter touching upon the area of EU competence and national sovereignty and carries the potential of becoming a real battlefield in the context of rule of law enforcement against the Member States. In particular, EU involvement in national affairs begs for compatibility with the principle of conferral, national identity and the ultra vires limits of EU law intervention as set by national constitutional courts (especially the famous *Solange* decision of the German Constitutional Court—the BVerfG).[26] Having said that, one has to approach competence delimitation

---

[20] For instance, the European Parliament has oversight over the Council, through the consent procedure viz the determination or a clear risk of a serious breach of EU common values.

[21] See M Martin, 'Expulsion of Roma: the French Government's Broken Promise', *Statewatch Analyses*, Vol 15, April 2013, available at www.statewatch.org/analyses/no-222-france-roma-expulsion.pdf; Y Maccanico, 'France Collective Expulsions of Roma People Undermines EU's Founding Principles', *Statewatch Analyses*, Vol 12, November 2010, available at www.statewatch.org/analyses/no-109-france-collective-expulsions-of-roma-people.pdf.

[22] See *MSS v Greece and Belgium*, no 30696/09, 21 January 2010; 4 November 2014; Joined Cases C-411/10 and C-493/10 *NS and ME* [2011] ECR I-13905. See also the implications of the EU's 'corrective fairness mechanism' in J Rankin, 'EU Executive to Propose Asylum Reforms and Approve Turkey Visa Deal' *The Guardian* 4 May 2016, available from www.theguardian.com/world/2016/may/03/eu-refugee-crisis-closed-door-countries-pay-solidarity-contributions.

[23] European Parliament Briefing, 'Member States and the Rule of Law Dealing with a Breach of EU Values', March 2015, available from www.europarl.europa.eu/RegData/etudes/BRIE/2015/554167/EPRS_BRI(2015)554167_EN.pdf.

[24] See initially on Art 7 TEU to get a general idea about the kind of violations this provision aims to address: G Budó, 'EU Common Values at Stake: Is Article 7 TEU an Effective Protection Mechanism', Barcelona Institute for International Affairs, Documents CIDOB, May 2014, available from www.cidob.org/ … /1/file/DOCUMENTS%20CIDOB_01_EUROPA.pdf (last accessed on 05.01.2016). Budó provides a brief analysis of past incidents in the Member States that could have triggered resort of Art 7 TEU—eg the 'Haider case' in Austria, the Constitutional Reform in Hungary, the Roma expulsions in France, and the political struggle between President Basescu and Prime Minister Ponta in Romania. See for more detail Ch 5.

[25] 'Commission Statement: EU framework for democracy, rule of law and fundamental rights', Speech of First Vice-President Frans Timmermans to the European Parliament, Strasbourg, 12 February 2015. Available from http://europa.eu/rapid/press-release_SPEECH-15-4402_en.htm.

[26] *Solange II*, October 22, 1986, BVerfGE 73.

in EU law with a certain dose of pragmatism taking into account the fact that 'the difference between purely national and EU-related can be so blurred, that even the experts are at times puzzled, making such determinations difficult if not impossible.'[27]

Notwithstanding any 'competence limitations' of rule-of-law enforcement, in 2014, the Commission announced a 'new EU framework to strengthen the rule of law' which commenced a dialogue between the Commission and the Member States, while the Council kick-started, in December 2014, an annual dialogue, in the General Affairs Council, on the rule of law in the Member States. Both the Commission's framework and the Council's dialogue revolve around the function of Article 7 TEU. Most notably, the Commission has even laid down a set of commonly shared rule-of-law principles that include a mixture of formal and substantive qualities about the rule of law:

i.   legality, which implies a transparent, accountable, democratic and pluralistic process for enacting laws;
ii. legal certainty;
iii. prohibition of arbitrariness of the executive powers;
iv. independent and impartial courts;
v.   effective judicial review including respect for fundamental rights; and
vi. equality before the law.[28]

The Commission's effort to list the principles akin to the EU rule of law demonstrate seriousness from the part of the EU institutions to safeguard EU values as well as eagerness to frame the rule of law debate according to a rather broad set of legal values. In the same direction, it is telling that the portfolio of Frans Timmermans as the Vice-President in charge of rule of law consists of 'Better Regulation, Interinstitutional Relations, the Rule of Law and the Charter of Fundamental Rights'. His job title shows the more general context in which the Commission perceives the rule of law—ie placed next to directions for law—and rule-making, institutional relations and fundamental rights: a mixed bag of different yet connected legal elements. This all-encompassing understanding of the rule of law akin to procedural virtues and human rights protection has also been promoted by other institutions such as the European Parliament which places emphasis on rights protection as key to the preservation of the rule of law.[29] Some commentators have stressed that it is of no coincidence that the EU institutions'

---

[27] P Bard et al, 'An EU Mechanism on Democracy, the Rule of Law and Fundamental Rights', CEPS Paper in Liberty and Security in Europe, No 91/ April 2016, 69.
[28] Commission Communication to the European Parliament and the Council, 'A new EU Framework to strengthen the Rule of Law', 11.03.2014, COM (2014) 158 final.
[29] See for instance: European Parliament resolution of 3 July 2013 on the situation of fundamental rights: standards and practices in Hungary (pursuant to the European Parliament resolution of 16 February 2012) [2016] OJ C 75/52; European Parliament resolution of 10 June 2015 on the situation in Hungary [2015] OJ C 407/46; European Parliament resolution of 21 May 2013 on the EU Charter: standard settings for media freedom across the EU [2016] OJ C 55/33.

understanding of the rule of law revolves around areas such as fundamental rights enforcement where the EU seems to have a more solid grounding.[30] This is compared, for instance, to enforcing democracy in the Member States—a value which has always raised national concerns about the EU's accountability and legitimacy.[31]

B. The Addressees of the EU Rule of Law

As it transpires, the modern debate about the EU rule of law has been monopolised by its disciplinarian flavour and concerns over the conduct of the Member States within the EU, inclusive of the implementation of EU law and mutual recognition and enforcement of civil and criminal judgments across Europe. EU legal scholarship is currently preoccupied with the EU's oversight of rule of law crises in the Member States.[32] There is also growing commentary on the institutional priorities regarding the modalities of disciplining 'systemic deficiencies' in the Member States.[33] Hence, for the spectator, the current EU rule of law discourse points to the Member States as the main addressees of the EU rule of law and also the main culprits of violating its tenets. There is a good reason why this is happening. EU law is often construed on the (false) premise that Member States will apply its norms properly. It is established that since the content of the principles and standards stemming from the rule of law may vary at national level, depending on each Member State's constitutional system, diverse standards may apply throughout—some of them lower than others. There is also an impending danger that national mechanisms may at times malfunction or cease to operate effectively. Some commentators, in particular, have made a case of 'constitutional loopholes' in certain Member States.[34] As such the EU has taken interest in protecting the rule of law as a common EU value based on reciprocal respect.[35]

While establishing that the notion of the rule of law is becoming universal by virtue of states' international obligations under their EU membership, the EU

---

[30] See on the protection of human rights in Europe by the CJEU the various contributions in: K Dzehtsiarou, T Konstadinides et al (eds), *Human Rights Law in Europe: The Influence, Overlaps and Contradictions of the EU and the ECHR* (London, Routledge, 2014).

[31] M Bonelli, 'Safeguarding Values in the EU: The European Parliament, Article 7 and Hungary', School of Government Luiss Guido Carli, Working Paper Series, SOG-WP28/2015, available from http://sog.luiss.it/sites/sog.luiss.it/files/SOG%20Working%20Papers%20WP28-2015%20Bonelli%20 -%20MB%20(3).pdf.

[32] See C Closa and D Kochenov (eds), *Reinforcing Rule of Law Oversight in the European Union* (Cambridge, Cambridge University Press, 2016); C Closa, D Kochenov and JHH Weiler, 'Reinforcing Rule of Law Oversight in the European Union', EUI working papers, RSCAS 2014/25, March 2014.

[33] See Special Rule of Law issue (2016) 54 (5) *Journal of Common Market Studies* 1043–259.

[34] See for instance: A Von Bogdandy and P Sonnevend, *Constitutional Crisis in the European Constitutional Area: Theory, Law and Politics in Hungary and Romania* (Oxford, Hart Publishing/Bloomsbury, 2015).

[35] See EMH Hirsch Ballin, 'Mutual Trust: The Virtue of Reciprocity. Strengthening the Acceptance of the Rule of Law through Peer Review' Tilburg Law School Research Paper No 14/2015, available from http://ssrn.com/abstract=2649856.

institutions have set for themselves an arduous task to complete: first, they need to set clear conceptual boundaries to the rule of law so that when a Member State disregards the EU's fundamental principles it can be clearly seen whether it is testing or violating them. Second, they must treat all Member States equally and avoid double standards or at least ensure that when a Member State's erratic behaviour is tolerated and another Member State starts acting in a similar manner, no adverse precedent is created that can potentially erode the rule of law. Third, the EU institutions need to draw a line as to how far they can intervene to prevent systemic risks in the legislation of the Member States without impinging upon the practicalities of their legal competence to do so under the Treaty.

Moving on, we need to establish that the EU institutions are also the addressees of the EU rule of law. What is often missing from the current debate monopolised by the discussion for a mechanism for a regular assessment of Member States' compliance with the rule of law is an *aide-memoire* that the above principles identified by the Commission as 'common' (legality, legal certainty, etc) also bind the EU institutions in that all their decisions can be challenged by those affected by them. The rule of law is applicable to the Member States as much as it is to the EU institutions. As mentioned, we tend to perceive the EU rule of law from a top-down perspective, as a requirement placed on the governments of the Member States: ie they must exercise their powers through the application of general rules; they must make those rules public; they must limit the discretion of their civil servants; they must not impose penalties on people without due process; and so on. But we will be illustrating in Chapter 4 that these responsibilities relevant to the rule of law also apply to the EU institutions. As Haljan puts it: 'Not only does the rule of law bind addressees but also the authors. It bears constant reminder that the rule of law has the bilateral nature of relating author and addressee through the legal order. Both are equally bound to the law, and to compliance therewith'.[36] What is more, to paraphrase from Kochenov, the idea of the subordination of the EU *acquis* to another source of law, external to the EU legal order and, therefore, one which is not for the EU institutions to change at will, is key to the rule of law discussion at the EU level.[37]

On the same token we need to consider that both the EU legislative *acquis* and the CJEU's interpretation of it not always do justice to EU citizens nor do they safeguard the rule of law properly. Take for example the field of EU criminal justice. The EU criminal law *acquis* contains examples to illustrate that EU intervention through legislative action or mutual recognition is occasionally futile. On the

---

[36] D Haljan, 'Is the Rule of Law a Limit on Popular Sovereignty' in E Claes et al (eds), *Facing the Limits of the Law* (Berlin, Springer, 2009) 278.

[37] Kochenov contends, for instance, that '[h]aving no problem with finding its *gubernaculum* (the law made in compliance with the principle of legality in accordance with all procedural requirements, which is the body of the *acquis* in the EU context)—the question is: where is the EU's *jurisdictio* (ie the law to check the acquis against)?' D Kochenov, 'EU Law without the Rule of Law' [2015] *Yearbook of European Law* 1, 10.

one hand, EU legislation in substantive criminal matters is at times equated with internal market harmonisation—paying little attention to the fact that criminal procedure in the Member States differs substantially in form and substance.[38] On the other hand, mutual recognition does not imply mutual respect for each other's criminal laws so that, for the sake of uniformity, they are treated as domestic.[39] The rule of law is, therefore, potentially threatened as EU criminal law (in whichever of the two above-mentioned forms is manifested) may have a negative effect upon individuals' rights, such as human dignity and privacy.[40]

Having said that, we must acknowledge that the CJEU has recently made noble attempts to mitigate any miscarriages of justice in the field of criminal or security law in general. It has achieved 'justice' in two ways. First by imposing caveats upon mutual recognition across the EU-28. The judgment of *Aranyosi and Căldăraru* constitutes a good example of this approach where the CJEU held that the execution of a European Arrest Warrant (EAW) must be deferred if there is a real risk of inhuman or degrading treatment because of the conditions of detention of the person concerned in the Member State where the EAW was issued. Second the CJEU has reinforced the importance of EU data protection law that poses positive obligations on its recipients. In *Google Spain*, for instance, the Luxembourg Court established that individuals have the right—under certain conditions—to ask online search engines to remove links with personal information about them. Hence, it held that EU data protection law (Directive 95/46/EC, in particular, on personal data and free movement of such data) applies to Google and so does the right to be forgotten.[41] Likewise, the CJEU held in *Tele2 Sverige AB* that Directive 2002/58/EC concerning the processing of personal data and the protection of privacy in the electronic communications sector must be interpreted as precluding national legislation which, for the purpose of fighting crime, provides for general and indiscriminate retention of all traffic and location data of all subscribers and registered users relating to all means of electronic communication.[42]

Despite the positive atmosphere generated by the above judgments, one cannot help but pick the following general trend in the enforcement of EU law: the incremental 'Europeanisation' of policy areas is often followed by an unequal division

---

[38] Mitsilegas argues that 'while market efficiency requires a degree of flexibility and aims at profit maximisation, clear and predictable criminal law principles are essential to provide legal certainty in a society based on the rule of law.' See V Mitsilegas, *EU Criminal Law* (Oxford, Hart Publishing, 2009) 118. See also the German Constitutional Court's Press Release No 4/2016, 'Protection of Fundamental Rights in Individual Cases is Ensured as Part of Identity Review', 26 January 2016. The BVerfG relied heavily on national identity as a means of protecting fundamental rights enshrined in the Constitution against the tidal effect of the principle of mutual recognition in criminal matters.

[39] See V Mitsilegas, *EU Criminal Law after Lisbon: Rights, Trust and the Transformation of Justice in Europe* (Oxford, Hart Publishing, 2016).

[40] See S Douglas-Scott, 'Justice, Injustice and the Rule of Law in the EU' in G De Búrca et al (eds), *Europe's Justice Deficit? Beyond Good Governance* (Oxford, Hart Publishing, 2014). Available at SSRN: http://ssrn.com/abstract=2457266.

[41] Case C-131/12 *Google Spain* [2014] ECLI:EU:C:2014:317.

[42] Case C-203/15 *Tele2 Sverige AB* [2016] ECLI:EU:C:2016:970.

of workload between the European and the national courts which do not always guarantee the possibility of judicial avenues for redressing grievances against the state and the EU.[43] Beyond question, EU law leaves more manoeuvring space to the Member States on procedural than on substantive issues. Thus, national courts often need to establish the consequences of EU law breaches by state organs or private parties. This includes ensuring access to justice and the availability of remedies (the hallmarks of the rule of law) when individuals challenge EU law. From an integrationist perspective, this approach denotes synergy between national courts and the CJEU operating under a single judicial web. Yet, there are problems with this model because its success depends on all Member States being law-abiding, loyal and operating in good faith. For instance, the expectation from the side of the EU is that everyone, including rule-of-law backsliding Member States, is responsible for establishing a system of procedures and remedies in order to guarantee the full effectiveness of EU law. The expectation is no different when, for instance, there are pending allegations against a Member State that its respective government in power has dismantled the country's democratic institutions.

Going back to the question of who are the main addressees of the EU rule of law, we shall mention that apart from the Member States and the EU institutions, the rule of law also concerns and addresses the individual. In this context, the EU rule of law is freedom-oriented and includes both economic and social rights. At the same time it promotes self-responsibility and requires the EU citizen to obey the laws that apply to her. Likewise, the expectation is that she should be alert to changes in EU law and she should arrange for her legal representatives to inform her about her rights and obligations in a case at hand. Equally, she should not act in any way that undermines or jeopardises the operation of the EU legal system. The importance of positive obligations with regard to EU law has seen an increase in recent years—not only do Member States need to protect their citizens and, therefore refrain from interfering with their Treaty rights, but equally individuals must not abuse these rights.[44]

C. An EU Rule of Law as Opposed to a National Rule of Law

The discussion about how the rule of law is manifested and enforced at the EU level owes a lot to the hallmarks of adherence to the rule of law in its traditional form. In the UK, for instance, the late Lord Bingham laid down eight principles of the rule of law and illustrated that the concept generally implies that everyone is bound by and entitled to the benefit of accessible, non-arbitrary, prospective,

---

[43] More often than not individuals are referred to the national courts unless they are challenging an EU act which is addressed to them or is of direct and individual concern to them.

[44] See for instance Dir 2004/38 on the right of citizens of the Union and their family members to move and reside freely within the territory of the Member States [2004] OJ L 158/77. Art 35 authorises Member States to adopt measures to prevent abuse and fraud, such as marriages of convenience.

rights-conferring and justiciable laws.[45] EU law aspires to embrace and enforce such universal standards of justice and fairness. But this is not the end of the line for the EU rule of law. More often than not, the EU rule of law applies where the (national) rule of law already exists. Hence, while studying EU law one has to be mindful of elements of the rule of law which are intimate to the state and cannot, therefore, be 'stretched' and applied in a supranational context. Lord Bingham was, for instance, emphatic that judges should be subservient to parliamentary sovereignty. This is a distinctive feature which reflects the UK's original constitutional nature. Yet, in his seminal book on the very subject matter of the rule of law,[46] the contradictions between parliamentary sovereignty and the rule of law were, as noted by Gearty, 'rather glossed over (even though he sensibly sees that Parliament needs to trump judicial will)'.[47]

Having said that, and to his defence, Bingham's book contextualises the extent to which parliamentary sovereignty is absolute in the light of the UK's participation in international organisations. His Lordship's 'eighth principle of the rule of law' requires compliance by the state with its obligations under international law (inclusive of EU law—we may argue—as sub-species of international law).[48] As we juxtapose parliamentary sovereignty against the doctrine of EU law primacy, we will conclude that the latter has restricted the absolute authority of parliament to legislate as it wishes.[49] But does the constitutional authority of the EU and the changes it has generated to the power configuration in the Member States marginalise the ideal of the rule of law? The answer is in the negative since there is often nothing in the rule-of-law expressions that indicates that the law by which the state is governed is strictly confined to its own domestic law. On the contrary, the rule of law has placed an obligation on national governments to operate in par with their international obligations that spring out of the text of the Treaties that they voluntarily signed.[50]

The quality of the domestic rule of law is therefore affected when entering an international organisation. To use the British example again, the European Communities Act 1972—a constitutional statute—made the necessary changes to domestic law that were required as a result of the UK's EU membership. These changes have produced a form of law which is—insofar as it is accepted by national

---

[45] T Bingham, House of Lords, Sixth Sir David Williams Lecture, 'The Rule of Law', University of Cambridge, Centre for Public Law, 2006, available from http://netk.net.au/RuleOfLaw/Bingham1.asp. See P Craig, Select Committee on Constitution, 6th Report, App 5: The Rule of Law, available from www.publications.parliament.uk/pa/ld200607/ldselect/ldconst/151/15115.htm.

[46] T Bingham, *The Rule of Law* (London, Penguin, 2011).

[47] C Gearty, 'The Rule of Law by Tom Bingham' *The Guardian* 7 February 2010, available from www.theguardian.com/books/2010/feb/07/rule-of-law-thomas-bingham.

[48] See the Bingham Centre mission statement for a summary of Lord Bingham's eight rule of law principles: http://binghamcentre.biicl.org/about-us.

[49] S 2(1) when read with s 2(4) European Communities Act 1972.

[50] Having said that the updated UK Ministerial Code of 15 October 2015 removed the reference to international law from the code. See 'Ministerial code: No 10 "showing contempt for international law"' *The Guardian* 26 October 2015, www.theguardian.com/law/2015/oct/26/ministerial-code-no-10-showing-contempt-for-international-law.

courts—superior to domestic law. EU law has enriched UK law with rights, obligations and liabilities which may be altered or cease to have effect only once notice is given under Article 50 TEU and the UK has renegotiated its position outside the EU. It follows that the quality of the rule of law would be negatively affected when the UK decides to leave the EU due to the effect of such departure upon, for example, EU-conferred rights in relation to, inter alia, data protection law, the right to be forgotten, the right to a fair trial and the right to family life.[51] As we witnessed, the modalities of exit from the EU also invited a rule of law discussion at home regarding procedure and separation of powers viz which institution has the power to begin the departure process. Specifically, as both the UK High Court and the UK Supreme Court established in *Miller*, the executive cannot use the power under the Crown's prerogative to give notice pursuant to Article 50 TEU for the UK to withdraw from the EU and therefore remove (without the intervention of Parliament) statutory rights of individuals.[52] British judges highlighted both the principle of parliamentary sovereignty as the bedrock of the British Constitution and the constitutional limits on the prerogative powers set by common law. Accordingly, they held that 'the subordination of the Crown (ie executive government) to law is the foundation of the *rule of law* in the United Kingdom.'[53]

Reflecting on the above thoughts it emerges that under EU membership, Member States have compromised their constitutional peculiarities or identity consistently with constitutional principle. Such a compromise fulfils the commitment to give 'loyal effect' to EU law.[54] But to what avail? Jacobs stresses that the 'ultimate source of authority is no longer the sovereign in the shape of a monarch, or even in the shape of a Parliament; but rather certain values, or certain fundamental principles, which form an inherent part of a well-functioning legal system.'[55] It follows that these values would be weakened if Member States decided to systematically undermine them or left the EU altogether. Following Jacobs' trail of thought one may attempt to get closer to a more transnational conception of the 'rule of law' in the EU which concerns the manner in which the law is enacted as well as ideals of fairness, rights and remedies. The foundations of such a transnational approach would lie on what is often referred to as common or 'shared traits' between the Member States.[56] In this respect, the EU rule of law is perceived more as a homecoming and less as a 'foreign invasion'. But one needs to remain open-minded

---

[51] See T Lock, 'Human Rights in the UK after Brexit' (2017, with the author).

[52] See *R (Miller) v Secretary of State for Exiting the European Union* [2016] EWHC 2768 (Admin) and [2017] UKSC 5 respectively. Both Courts considered the sovereignty of parliament to be critical, and stated the Crown was not entitled to change domestic law through exercise of its prerogative powers. Instead the executive requires an Act of Parliament to proceed with a notice pursuant to Art 50 TEU.

[53] This is a direct quote from the High Court's judgment, [2016] EWHC 2768 (Admin) para 26 (emphasis added).

[54] See *Thoburn v Sunderland City Council* [2002] EWHC 195 (Admin), para 59; *R (HS2 Action Alliance Ltd) v Secretary of State for Transport* [2014] UKSC 3; para 206.

[55] Jacobs, *The Sovereignty of Law: The European Way* (n 11) 62.

[56] See for a detailed discussion on the EU rule of law 'shared traits': L Pech, 'The Rule of Law as a Constitutional Principle of the European Union' Jean Monnet Working Paper 04/09.

and take account of the fact that the EU rule of law legitimately displaces certain national constitutional idiosyncrasies. The worry is, of course, that it permanently replaces them with its own, much to the demise of the domestic Constitution.

Moving forward, we shall appreciate that the EU rule of law presents distinctive features which reflect the arrangements of the EU's constitutional ecosystem. It follows that these features have generated changes in the Member States and have contributed to the reconfiguration of the very core of the relationship between the people and the state (as subjects and rulers). For instance, Oliver claims that nowadays the 'duties of judges are not limited to upholding individuals' rights. They include ensuring the practical working of constitutional arrangements, for instance relationships with the EU and between the UK and devolved bodies, which in turn facilitate the rule of law.'[57] This view acknowledges the extent of the UK's participation within a federal structure based on the devolution of powers, which of course is bound to change significantly after Brexit.

Against the notion of a self-proclaimed 'EU rule of law', we support the idea that national understandings of the rule of law feed into the Treaty's conceptions of the rule of law. As mentioned, it is impossible to establish a unitary conception of the rule of law at the EU level which is 'cloned' in all 28 legal systems. We will rather take as a starting point the fact that there are generally common characteristics of the rule of law in the Member States which are influenced by the fact that EU law rules directly over the activities of the Member States: it regulates, inter alia, the conduct of the administration, the content of individual decisions, the operating of their judicial review and formulation of judicial precedent. We acknowledge, of course, that despite their commonalities the EU and national 'rules of law' are likely to be different across a wide range of attributes and policy areas. This is particularly important when the Member States are acting outside the scope of EU law. Within the realm of EU law, however, the integrative conception of the EU rule of law has occupied a special place in the national legal tradition and it is a key driver for the continuity and development of every national constitution.[58] Lord Mackenzie Stuart's opening line of his Hamlyn Lecture back in 1977 has survived the test of time:

> From an observation post in the Grand Duchy of Luxembourg there is a danger that one may take too Copernican a view of Community law. Perhaps the then Lord Chancellor, Lord Dilhorne, was right when in 1962 he said: 'I venture to suggest that the vast majority of men and women in this country will never directly feel the impact of the Community made law at all.' Nonetheless, it seems to me that the impact of Community law on daily life is increasingly evident. I do not mean only the effect of the dominant themes of the Treaty of Rome: the removal of trade barriers; the prevention of distortion of international trade, the encouragement of workers to move from one country to another

---

[57] D Oliver, 'Parliamentary Sovereignty: A Pragmatic or Principled Doctrine?' UK Constitutional Law Association, 3 May 2012, available from https://ukconstitutionallaw.org/2012/05/03/dawn-oliver-parliamentary-sovereignty-a-pragmatic-or-principled-doctrine/.

[58] See Barber (n 15).

in search of employment and the adoption of a common policy in agriculture. I mean more.[59]

Our starting point in this book is the normative conceptualisation of non-arbitrariness which is more often than not manifest in legal theory texts studying the purpose of the rule of law than in the context of public or private law.[60] Non-arbitrariness as a normative objective suggests that the 'law' should govern (as opposed to arbitrary rule) and protect the citizen from those in authority from exercising wide, arbitrary or discretionary powers. Krygier, a keen rule of law 'partisan',[61] has repeatedly argued that this is perhaps the most prominent shared point of connection viz the rule of law which places emphasis upon the existence of safeguards against the abuse of public power.[62] Indeed, there is an explicit understanding in every democratic Constitution that the rule of law is aimed at reducing the discretion of public administration by posing effective controls against any arbitrary exercise of power.[63] Krygier notes that:

> After all, those most urgently seeking the rule of law are in the end concerned not with a package of legal techniques but with an outcome: a salutary state of affairs where law counts more than it does or has in many places, at least as a reliable constraint on the exercise of power, and in particular as a brake on the possibility of arbitrary exercise of power. Unless that goal is kept in the forefront of attention, we can tinker as much as we like but still lose sight of why the tinkering might matter.[64]

Krygier's rule of law conception dovetails with the CJEU's understanding of the EU rule of law as a means for reviewing the legality of the EU institutions' actions, in compliance with the Treaties. Accordingly, the Member States are also subject to the jurisdiction of the CJEU viz any EU law infringement. As Jacobs remarks,

---

[59] Lord Mackenzie Stuart, *The European Communities and the Rule of Law*, The Hamlyn Lectures, 29th Series, (London, Stevens & Sons, 1977).

[60] See W Lucy, 'The Rule of Law and Private Law' in LM Austin and D Klimchuk, *Private Law and the Rule of Law* (Oxford, Oxford University Press, 2014), also available from http://dro.dur.ac.uk/13907/1/13907.pdf. Lucy argues at 6, fn 12, that, 'in our English public law textbooks, neither "arbitrariness" nor "arbitrary" exercises of power receive much sustained attention (for an exception, see T Endicott, Administrative Law (Oxford: Clarendon 2009), 49), it seemingly being taken for granted that lawyers will know arbitrariness when they see it. The notion also sometimes crops up in more jurisprudential discussions of the rule of law, albeit almost always rather fleetingly. Two examples are D Dyzenhaus, The Constitution of Law (Cambridge: CUP 2006) 2 and TRS Allan, Constitutional Justice (Oxford: Clarendon Press 2001) at 2-3, 11-12 and 15.'

[61] M Krygier, 'Four Puzzles about the Rule of Law: Why, what, where? And who cares?' (18 June 2010) UNSW Law Research Paper No 2010-22, 1, available at SSRN: http://ssrn.com/abstract=1627465.

[62] This characteristic of the rule of law—ie tempering arbitrariness—is a recurrent theme in Martin Krygier's work. See M Krygier, 'The Rule of Law. Legality, Teleology, Sociology' in G Palombella and N Walker (eds), *Relocating the Rule of Law* (Oxford, Hart Publishing, 2009). See also his other work available on SSRN: http://papers.ssrn.com/sol3/cf_dev/AbsByAuth.cfm?per_id=102666.

[63] See more on a theory of the EU rule of law: T Konstadinides, 'An EU Concept of Rule of Law: Theory and Practice' (2016) Copy with the author.

[64] M Krygier, 'The Rule of Law and "the Three Integrations"' (2009) 1 *The Hague Journal of the Rule of Law* 1, 10.

'the rule of law is applicable both to the institutions and to the Member States.'[65] This is important for our comprehension of the EU rule of law because for a long time the CJEU was the only EU institution that conferred an opinion on the matter. Yet, while the interpretation of the EU rule of law by the CJEU has been persuasive, it carries serious ramifications for the territorial limits of the CJEU's jurisdiction. For instance, the incremental human rights culture developed within the CJEU which has expanded the types of questions falling within jurisdictional boundaries of that Court has been an important driver for resentment towards its judgments in some Member States. Some individuals may also resent the CJEU given that, in their capacity as claimants against the EU institutions, they are often unable to place the substantive issues of their case before the Luxembourg judges. Having said that, the importance and potential constitutional impact of granting access to judicial review before the European Courts has never been played down by the CJEU. By contrast, the Luxembourg Court has stressed its pivotal role in upholding the rule of law by checking whether EU and national acts are in conformity with the EU 'constitutional charter', the Treaty.

II. ARGUMENTS AGAINST THE EU RULE OF LAW

There are numerous arguments that can be made against the EU rule of law. We focus on two main arguments here. First, despite the EU's efforts to mainstream the rule of law, the concept suffers from an imposter syndrome or prejudice. One may be suspicious about the motives of the EU to promote the rule of law. A criticism that can be made is that the EU rule of law forms partly a mere rhetoric and partly a conceptual basis to legitimise sweeping new powers and policies in the name of more integration. We call this the 'competence creep argument'. Second, the previous argument has a profound impact upon the legitimacy of EU action, particularly in the context of the multiple crises that Europe is facing which affect the individual— what we call the 'crisis resilience argument'. Both arguments are important to discuss here because they make the question of whether the rule of law (and which conception of the rule of law) should be enforceable in the first place more pertinent. They touch upon issues that explain Member States' resort to instruments of national democracy, such as referenda, as a way out of their EU law obligations. They finally inform the debate about the increase in support for Eurosceptic movements and decrease in European solidarity. Let us observe both arguments in turn.

A. The Competence-creep Argument

The argument here is two-fold. First, the rule of law can be conceived as a conceptual green light to expansive EU policies in areas where EU competence is questionable.

---

[65] Jacobs, *The Sovereignty of Law: The European Way* (n 11) 36.

This old 'competence-creep' argument[66] coheres around the relationship between 'constituent (constituting) and constitutional (constituted) power'. As it has been argued 'this distinction has proven to be central to discussions on democracy, the rule of law and the relationship between law and politics.'[67] Creeping competences also carry operational ramifications for the enforcement of the rule of law. Not only do EU institutions go beyond their mandate, but the internal mechanisms in place that require them to justify why they took action and the judicial mechanism available to review such actions are rigid and sometimes impenetrable.

What is more, the rules and procedures available so that the EU institutions can hold Member States to account for not applying EU law properly appear incomprehensive. Beyond the sanctioning of breaches of EU common values, rule-of-law action also grants permission to the EU institutions to sanction Member States in the event of a breach in an area where the latter have acted autonomously—outside the scope of EU law.[68] All in all, the enforcement of the rule of law has been influenced by an institutional interest to promote constitutional 'integration'—translated according to the circumstances into procedural constraints (usually manifest in challenges against the EU institutions for breaches of EU law) or enablements (evident in challenges against Member States for breaches that have occurred outside the strict scope of EU law). It is argued that the uncertainty over the application of these constraints and enablements may have an adverse effect upon the rule of law as the ultimate backstop to our behaviour as EU citizens.

Understandably, the discussion of Member State compliance with the rule of law is often shaped around an argument based on the scope of EU law. Accordingly, the EU institutions' supervisory role is restricted to the areas of EU competence and cannot, therefore, interfere with the internal structures of the Member States and their capacity to exercise power against their subjects.[69] This is a rather

---

[66] See T Konstadinides, 'The Competences of the European Union' in R Schütze and T Tridimas (eds) *The Oxford Principles of European Union Law, Vol. 1: The European Union Legal Order* (Oxford, Oxford University Press, 2017); L Azoulai (ed), *The Question of Competence in the European Union* (Oxford, Oxford University Press, 2014); T Konstadinides, *Division of Powers in European Union Law: The Delimitation of Internal Competence between the EU and the Member States* (The Hague, Kluwer Law International, 2009); S Weatherill, 'Better Competence Monitoring' (2005) 30 (1) *European Law Review* 23; S Weatherill, 'Competence Creep and Competence Control' (2004) 23 *Yearbook of European Law* 1; FC Mayer, 'Competences—Reloaded? The Vertical Division of Powers in the EU after the New European Constitution' WHI—Paper 19/04, available from www.whi-berlin.eu/documents/whi-paper1904.pdf.

[67] L Corrias, 'Paradigms of Constitution-Making, or Two Tales of One Dualism' in *The Passivity of Law Competence and Constitution in the European Court of Justice* (London, Springer, 2011) Ch 2, 25.

[68] European Commission, Communication from the Commission to the Council and the European Parliament on Art 7 of the Treaty on European Union. Respect for and promotion of the values on which the Union is based, COM (2003) 606 final, 5.

[69] It is acknowledged that only the sanctions relevant for breach of EU law and of the EU Charter of Fundamental Rights fall squarely within the jurisdiction of the CJEU (although the CJEU has been criticised for going beyond EU competence in relation to the Charter). At the same time, while the migration and security (terrorism) crises have an EU dimension, they are closely related to external factors and domestic politics.

grey and nascent area but one where the EU seems to have secured a vague consensus from the part of the Member States. Besides, the CJEU's recent human rights jurisprudence reveals that competence is not an absolute limitation when it comes to protecting EU values. Although the link between EU law and a case at issue may appear to be tenuous, it may still trigger—subject to limitations—the application of EU law. Such was the application of the EU Charter of Fundamental Rights in *Åkerberg Fransson* in order to invoke the *ne bis in idem* principle in relation to penalties for infringement of VAT.[70] Still, however, the position of the EU institutions as rule-of-law enforcers is delicate. Not only are they confronted with different levels of rule of law protection in some Member States. They also have to address the position of EU law with regard to substantial constitutional reforms introduced by certain national governments that may contravene the common values enshrined in the Treaty.

Textually, the position seems fairly clear: if a Member State does something against the rule of law which breaches substantive EU obligations, the Commission can respond using enforcement proceedings under Articles 258–260 TFEU by detoxing specific disputes.[71] If the Member State does something against the rule of law outside the scope of substantive EU law, Article 7 TEU provides the appropriate response. There are still questions, however, as to whether the EU can and should go further—either based directly on Article 2 TEU or some general notion of mutual trust between the Member States. A convincing case is yet to be made with regard to the legal basis for such powers, their corresponding procedure or indeed the nature of the Member State's obligation and the consequences of non-compliance. Not only is this suggestion premature but it also clashes with the argument often made against the EU institutions, ie that they should be wary of adopting an unduly expansive conception of their own powers in a way that might rightly antagonise the Member States concerned about the principle of attributed powers.

On a different note, recent focus on the rule of law (and especially on Article 7 TEU) may have legitimised the expanding jurisdiction of the EU institutions but it has not put forward a convincing case of infinite rule-of-law compliance by the EU institutions themselves. On the contrary, the rule of law is not always effectively guaranteed by the monitoring role of the EU institutions or the wide jurisdiction conferred on the CJEU as an active and independent court. More specifically, there are recent issues in relation to the EU institutions' rule of law compliance viz their

---

[70] Case C-617/10 *Åkerberg Fransson*, EU:C:2013:105; Case C-206/13 *Siragusa*, EU:C:2014:126. F Fontanelli 'Implementation of EU Law through Domestic Measures after Fransson: the Court of Justice buys Time and "Non-preclusion" Troubles Loom Large' (2014) *European Law Review* 682.

[71] See Case C-286/12, *Commission v Hungary* EU:2012:687. See comment by U Belavusau, 'On Age Discrimination and Beating Dead Dogs: *Commission* v *Hungary*' (2013) 50 *CML Rev* 1145–60. In the absence of legislative competence over the independence and impartiality of national judiciaries, the Commission took action against Hungary under Art 258 TFEU. In order to put Hungary back on track, it relied on the EU principle of non-discrimination on the ground of age which falls squarely within the EU's competence.

action or inaction in breach of EU values in the realm of migration or in relation to the Euro crisis. What is more, in challenges against EU legislation, the CJEU jurisprudence has gone to great lengths to preserve and often impose EU legal doctrines such as primacy and mutual recognition (inherent in the idea of a Union based on the rule of law). In this light, the CJEU becomes complicit to EU competence creep. It can be criticised for risking becoming less attentive to other needs (such as protecting access to courts or the right to judicial review) which may be implicated in the same case and which have a close resonance with the rule of law.

Taking the above into consideration, it can be contended that CJEU practice should be sensitive to the extent that the national level can 'see' the rule of law. In particular, foreseeability and accessibility are qualitative requirements by which the CJEU shall be restrained from acting arbitrarily. If the individual is to know the wording of the relevant EU provision and, if necessary what acts and omissions would make her liable, it is crucial that she has also confidence in the CJEU's interpretation of it, as the guardian of the rule of law. This is particularly important since numerous principles founded by the CJEU which relate to both procedural (eg individual standing in actions for annulment discussed in Chapter 4) and substantive points (such as the case law on fundamental rights, also mentioned in this book), have found their way into the Treaty. Those against the CJEU's dynamic interpretation of the Treaty would be relieved to discover that the CJEU will have a very limited role in Article 7 TEU proceedings. According to Article 269 TFEU, the Luxembourg Court can be called upon by the Member State concerned to review only the procedural requirements of Article 7 TEU. In some cases it may also decide that the procedure before it shall also include a hearing which all those concerned shall be given notice to attend.[72] As such, the CJEU's future case law on adherence to the rule of law in the Member States will not be as decisive in facilitating majoritarianism within the EU process.[73]

B. The Crisis Resilience Argument

The above competence-creep concerns take place in the midst of multiple crises in Europe and emerging EU crisis management initiatives. Indeed, the term 'crisis'

---

[72] See for more detail Art 206 of the Rules of Procedure of the Court of Justice regarding requests under Art 269 TFEU, [2012] OJ C 337/42.

[73] See European Parliament Briefing, 'Member States and the rule of law Dealing with a breach of EU values', March 2015, available at www.europarl.europa.eu/RegData/etudes/BRIE/2015/554167/EPRS_BRI(2015)554167_EN.pdf. It is argued inter alia about Art 7 TEU that 'some argue that possible EU intervention needs to be based on a legally founded decision subject to review by the Court of Justice of the EU (CJEU). This would reduce the risk of, on the one hand, discretionary and opportunistic decisions, and on the other, Member States refusing to act against each other. Others claim that legal criteria alone cannot determine whether there is a breach of values, so legitimising EU intervention, and see the more political approach as a step towards democratisation of the Union through its politicisation.'

has a special place in this book. The idea for this book was conceived while multiple crises hit the continent and generated serious financial, security and humanitarian complications. It was also triggered by the EU institutions' responses to these 'multi-crises' which sometimes tested the EU's capacity to do justice to its citizens. Most importantly, while writing this book certain Member States, like Hungary and Poland, began to demonstrate deficiencies as regards the independence of the justice system or other aspects of the rule of law, and for the first time in the course of European integration there were allegations that the EU was confronted with a 'rule of law crisis' of sorts.[74] It is in the backdrop of these systemic challenges in the process of European integration that the instabilities of the rule of law in the EU are confronted and recorded almost as historical artefacts. This is because the respected state of affairs to which the law contributes has been shaken by the crisis of values in the EU triggered by different causes—whether we are facing a growing humanitarian crisis in Europe caused by the migration crisis or a situation involving a government's political interference in the independence and authority of a Member State's constitutional court.[75]

Notwithstanding the influence of the multiple crises in Europe upon the quality of the rule of law in Europe, Habermas has cautioned that we shall not 'become narrowly focused on the immediate expedients for resolving the current banking, currency and debt crisis and as a result [lose] sight of the political dimension.'[76] On a similar note, Kilpatrick challenges the view that 'the EU sovereign debt response is a rule of law crisis because of its incompatibility with the EU Treaty provisions on Economic and Monetary Union.'[77] The argument that through, for instance, the European Stability Mechanism (ESM) and the European Central Bank (ECB)'s Outright Monetary Transactions (OMT) programme the EU institutions have taken a rule-of-law leap has not enjoyed unanimous scholarly support. By contrast, the case for constitutional change through these mechanisms is not proven.[78]

Having said that, we may agree that the varying crises in the continent have exposed the vulnerabilities of the European constitutional project viz its design and procedures. They have also been met with disjointed responses from the Member States. For instance, in light of the migration crisis, a strong case can be made for Member States to ensure more equitable sharing for asylum seekers.

---

[74] von Bogdandy and Sonnevend (n 34).

[75] Kochenov stresses that 'the crisis of values in the EU is very different from other obstacles faced by the EU in the past in a number of important respects, hitting at the very core of what the Union— and its law—is about.' D Kochenov, 'Europe's Crisis of Values' (2014) 48 *Revista catalana de dret públic* 106, 118.

[76] J Habermas, *The Crisis of the European Union: A Response* (Cambridge, Polity, 2012) 3.

[77] C Kilpatrick, 'On the Rule of Law and Economic Emergency: The Degradation of Basic Legal Values in Europe's Bailouts' (2015) 35 (2) *Oxford Journal of Legal Studies* 325. See 326 where Kilpatrick distinguishes this rule of law argument from her own.

[78] B De Witte, 'Euro Crisis Responses and the EU Legal Order: Increased Institutional Variation or Constitutional Mutation' (2015) 11 (3) *European Constitutional Law Review* 434–57.

Reporting on the migration crisis on its website, Human Rights Watch criticises that:

> Border closures and a March 2016 deal with Turkey led to a significant decline in arrivals of migrants and asylum seekers by sea to Greece compared to 2015, while boat migration from North Africa to Italy kept pace with previous years. By mid-September, over 290,000 people had made the crossing since the start of 2016, while more than 3,200 died or went missing in the attempt. European Union countries failed to take collective action to share responsibility equitably for asylum seekers or to create safe and legal channels to Europe.[79]

But even when national governments decide to act together under the EU masthead (eg through initiatives that promote solidarity and a fair sharing of responsibility within the EU), they can resort to unclear and unstable laws and practices or perhaps achieve too little justice, too late.[80] The above are only a few examples that have triggered a case for a rule-of-law deficit at the heart of the EU—a claim of an endemic systemic problem that goes both ways—it affects the Member States as much as it affects the EU. Litigation has been unavoidable in the backdrop of the crises in Europe and handling liability issues as well as damages, fines, settlements and litigation costs has proved a sensitive matter for both the CJEU and national courts. Accordingly, since the crises will inevitably further question the constitutional soundness of the EU project in the court room, the CJEU has to act in a politically sensitive way in order to preserve the balance between the Member States and EU institutions and protect the freedom and well-being of the individual.

Of course the EU cannot offer a panacea for the ills of Europe—whether these are derivative of EU policy (eg the Eurozone crisis) or triggered by external factors (eg the migration crisis). Accordingly, it transpires that the institutional contribution to rule-of-law protection has been constrained or expanded by the circumstances of European integration. There are times when the EU institutions are out of place in protecting the rule of law when it comes to breaches that occur outside areas of conferred competence. But even within their respective jurisdiction, different EU institutions have different mandates. For instance, European judges appear to be far more constrained in the considerations they use as compared to the legislative EU institutions. This was manifest when it came to determining the legal consequences related to post-financial crisis EU measures. These measures called into question the old balance between Member States and EU institutions and raised the prospect of action of 'apolitical' institutions such as the ECB.[81]

---

[79] Human Rights Watch, 'Europe's Migration Crisis', 2016, available from www.hrw.org/tag/europes-migration-crisis.

[80] Douglas-Scott (n 40).

[81] See P Eeckhout and M Waibel, 'The Economic and Monetary Union: Constitutional and Institutional Aspects of the Economic Governance within the EU', UK National Report, FIDE 2014, available from www.ukael.org/associates/associates_60_931463614.pdf; S Peers, 'Towards a New Form of EU Law?: The Use of EU Institutions outside the EU Legal Framework' (2013) 9 *European Constitutional Law Review* 37.

Nonetheless, the CJEU appeared unwilling to interfere with the EU legislative process and decided the relevant cases against the individual applicants.

The unsuccessful challenge against the ECB's stimulus measures is perhaps only one indication of a wider trend.[82] There the CJEU regressed to a narrow interpretation of the law choosing abstention from making political decisions. Clearly, the CJEU does not desire to be seen to be interfering in the EU legislative activity and, with a few exceptions, this has resulted in a looser and more formalist understanding of the rule of law at the EU level. There are other times, however, where the CJEU has adopted a different attitude. Indeed, when the politico-socio-economic milieu mandates a more proactive approach, the Luxembourg judges appear prepared to go to extensive lengths to uphold the rule of law, sometimes marking a retreat from their previously established jurisprudence which appeared detached from social reality and the relevant jurisprudence of national courts in the Member States. For instance, the CJEU has demonstrated a notable concern for ensuring protection of individual rights within the application of the European Arrest Warrant, especially in relation to procedural (fair trial) rights;[83] in absentia trials;[84] detention length;[85] and detention conditions.[86]

No doubt, the above mixture of judicial responses raises questions about what it means for the rule of law to exist in the EU. There is currently certain confusion about the degree Member States can be held to the rule of law and about whether the concept enjoys uniform application in all EU institutions and policies. The rule of law's increasing monitoring is a particularly interesting development in the midst of the general lack of clarity of the obligations that the rule of law imposes upon all actors that partake in European integration; the means available to the EU institutions to ensure observance to the rule of law throughout the duration of Member States' EU membership; and generally speaking, the normative content of

---

[82] See Case C-62/14, *Gauweiler and Others v Deutscher Bundestag* [2015] ECLI:EU:C:2015:400; I Glinavos, 'Whatever It Takes vs Whatever Is Legal: The ECB's Problematic Relationship with the Rule of Law' (21 June 2016) available at SSRN: http://ssrn.com/abstract=2798692.

[83] See Case C-216/14 *Covaci* [2015] ECLI:EU:C:2015:686 on the right to interpretation and translation in criminal proceedings and the right to be informed of the charge.

[84] Case C-108/16 PPU *Dworzecki* [2016] ECLI:EU:C:2016:346. On a sentence handed down in absentia, the CJEU held that the concepts of 'summons in person' and 'official notification by other means' (pursuant to Art 4a(1)(a)(i) of the Framework Decision 2002/584/JHA on the EAW—as amended by Framework Decision 2009/299/JHA) are autonomous concepts of EU law and thus must be interpreted uniformly throughout the EU.

[85] See Case C-237/15 PPU *Lanigan* [2015] ECLI:EU:C:2015:474 on keeping the requested person in detention.

[86] See Joined Cases C-404/15 and C-659/15 PPU *Aranyosi and Căldăraru* [2016] ECLI:EU:C:2016:198 where the CJEU revisited the principle of mutual recognition in the context of the European Arrest Warrant (EAW). By contrast to its previous case law, the CJEU held that the execution of a EAW 'must be deferred if there is a real risk of inhuman or degrading treatment because of the conditions of detention of the person concerned in the Member State where the warrant was issued'. The CJEU added that 'if the existence of that risk cannot be discounted within a reasonable period, the authority responsible for the execution of the warrant must decide whether the surrender procedure should be brought to an end.' See press release No 36/16, Luxembourg, 5 April 2016.

the rule of law as understood at the EU level and as adhered to also by the EU institutions themselves. As highlighted, the EU institutions should set a good example for the Member States' authorities—one thing is to measure others' compliance to the rule of law, another is to have clear rules about holding yourself (charged with the task of upholding the rule of law) to the law itself.

But why is the rule of law good for the EU and why has it gained such prominence recently? What is it thought to do and facilitate in times of crisis? Since the EU occupies a big part of our lives, often promoting itself as a paradigm actor, it is imperative to conceptualise the rule of law as it applies in the EU and identify its morphology—its procedural and substantive dimension. Additionally, it is equally important to identify what value or end it serves. The factual background of a crisis-struck Europe makes a fresh analysis of the rule of law relevant because, to paraphrase Krygier, even if the EU structures are present and are just but the law fails to rule we may be deprived of the rule of law.[87] This is why this book has set out to examine how the components of the rule of law manifest themselves in EU law, how responsibility is spread out at the supranational level and how rule-of-law breaches by the EU institutions and the Member States are disciplined within that 'law'. Beyond these morphological aspects, a rule-of-law discussion at the heart of the EU helps the individual as an addressee of the rule of law to identify 'whether a certain sort of valued state of affairs, to which law contributes in particular ways, exists'[88] or can be reinstated at the EU level. This is so that the rule of law flourishes and the possibility of arbitrary exercise of power (an end embedded in the rule-of-law tradition) is strongly constrained in the EU.

Apart from the multi-crises in Europe, there are other causes to draw attention to the rule of law and its misgivings at the EU level. Some of them fall outside the scope of this book and deserve further study. First and foremost, the rule of law does not always meet the needs of the European polity. On the one hand, EU law has affected national law and has also pushed political and public opinion towards a progressive attitude with regard to, inter alia, pluralism and fundamental rights protection. On the other hand, as mentioned, the rule of law as a distinctive virtue of the EU legal system is not always of a satisfactory standard—sometimes failing to deliver its promise to European citizens, whether that is market building, security or justice. Past studies have also revealed that the rule of law manifests itself differently in diverse areas of EU law making—eg from being a yardstick in EU enlargement policy to enforcing discipline in the application of EU sanctions against individuals and third countries.

Last but not least, the rule of law applies with different intensity in the EU. For instance, there are aspects of EU law, such as the limited jurisdiction of the CJEU in Common Foreign and Security Policy (CFSP) matters, that do not fully comply

---

[87] M Krygier, 'The Rule of Law: Pasts, Presents, and Two Possible Futures' UNSW Law Research Paper No 2016–31, available at SSRN: http://ssrn.com/abstract=2781369.
[88] ibid, 7.

with commonly cited components of the rule of law.[89] The same applies to more complex matters of law, which can be too technical even for lawyers to comprehend. Take for example the ambivalent application of the EU Charter of Fundamental Rights in relation to the European Stability Mechanism (ESM)[90] or to Commission and ECB actions in the context of financial assistance programmes.[91] The above drawbacks may carry serious implications for EU's rule-of-law outcomes, especially with regard to the legal measures enacted by the EU institutions and Member States to respond to future crises in fields where the EU's commitment is already vague or questionable.

III. THE RULE OF LAW AS A STRETCH CONCEPT

An important question that emerges in the debate about the EU rule of law is whether the rule of law in its classic form (ie akin to the rule-of-law state idea) is susceptible to conceptual stretching. In other words, can the rule of law perform a valuable function for the EU? According to Sartori, 'the wider the world under investigation, the more we need conceptual tools that are able to travel'.[92] If the world under investigation is, therefore, the EU legal order and the conceptual tool is the rule of law, then the question is how far can the rule of law 'travel' with the help of the available legal vocabulary. Sartori illustrates that the 'larger the world, the more we have resorted to *conceptual stretching,* or conceptual straining, ie to vague, amorphous conceptualisations.' There, he warns, 'our gains in extensional coverage tend to be matched by losses in connotative precision'.[93]

A Sartorial interpretation of the EU rule of law, therefore, requires some leap of faith. Indeed, the rule of law as it manifests itself in all Member States may enjoy common characteristics that can be 'stretched' and applied across the board. But

---

[89] Cremona notes that 'With two exceptions (Articles 40 TEU and 275 TFEU) the jurisdiction of the CJEU is excluded from CFSP provisions. The exceptions are however significant. For example, the CJEU may need to determine CFSP objectives in order to determine the correct legal basis of a Union act.' See: M Cremona, 'Implementation of the Lisbon Treaty Improving Functioning of the EU: Foreign Affairs', DG For Internal Policies, 2015, PE 5236.475, 7.

[90] The ESM is a crisis resolution mechanism for countries of the euro area. It is an intergovernmental treaty signed by the Euro-area Member States on 2 February 2012. See Treaty establishing the European Stability Mechanism 2012 (Brussels, 02/02/2012); F Fabbrini, 'The Euro-Crisis and the Courts: Judicial Review and the Political Process in Comparative Perspective' (2014) 32 (1) *Berkeley Journal of International Law* 64; B de Witte and T Beukers, 'The Court of Justice approves the creation of the European Stability Mechanism outside the EU legal order: Pringle' (2013) 50 *Common Market Law Review* 805.

[91] Joined Cases C-8/15 P *Ledra Advertising v Commission*, 20 September 2016; Joined Cases C-105/15 P to C-109/15 P *Mallis*, 28 October 2016.

[92] G Sartori, 'Concept Misinformation in Comparative Politics' (1970) 64 (4) *American Political Science Review* 1033, 1034.

[93] ibid, 1034 and 1035 respectively. Conceptual stretching describes the distortions that result when established concepts, such as the rule of law, are introduced to new cases without the required accompanying adaption. As new definitions and meanings are assigned to the concept it begins to distort and 'stretch' until it begins to resemble nothing more than a vague generalisation.

still, these traits, although shared, do not form a rigidly integrated whole. Additionally, they are subject to contemporary politico-socio-economic forces which manifest themselves differently in the Member States. What is more, beyond the existence of common characteristics, the rule of law, as manifested in each Member State, maintains properties which are unique only to that State and are deeply embedded in its constitutional history and tradition. We argue that such 'constitutional properties' are immune from 'stretching' and, although the EU shall be aware and respectful of them, it can hardly adopt them as components of its quasi-federal system.

For instance, although the UK and Germany may agree that the prohibition of arbitrariness is inseparable from the rule of law (as a common trait in their legal orders), we cannot overlook the fact that the English principle of the absolute legislative sovereignty of Parliament has no match in Germany, which instead favours a model of constitutional sovereignty. In other words, in the UK we seem to prefer democratically elected politicians rather than appointed judges to have a final say when it comes to upholding the Constitution.[94] Equally the principle of separation of powers in Germany is not as rigidly expressed in English law and so on. These formal rule of law attributes which are historically embedded in the constitutional heritage of these Member States undermine any effort to conceptualise the EU rule of law as a universal European concept. Finding shared traits between the Member States that can be stretched in order to create a state of (pan-European) rule of law euphony without distorting those States' legal heritage appears to be a more realistic option. It is also in line with the protection that EU law affords to the Member States' constitutional identity under Article 4 (2) TEU.[95]

While we may achieve some constitutional consonance at the EU level by mixing all common points about the rule of law in the Member States (eg relevant to the principle of separation of powers, judicial review, fair application of the law, and protection of fundamental rights) we may not always obtain the perfect nuance. For instance, the EU rule-of-law picture gets 'fuzzier' when we start adding into the mix supranational principles (such as the 'formal' aspects encompassed in the duty of consistent interpretation; the principle of direct effect; the principle of primacy of EU law; and the 'substantive' aspects epitomised in

---

[94] See a relevant discussion in the House of Commons Select Committee, Political and Constitutional Reform—Fourteenth Report, 'Constitutional role of the judiciary if there were a codified constitution—Political and Constitutional Reform', 8 May 2014, available from www.publications.parliament.uk/pa/cm201314/cmselect/cmpolcon/802/80202.htm.

[95] See on constitutional identity: L Besselink, 'National and Constitutional Identity Before and After Lisbon' (2010) 6 (3) *Utrecht Law Review* 36; A von Bogdandy and S Schill, 'Overcoming Absolute Primacy: Respect for National Identity under the Lisbon Treaty' (2011) 48 (5) *Common Market Law Review* 1417; B Guastaferro, 'Beyond the Exceptionalism of Constitutional Conflicts. The Ordinary Functions of the Identity Clause' (2012) 31 (1) *Yearbook of European Law* 263; J Sterck, 'The Nation's Own Genius: A European View of Irish Constitutional Identity' (2014) 37 *Dublin University Law Journal* 109; T Konstadinides, 'Dealing with Parallel Universes: Antinomies of Sovereignty and the Protection of National Identity in European Judicial Discourse' (2015) 34 (1) *Yearbook of European Law* 127.

guaranteeing the effective enjoyment of EU freedoms and rights) which apply within the Member States by virtue of EU law. The bystander's question is a fair one: how do these principles sit next to the Member States' 'constitutional properties' we discussed previously?

As we know, in the UK there is a parliamentary mandate created by the European Communities Act 1972, as interpreted by domestic courts, which instructs state bodies to keep UK legislation in line with the country's EU obligations—inclusive of adherence to principles which are unique to the EU legal order.[96] The emphasis placed on these principles in the course of European integration has triggered criticism about the autonomous encroachment of EU law upon established notions of the rule of law in the Member States. To the critical eye, the alleged 'Europeanisation' of national law has spawned a genre of supranational rule of law which is not only different in scope, but also contains an alternative hierarchy of norms, thus running under its own stream.

The above argument is, at least in theory, rebutted by the language of the Treaty which establishes that the EU still derives authority from the Member States. As such, the principle of EU law primacy does not take effect in an autonomous manner imposed by the EU institutions against the will of national legislatures.[97] As mentioned, in the UK, the country's fundamental constitutional basis still remains the principle of parliamentary sovereignty. At the same time, however, it has to be acknowledged that 'the European Communities Act is a very short Act, and EU law is very complex ... Therefore, there is the European dimension which cannot simply be controlled by the European Communities Act.'[98] This 'European dimension'—whose scope of application is not always predictable—is crucial to our understanding of how the rule of law applies in the Member States. For instance, the UK's compliance with common law principles, and commitments springing out of the EU, is a requirement of the rule of law as understood by national judges and it is binding upon all state bodies. Yet, as we will observe, there are complex technical and jurisdictional arrangements which arise from EU membership and which occasionally generate 'hard cases' where value judgments have to be made at the supranational level. In those 'hard cases' cases, European judges are asked to determine between different versions of law, hence a risk of arbitrariness and the imposition of EU values is not far from sight.

A concern about constitutional impermissible risks of arbitrariness in the Member States can be supported by the fact that EU law does not merely concern a number of objectives inherent in the Treaties but is also about judicial arguments as to what these objectives should entail. Indeed, the CJEU is commonly

---

[96] See *R v Secretary of State for Transport, ex parte Factortame (No 2)* [1990] 3 WLR 818 and *R v Secretary of State for Employment, ex parte Equal Opportunities Commission* [1995] 1 AC 1.

[97] See on the principle of primacy of EU law: Konstadinides, *Division of Powers in European Union Law* (n 66) Ch 3.

[98] See A Bradley's evidence to the European Scrutiny Committee, 'The EU Bill and Parliamentary sovereignty', 25.11.2010, available from.www.publications.parliament.uk/pa/cm201011/cmselect/cmeuleg/633ii/10112502.htm.

confronted with 'hard cases'. The much-discussed *Viking* dicta offers an interesting example of how the CJEU sets out to tackle hard cases: it favoured its classic market template in a horizontal situation of trade unions against the individual building companies and workers.[99] *Viking* was a 'hard case' because, on the one hand, the CJEU had to ensure that free movement was complied with and make sure that national protectionism was avoided at all costs. On the other hand, there were sensitive labour law and social protection issues at stake which tally with substantive notions of the rule of law. In the end, in what can be described as an act of pragmatism, the CJEU chose to uphold free movement law. Besides *Viking*, it has been argued elsewhere that most of the early cases in European integration (where the CJEU had to establish the autonomous legal nature of the EU legal system) were all hard cases.[100]

Revisiting the question about a working definition of the EU rule of law as a stretch concept, the following suggestion can be made: drawing inspiration from Sartori's methodological framework, the researcher can collect a sample of rule of law definitions from different sources; distil their characteristics and class those characteristics and subcomponents. However convenient this may sound, it shall be acknowledged that this method may not always provide most accurate results. For instance, Sartori believes that conceptual classes, regardless of level of generality, must contain at least one clearly specified attribute. A rule-of-law purist may argue that this is particularly difficult to obtain for concepts like the rule of law for which there are multiple competing definitions available. Accordingly, this line of argument suggests that we cannot arrive at a succinct definition of the EU rule of law unless we know precisely what the concept entails in its classic form.

On the other hand, however, we shall acknowledge the existence of common denominators (clearly specified attributes) that all definitions of the rule of law share. We may agree that whether in the form of the Latin *imperium legum* ideal or in its more recent *Rechstaat* legalism, the rule of law constitutes an objective— a measuring stick. It is often presented as a concept that serves several traditions under a similar name and as a value which denotes certain formal and substantive qualities about the law. For instance, the rule of law generally advocates that the law has to be a safeguard against arbitrary governance providing that there must be equal justice before the law. It is akin to judicial independence and central to protecting justice from the executive's interference (inclusive of fairness of the political process).[101] It is also committed to fundamental rights protection and

---

[99] Case C-438/05 *Viking* [2007] ECR I-10779. See for comment: ACL Davies, 'One Step Forward, Two Steps Back? The *Viking* and *Laval* Cases in the ECJ' (2008) 37 (2) *Industrial Law Journal* 126.

[100] E Herlin-Karnell and T Konstadinides, 'The Rise and Expressions of Consistency in EU Law: Legal and Strategic Implications for European Integration' (2013) 15 *Cambridge Yearbook of European Legal Studies* 139.

[101] See Lord Thomas of Cwmgiedd, Lord Chief Justice of England and Wales, 'The Judiciary, the Executive and Parliament: Relationships and the Rule of Law', 01.12.2014, available from www.judiciary.gov.uk/wp-content/uploads/2014/12/institute-for-government.pdf, 3.

legal enforcement (inclusive of substantive human rights) and due process (even in times of emergency). Last, but not least, the rule of law is a promoter of democratic government and justice.

Likewise, adherence to the rule of law ensures a particular state of destination—one characterised by certainty, consistency and protection against abuse of power. It is a means of enabling the individual to plan her life productively and securely. We may agree that this is 'more or less' what the rule of law is about—ie certain requirements of the law which are crucial in establishing its legitimacy and ensuring its observance. Equally, the above characteristics would hardly be absent from any liberal democratic legal system in Europe and beyond. As former Advocate General Jacobs pointed out, 'the rule of law embodies certain values which seem, at least in Europe, widely accepted as essential to modern social and political life; and that we shall be able to identify some of those values.'[102] Yet the mere existence of these attributes does not guarantee their adherence. It would be unrealistic, for instance, to think that the common characteristics identified in national legal orders are interpreted in the same manner and are observed with the same intensity and at the same moment in time by all Member States. What is more, the more demanding the EU rule-of-law definition becomes by adding a multiplicity of components and their subcategories, the less operational it becomes. This is not least because of the potential resistance it may encounter in the Member States it addresses.

As the phrase goes, the law in the books is often different from the law in practice. There are variables, such as inequality, corruption and weak and dysfunctional institutions that are present in some Member States and can degrade the rule of law despite the good intentions manifest in the narrative of their national Constitutions or their pledge to the EU to respect the values listed in Article 2 TEU. For instance, despite pre-accession conditionality and tailored cooperation and verification mechanisms, the EU has been unsuccessful in assisting the management of corruption in certain Member States like Bulgaria.[103] Of course, this is a symptom often found in federal regimes and does not negate the EU's collective adherence to the rule of law merely because one of its limbs defaults. In this regard, it is important to examine whether the EU rule of law (as enforced by the other 'non-defaulting' Member States who agree on a set of common rule-of-law characteristics) has a corrective function vis-a-vis restoring justice in the 'defaulting' Member States.

Furthermore, we need to be mindful of the limits of the rule of law as a value which make it hardly an enforceable panacea for all the problems that the EU is currently facing. This is particularly relevant, for example, when ascertaining the rights of individuals in the context of the EU economic adjustment programmes, and the protection of these rights in claims litigated by private individuals against

---

[102] Jacobs. *The Sovereignty of Law. The European Way* (n 11) 8.
[103] S Pavlovska-Hilaiel, 'The EU's Losing Battle Against Corruption in Bulgaria' (2015) 7 *Hague Journal on the Rule of Law* 199.

their state or against the EU institutions. Despite the fact that the EU rule of law is primarily based on the idea of a complete system of legal remedies and procedures designed to ensure judicial review of the legality of EU acts, the CJEU has largely left the matter of liability in the hands of national courts. On their part, national courts have been reluctant to impose liability on national authorities for measures adopted as part of the relevant financial assistance programmes.[104] This is despite criticism that the austerity policies have had a far-reaching impact on human rights in the debt-laden Member States. These include adverse effects on minimum wages, encroachment on pension systems, collective bargaining, aggressive privatisation, and cuts in social security schemes, education and health care. The extent to which these effects have been adjudicated by courts is relevant to the EU rule-of-law repositories.

But still, as Sartori and especially Krygier (speaking about the rule of law) submit about scientific enquiry, 'the proper way to *begin* in thinking about the rule of law is to ask what value or ideal is particularly associated with it, what is its distinctive, specific "virtue" as Raz once put it ..., why we should care about it.'[105] In particular, Krygier's normative claim of reduction of the possibility of arbitrary exercise of power and the institutionalisation of power-restraints is attractive as a starting point viz providing a useful compendium about the central target to the rule of law, tempering power and doing justice to all actors that partake in the polity—'legal justice' that is.[106] Fixing our gaze to the target of the rule of law rather than the forms that it takes ('thin' or 'thick') may enhance our understanding of its substantive (and often self-fulfilling) objectives at the EU level whether that is to promote integration between European nations, protect the mobility rights of EU citizens, enhance security in the continent and counter terrorism or augment the EU's global profile as a trade and civilian power. We shall of course temper our approach with a dose of realism viz the broader context from which the EU rule of law emerges and to which it currently responds and tread accordingly.

We shall conclude this chapter by acknowledging that while recognising the value of the rule of law we often tend to be skeptical as to its achievability. Yet we are all up for it. We take the view that the rule of law has to be adhered to and enforced not because it is capable of giving us all the answers we need to hear ex post and ex ante but more as a matter of principle—ie in order to obtain 'the law's

---

[104] On litigation regarding the compatibility of macroeconomic adjustment programmes with fundamental rights see A Karatzia and T Konstadinides, 'Who is Responsible? Effective Judicial Protection in the Context of EU Macroeconomic Adjustment Programmes and Austerity Measures' (2017) copy with the authors.

[105] M Krygier, 'Still a Rule of Law Guy' (2013) *Recht der Werkelijkheid* 1, 3, available at http://ssrn.com/abstract=2311858.

[106] M Krygier, 'Tempering Power' in M Adams et al (eds), *Bridging Idealism and Realism in Constitutionalism and Rule of Law* (Cambridge, Cambridge University Press, 2016). S Douglas-Scott, *The Law After Modernity* (Oxford, Hart Publishing, 2013) 220. Douglas-Scott notes at 227 that 'Human rights operate both as constraints on power and as preserving shields for individual autonomy and liberty—thus also fulfilling the essential functions of the rule of law.'

promise to do justice'.[107] The rule of law is important if nothing else as an ideal in the current period of multiple crises which have discredited the EU's neo-liberal paradigm. Beyond idealism, we accept that the ability of EU law (and national law) to do justice to every individual affected by its laws and regulations applicable in its territory is simply impractical and unattainable.[108] In the context of European integration we acknowledge the difference between absolute and relative gains and claim that it is often the latter that have to be made before states choose to cooperate at the EU level. This is an ideological precondition often made by the international relations theory of realism. While realism's main focus is based on security and defence policy—the main justification for European integration according to realists—it does gives us some insight about the politicisation of the rule of law at the EU level.[109]

---

[107] Douglas-Scott, ibid 220.

[108] See S Douglas-Scott, 'The Problem of Justice in the EU' in J Dickson and P Eleftheriadis (eds), *The Philosophical Foundations of EU Law* (Oxford, Oxford University Press, 2012).

[109] See for instance in the context of EU external relations: T Dyson and T Konstadinides, *European Defence Cooperation in EU Law and International Relations Theory* (Basingstoke, Palgrave Macmillan, 2013).

2

Conceptualising the EU Rule of Law

I. INTRODUCTION

THE RULE OF law is recognised internationally as the foundation of political stability—it has been characterised as 'the preeminent political ideal of contemporary Western liberal democracies, notwithstanding disagreement about what this ideal means.'[1] But still, it is difficult to speak of measuring the rule of law or degrees of the rule of law until we have defined what it is and what it is not. At the same time, as some commentators have noted, we have to live with the fact that the rule of law suffers from certain conceptual ambiguity.[2] Our additional challenge in this book is that the rule of law is a concept that has 'travelled' considerable distance (from the national to the regional and global level). Not only has the rule of law as a national construct 'travelled' but it has also been 'stretched' to such a degree that it is now inextricably connected to the European and international legal sphere.[3] This chapter, therefore, serves as a flashback to the rule-of-law narrative. It looks, in particular, into the origins of the rule of law relationship with the idea of reduction of arbitrariness and the historical attempt to incorporate political morality (formal and substantive aspects) into its meaning. It then turns to examine its adjustment or 'stretching'—ie the rule of law's connotative distortion that derives from the effort to fit it within the global and EU legal order by widening its intension.

The emphasis on the universality of the rule of law is not a new trend. Already in 1932, Jennings contended that the rule of law 'is either common to all nations or does not exist'.[4] Although this view may be convenient today to EU integrationists, we have to remind the reader that in international activities the rule of law did not figure centrally until probably the late 1980s. Especially in Europe, the collapse of Communism became a catalyst for the rule of law. Not only new democratic

---

[1] B Tamanaha, *Law as a Means to an End: Threat to the Rule of Law* (Cambridge, Cambridge University Press, 2010) 130.

[2] J Møller and S Skaaning, *The Rule of Law: Definitions, Measures, Patterns and Causes* (London, Palgrave, 2014) Ch 1.

[3] G Sartori, 'Concept Misformation in Comparative Politics' (1970) 64 (4) *The American Political Science Review* 1033. Sartori warns against over-extension or the 'sea of empirical and theoretical messiness' that may result from 'conceptual stretching'.

[4] WI Jennings, 'The Report on Ministers' Powers' (1932) 10 *Public Administration* 333, 343.

constitutional arrangements substituted the previous instrumentalist approach to law in Central and Eastern Europe, but more notably, the Constitution-making process that took place in the 1990s in these countries was driven by the political incentive to accede to the EU as a 'post-national constellation' of states and people.[5] At the same time, however, although it can be argued that the rule of law was early imprinted in EU constitutional consciousness, it was not always textually obvious. More specifically, it was not until 1997 that the Treaty of Amsterdam expressly provided in former Article 6 (1) Treaty on European Union (TEU) that 'the Union is founded on the principles of liberty, democracy, respect for human rights and fundamental freedoms, and the rule of law, principles which are common to the Member States.' This is primarily why, prior to our analysis of the rule of law as a central concept in the EU legal narrative, we shall provide a warm-up into the origins and development of the rule of law in the light of the distinction between law and arbitrary power as a political process at the national level.

The advancing analysis involves a distinction between different styles of reasoning and theories of law. It will serve to reinforce existing knowledge and establish certain interesting parallels for the EU rule of law. For instance, we will aggregate some contradicting views and analyses which are relevant to the development of the EU rule of law inclusive of the desirability of moral criteria of legality as components of a legal system—or simply put, arguments about the justice or injustice of law. The overview provided in this chapter, which is by no means exhaustive, will also venture to provide a summary of the evolution of the international rule of law as a prelude to our discussion about the EU rule of law which 'is at the crossroads of different constitutional traditions.'[6] We will observe some diverse approaches to the EU rule of law which project varied images of the concept: an instrument of judicial review; and a theoretical device that provides insight to the EU constitutional project at a more abstract level viz the normative role of the EU as a community founded on justice and fairness.

II. THE RULE OF LAW, NOT THE RULE OF MAN

This section will discuss two main rule-of-law characteristics related to the purpose and characteristics of the concept: first, we will discuss the use-value or point of existence of the rule of law. Our focus will be on the subordination of arbitrary power. Law is not arbitrary if it is not discriminatory and safeguards the interests of its addressees and it is subject to their consent and control—in other words,

[5] See L Grenfell, *Promoting the Rule of Law in Post-Conflict States* (Cambridge, Cambridge University Press, 2013) 19; W Sadurski et al, *Spreading Democracy and the Rule of Law? The Impact of EU Enlargement on the Rule of Law, Democracy and Constitutionalism in Post-Communist Legal Orders* (Dordrecht, Springer, 2006) 194.

[6] M Fernandez Esteban, The Rule of Law in the European Constitution (The Hague, Kluwer, 1999) 3.

the common good. We will then look into the rule of law as a blend of both formal and substantive characteristics whose delineation is still ongoing amongst theorists.

A. The Rule of Law as a Restraint on Arbitrary Power

i. Background History

The reduction of arbitrariness illustrates one of the important values that the rule of law serves. According to Krygier it is the key aim of the rule of law.[7] The reduction of arbitrariness has always been at the epicentre of the history of the rule of law. Arbitrariness explains the state of affairs where the will of the power-wielders grows into the sole justification for the exercise of power. Its reduction as a condition that has to be satisfied for a legal system to flourish, is reminiscent of the principle of legal certainty—i.e. the law must provide its subjects with the ability to regulate their conduct in order to protect themselves from the arbitrary use of the state power. The first ideas of normative reduction of arbitrariness can be traced in the writings of Greek and Roman philosophers as well as to the British philosophers, and the French Enlightenment. In its most basic form, it embodies the rule-of-law principle that no one is above the law. Indeed, the Aristotelian 'government by laws and not by men' is a crucial underpinning of a society free from arbitrary rule.[8] Aristotle's much cited maxim 'the rule of law not the rule of men' set the sails for the development of the rule of law as a basis for formal equality and as a restraint to governmental authority.[9] It was an absolute theory of law whose traces can be found in the way states initially adopted the rule-of-law concept in their legal system.

Focusing on the reduction of arbitrary rule as the main purpose of the rule of law, Cicero, writing almost three centuries after Aristotle, was particularly critical of arbitrariness in relation to judicial discretion.[10] His *omnes legum servi sumus ut liberi esse possumus*, openly translated as 'we serve the law to be free', became almost synonymous with the ideal of liberty under the law (ie we are only free when the law rules). It was not, however, until a thousand years later that the rule

---

[7] M Krygier, 'The Rule of Law: An Abuser's Guide' in András Sajó (ed), *The Dark Side of Fundamental Rights* (The Hague, Eleven International Publishing, 2006).

[8] BZ Tamanaha, *On the Rule of Law: History, Politics, Theory* (Cambridge, Cambridge University Press, 2004). Tamanaha provides a very useful overview of the history of the rule of law tracing its origins back to classical Greek natural law theory according to which the law was consistent with virtue and, accordingly, good laws reigned supreme. See also M Loughlin, *Swords and Scales: An Examination of the Relationship Between Law and Politics* (Oxford, Hart Publishing, 2000) Ch 5.

[9] Aristotle, Politics III and XVI, 1257a: 'it is more proper that law should govern than any one of the citizens'.

[10] This expression influenced inter alia Voltaire, Montesquieu, and Kant and also featured in Hayek's writings, particularly, FA Hayek, *The Constitution of Liberty* (Chicago, The University of Chicago Press, 1978) 462.

of law discourse took root. Characteristically, Tamanaha provides a sequence of events that helped the West untangle from the Dark Ages.

> The rediscovery of Aristotle's works (which had been preserved by the Muslims) and the Justinian Code, in the twelfth and thirteenth centuries, coincided with a substantial rise in the number of educated men—the founding of the University of Bologna (for law) and the University of Paris, the beginnings of Oxford and Cambridge Universities, and others.[11]

As the application of the Roman canon during medieval times attempted to restrain the essentially arbitrary punishment of the Dark Ages, non-arbitrariness became entangled with the use-value of the rule of law—an emerging concept in philosophical tradition. Likewise, the scholastic Thomas Aquinas embraced Aristotelian eudemonism and combined it with Christian theology. He became the classic proponent of Christian natural law theory predicated on the axiom that a law is only just if it promotes the common good as its purpose.[12] The common good can be briefly defined as the sum of conditions that allow individuals to reach their fulfilment. Likewise, for Aquinas, moral virtues were vital to reaching *eudemonia*, not the least as motivators to seeking it. Likewise, legislation for the 'common good' constituted for Aquinas a moral concern. But still, the rule of law was revived at a time where the arrogation of ultimate power by popes and kings was commonplace—both unrestrained and autocratic in the use of authority. Still, the ideal of the 'common good' was somewhat mitigated with the monarchs' oath to power which included an express allegiance to the 'law'. Enforceable restraints to the powers of the monarchs were included in various feudal documents forced upon them by the privileged noble class.[13] Perhaps the most celebrated charter viz a factual reduction of arbitrariness is the Magna Carta, or the 'Great Charter', signed in 1215 between King John and the barons of Medieval England.[14]

The Magna Carta was created as a break on arbitrary rule. As it is well-documented, Clause 39 (later renumbered to Clause 29) of the Magna Carta is the ancestor of many due process clauses.[15] Hence, although the Magna Carta was a short-lived solution to a feudal dispute between the king and his barons, it is captivating for what it meant at the time—ie a curb on arbitrary royal authority. In the next 400 years or so it transcended its original context and became a key reference point for jurists who successfully distilled a number of substantive restrictions

---

[11] See Tamanaha (n 8) 18.

[12] Aquinas' axiom on natural law and natural rights was revived by John Finnis' 'neo-naturalism'. See J Finnis, *Natural Law and Natural Rights* (Oxford, Clarendon Press, 1980).

[13] ibid 22.

[14] The Magna Carta recently completed its 800th anniversary. See for information: *The Magna Carta Project*, available from http://magnacarta.cmp.uea.ac.uk.

[15] It stressed that that 'no free man is to be arrested, or imprisoned, or disseised, or outlawed, or exiled, or in any other way ruined, nor will we go against him or send against him, except by the lawful judgment of his peers or by the law of the land.' See for a short summary of the Magna Carta: AE Dick Howard, *Magna Carta: Text & Commentary* (Charlottesville, University of Virginia Press, 1998). For further reflection see: D Carpenter, *Magna Carta* (London, Penguin, 2015).

from Clause 39 and 40 such as the idea of procedural due process, fair trial and access to justice. For Coke, for instance, the Magna Carta provided the necessary ammunition to oppose the Stuart claims of royal prerogative by conceptualising the idea of the mythical ancient Constitution (or customary law) of which the Magna Carta allegedly formed a significant part.[16]

The Magna Carta paved the way for further developments in English law in subsequent reigns. In particular, the Glorious Revolution and the English Bill of Rights of 1689 established a representative government and made parliament more powerful than the king. Especially, Article 9 of the Bill of Rights 1689 which precludes the impeaching or questioning in any court of debates or proceedings in parliament still constitutes 'one of the pillars of constitutional settlement which established the rule of law in England in the 17th century.'[17] Article 9 of the Bill of Rights has also shaped the constitutional relationship between the UK and EU law, which can only be established by common law in the light of domestic statutes and not by the Court of Justice of the European Union (CJEU) holding, for instance, that national courts are obliged to scrutinise parliamentary process in order to comply with EU secondary legislation.[18]

Needless to say that the legacy of the Magna Carta regarding the idea of limited government was not confined to the UK. The original foundational precepts of the Magna Carta and, in particular Clause 39, grew over time and were captured, inter alia, in the French Declaration of Rights of Man and Citizen of 1789, which is part of the French Constitution, as well as the Fifth and the Fourteenth Amendments to the American Constitution which limit the power of the federal and state governments to discriminate by placing emphasis on inherent rights. In more recent years, references to the Magna Carta featured in cases before the US Supreme Court, especially those concerning habeas corpus petitions submitted by the prisoners at Guantánamo Bay.[19] Indeed, the Magna Carta embodied the minimum content of the rule of law—that both the government as well as the governed are bound by the law. Yet, according to Pocock, Coke's typical common law view of the mythical ancient Constitution was evidence of ignorance of continental legal scholarship nourished in the civil law tradition.[20] As such,

---

[16] DM Jones, 'Sir Edward Coke and the Interpretation of Lawful Allegiance in Seventeenth-century England' (1986) 7 (2) *History of Political Thought* 321.

[17] See *R (HS2, Buckingham County Council and others) v Secretary of State for Transport* [2014] UKSC 3, at 203. See for a comprehensive case comment of *HS2*: P Craig, 'Constitutionalising Constitutional Law: HS2' (2014) 3 *Public Law* 373.

[18] See P Craig, *UK, EU and Global Administrative Law* (Cambridge, Cambridge University Press, 2015) 285–91.

[19] See for instance the strong reference to the Magna Carta made by Justice Kennedy in his opinion in *Boumediene v Bush* 553 US 723 (2008) relating to detention at Guantánamo Bay. He used the Magna Carta as an example to stress the point of illegal imprisonment of foreign nationals outside the US as sanctioned by the Military Commissions Act. Available from: https://supreme.justia.com/cases/federal/us/553/723/#annotation.

[20] JGA Pocock, *The Ancient Constitution and the Federal Law* (Cambridge, Cambridge University Press, 1987).

the Magna Carta's emotional and moral value was deemed to be greater than its legal or constitutional one.

While British legal mentality was divided between the authority of the statute as opposed to common law constitutionalism,[21] continental political theorists enquired about the compatibility of the rule of law with sovereign legislative authority and individual freedom under the law. Especially during the age of the Enlightenment, liberalism became a prominent ideology utilising passions for common good and the rule of law as opposed to absolutism in government. Variant conceptions of liberalism were introduced by some of the greatest thinkers of the seventeenth and eighteenth century such as Kant (on moral theory—categorical imperative), Locke (on authority circumscribed by law and moral community);[22] Montesquieu (on constitutional design and the separation of powers)[23] and Rousseau (on general will and the social contract) whose ideas can still challenge our contemporary and often instrumental understanding of the rule of law.[24] Despite their internal variations, liberals converged on the view that rationality, personal liberty and enforceability of rights were key to political obligation, in other words, the justification for obedience to the law. Any arbitrary interference constituted a limitation of liberty.

The rule-of-law discourse continued through the late eighteenth and early nineteenth century to unravel the riddle of what makes the law valid—whether it was created by the correct authority and whether that authority followed the appropriate procedures. Divine law and natural law became firmly separated from positive law. This development spawned 'positivism'—a meta-theory about theories of law which supported that law is essentially a matter of social fact. As such, its content must be determined by social sources such as legislation, custom, the Constitution and judicial decisions. Aloof from the ethical content of legal justice, positivism gathered momentum in the writings of utilitarian thinkers such as Bentham, Mill and Austin.[25] The latter developed the rather controversial 'command theory of law' which portrayed the law in terms of power—this saw the force of law as residing in commands backed by the threat of sanctions rather than in an acceptance of the sovereign's authority.[26] As such it is not surprising that Austin's theory was criticised as forcible, arbitrary and exclusionary—placing the mantel of the common good to one side in favour of conformity with rules. Kelsen, for instance, criticised that 'a command is binding, not because the individual commanding has

---

[21] On classical common law theory see the works of Edward Coke, Matthew Hale, and William Blackstone. See for a summary, M Davies, *Asking the Law Question* (Pyrmont, Thomson Reuters, 2002) Ch 2.

[22] J Dunn, *The Political Thought of John Locke* (Cambridge, Cambridge University Press, 1969).

[23] AM Cohler (ed), *Montesquieu, The Spirit of the Laws* (Cambridge, Cambridge University Press, 1989).

[24] JJ Rousseau, *The Social Contract* (London, Penguin, 1968).

[25] J Gardner, 'Legal Positivism: 5 1/2 Myths' (2001) 46 *American Journal of Jurisprudence* 199.

[26] J Austin, *The Province of Jurisprudence Determined and the Uses of the Study of Jurisprudence* (London, Weidenfeld & Nicolson, 1954).

an actual superiority in power, but because he is "authorized" or "empowered" to issue commands of a binding nature.'[27]

Modern legal positivism mutated further into the twentieth century maintaining its focus on what the law *is* (not what it *ought to be*) while, at the same time, growing more sophisticated. For instance, Austin's ideas of a sanction-backed sovereign command were also put to the test by Hart's rule of recognition.[28] Conversely, legal positivism was contested by Fuller, a natural law pragmatist, who focused on the narrow questions of internal morality and the reduction of arbitrariness. He laid down a set of precepts of legality that have to be satisfied for the existence of a legal system and claimed that the rule of law comprises a moral ideal. Accordingly, guaranteeing that laws are public, clear, non-contradictory, proscriptive and reliable are essential characteristics of a legal system that allows citizens to govern their interactions with one another with reference to rules.[29] Fuller contended that once these formal requirements are satisfied, the law can have any content. Additionally, he advanced that in the absence of any substantive concerns from the formal rule of law an instrumentalist understanding of law will prevail.

Such an instrumentalist understanding was developed later by the so-called 'realists' who inter alia developed their own theory about the judicial process.[30] In short, realists believed that judicial decision-making is a creative activity and as such judges 'legislate'. Fuller repudiated the realist paradigm, ie that the law is to be found in judicial practice and rejected the argument that legal theory shall be based on empiricism. His exposition of ideas was inspired by the illegality of the Nazi arbitrary and tyrannical regime, which in effect kept the democratic Constitution and ruled exclusively by invoking a state of exception for the sake of national security. Fuller's fidelity to the legality approach initiated a fruitful two-man debate with Hart about whether law and morality should be intertwined or rather mutually exclusive (as suggested by Hart's positive approach).[31] In the end, as it has been documented, Fuller's legal interpretation guided by the purposes of legal rules prevailed over Hart's explicit textualism. The latter's strict positivist model provided an unrealistic account about how judges decide cases since judges generally take the purposes of legal rules into account when applying them.[32]

---

[27] H Kelsen, *General Theory of Law and State* (A Wedberg trans, New Jersey, The Lawbook Exchange, 2009) 31. See also L Vinx, 'Austin, Kelsen, and the Model of Sovereignty: Notes on the History of Modern Legal Positivism' in M Freeman and P Mindus (eds), *The Legacy of John Austin's Jurisprudence* (Berlin, Springer, 2013).

[28] HLA Hart, *The Concept of Law* (Oxford, Oxford University Press, 1961).

[29] L Fuller, *The Morality of Law* (New Haven CT, Yale University Press, 1969).

[30] TM Benditt, *Law as Rule and Principle: Problems of Legal Philosophy* (California, Stanford University Press, 1978) Ch 2: 'Legal Realism and Rules of Law' 22.

[31] HLA Hart, 'Positivism and the Separation of Law and Morals' (1957) 71 *Harvard Law Review* 593; Lon L Fuller, 'Positivism and Fidelity to Law–A Reply to Professor Hart' (1957) 71 *Harvard Law Review* 630; P Cane (ed), *The Hart-Fuller Debate in the Twenty-First Century* (Oxford, Hart Publishing, 2010) 157.

[32] A Street, 'Judicial Review and the Rule of Law: Who is in Control?' The Constitution Society, 2013, available at www.consoc.org.uk/wp-content/uploads/2013/12/J1446_Constitution_Society_Judicial_Review_WEB-22.pdf.

As discussed in this historical overview, the broad requirement of non-arbitrary interference has occupied a large part of legal history pertaining to the rule of law. Indeed, most theories about the rule of law converge in that they examine the relationship between arbitrariness and compliance dependence as well as the protection of the individual against arbitrary interference by the state with her right to liberty and equality. The ideal of the rule of law—that governmental action should be controlled by known rules preventing arbitrariness—is something which has guided legal and political practice at the EU level.

ii. The EU against Arbitrary Exercise of Power

The rule of law as a restraint on power's arbitrariness provides a useful, although not exhaustive, doctrinal compendium about the central target to the rule of law in the EU—tempering power, promoting a just legal system within which individuals are adequately protected and enjoy fundamental rights and freedoms under the EU Treaties.[33] Yet, our focus on arbitrariness can be criticised for not addressing directly the legitimating capacity of EU institutions, which—to borrow from Krygier—are often treated as 'ends in themselves'.[34] A further criticism towards an arbitrariness-centric approach to the rule of law is that the interconnection between the rule of law and the notion of the common good 'only makes sense under a moralistic definition' while 'a robust enough notion of consent or control is not available.'[35]

Against the above criticisms it has been contended that the reduction of arbitrariness encompasses the idea that governance is restrained by some 'persuasive, rational, [and] impartial justification'. Hence 'to reduce arbitrariness is to enhance legitimating capacity.'[36] If we side with this view, EU law is only legitimate when its content corresponds to standards of justice and a conception of the common good that all EU citizens can reasonably be expected to agree by virtue of their adherence to the EU as a political community. Such an approach requires elaboration in a number of directions regarding, for instance, the role of institutional design (inclusive of processes that embrace incentives for generating public commitment and legitimisation) and the interaction of EU law and national norms that express certain moral, ethical or cultural values. These are key factors in facilitating human interaction and orientation towards the EU as well as fostering understanding of what is 'common good'.[37]

---

[33] M Krygier, 'Tempering Power' in M Adams et al (eds), *Bridging Idealism and Realism in Constitutionalism and Rule of Law* (Cambridge, Cambridge University Press, 2016).

[34] M Krygier, 'The Rule of Law: Legality, Teleology, Sociology' in G Palombella and N Walker (eds), *Relocating the Rule of Law* (Oxford, Hart Publishing, 2009) 58.

[35] A Sharon, 'Domination and the Rule of Law' in D Sobel et al (eds), *Oxford Studies in Political Philosophy* Vol 2 (Oxford, Oxford University Press, 2016) 145.

[36] K Soltan, 'A Social Science that does not Exist' in J Witteveen et al (eds), *Rediscovering Fuller: Essays on Implicit Law and Institutional Design* (Amsterdam, Amsterdam University Press, 1999) 404.

[37] F De Witte, 'Sex, Drugs & EU Law: The Recognition of Ethical and Moral Diversity in Europe' (2013) 50 (6) *Common Market Law Review* 1545. De Witte suggests that 'Such values, which might

It arises, therefore, that although the reduction of arbitrary exercise of power forms a reasonable justification as to why we need the rule of law as a driver in European integration, the prohibition of exercise of arbitrary rule as key to common good may not always serve us well. The problem is that arbitrariness is often broadly construed. For instance, the criticism of regional arbitrariness in the EU has become a standard of reference and is often not confined to specific examples in which arbitrary interference has been damaging. To use a classic example, it is often abstractly argued that the delimitation of competences at the EU level forms an illegitimate exercise—endorsed and imposed by the CJEU ('a rogue court') and its teleological interpretation of EU law—which has resulted in an incessant erosion of the sovereign authority of Member States.[38] This contention tries to stress the point that the rule of law has to be adhered to by the EU as the legal principle that the law should govern its legal order, as opposed to being governed by arbitrary decisions of individual EU institutions or Member States.[39] It also highlights the original meaning of the rule of law as a fundamental condition of the existence of legal systems. Yet, it falls short of offering constructive recommendations about the kind of procedural steps that need to be taken in order to reinforce a sense of constitutional order in the EU viz arbitrary interference—the path towards the common good.

What is more, the reduction of arbitrariness may be more relevant to the EU institutions exercising their legislative power over the Member States and their citizens. Conversely, it may not be as helpful an attribute in the context of examining a Member State's adherence to the EU rule of law. To be more specific, whereas the rule of law for the EU is often framed in terms of the principle of conferral, in the case of the Member States it is perceived in terms of compliance with the EU *acquis* (ie recognition of the authority of EU law to rule and compliance with EU law norms).[40] So are there two rules of law even within the EU? We need to be clear at this point that the EU's internal rule of law might be different to what is expected from the Member States. As such, we may agree that the idea of reduction of arbitrary exercise of power as a central tenet of the EU rule of law has to be

range from drugs policy to the patentability of human cells, and from the consumption of seal meat to abortion, have something important in common: they ascribe a normative quality to a particular type of life, and typically reflect a communal, political understanding of what is "good".

[38] R Thompson QC, 'Michael Gove's "Misleading Attacks" on the EU Court of Justice', *The Times*, 23 June 2016, available from www.thetimes.co.uk/article/michael-goves-misleading-attacks-on-the-eu-court-of-justice-90wstv3ft.

[39] See also for a short academic reflection on the CJEU's teleology: P Lindseth, 'The Quest for EU Reform after Brexit: Changes to the Role and Doctrines of the European Court of Justice', 24 June 2016, available from https://eutopialaw.com/2016/06/24/the-quest-for-eu-reform-after-brexit-changes-to-the-role-and-doctrines-of-the-european-court-of-justice/#more-2774. Lindseth argues that 'the Court should abandon its traditional "teleological" method of interpretation that seeks to maximize the powers of European institutions. This step would be especially important in augmenting judicial policing of the bounds of authority delegated to the supranational level.'

[40] Still, however, rule of law critiques of the Euro-crisis measures are not necessarily competence based. See for instance: C Barnard, 'The Financial Crisis and the Euro Plus Pact: A Labour Lawyer's Perspective' (2012) 41 (1) *Industrial Law Journal* 98.

adjusted in order to imply something meaningful that can be acted upon by the Member States—eg reducing the capacity of their executives to act independently out of whim, constitutional caprice, paying little or no regard for hard-earned EU legal values and with little consideration towards their counterparts.

As we will discuss in Chapter 5, the rule of law as a means of reducing the arbitrary exercise of power is important for Member States like Hungary or Poland where it can place their respective governments on check and reverse decisions concerning the retirement age of judges, and stopping the arbitrary reassignment of cases between courts. Yet we also have to appreciate that there are Member States that may allegedly jeopardise the EU rule of law without acting arbitrarily in the narrow or broader sense. Member States like Greece have been singled out as showing poor fiscal performance and other 'serious deficiencies' in terms of compliance with EU asylum law and the protection of rights under the European Convention on Human Rights (ECHR).[41] At the risk of over-generalising, there are 'failing states' in Europe with internal and endogenous problems, related to the maintenance of law and order, which have produced cross-border impact. The ideal of reduction of arbitrariness as a means of answering why we need the rule of law in the EU may be in short supply there.

While the idea of reasonable apprehension of the exercise of power is far from perfect as the main goal of the EU rule of law, it is useful in orienting ourselves towards adopting a solution-based approach against the political danger of arbitrariness. It follows that the EU rule of law shall contribute to the free interaction of citizens in pursuit of the European *res publica*. If positive laws or their enforcement serve other purposes there is a rule-of-law deficit that serves arbitrary power. Indeed, the 'common good' has been encapsulated in the idea of the Constitution as a basic framework for guaranteeing fundamental rights. As Burke remarked, the British Constitution is the legal framework aimed at the common good—'our island which uses and restrains its subject Sea'.[42] It can also be argued that the EU Treaty was also drafted with the European common good in mind—developing representative democratic institutions; offering the EU citizens an 'area of freedom, security and justice'; encouraging the judicial application of the EU Charter of Fundamental Rights; linking the rule of law to the principles of democratic governance and human rights protection. These developments have taken place albeit criticisms that in Europe the common good ideal has turned out to be only a temporary good and has recently receded into the background, replaced in the foreground by functional and instrumental impulses, especially in the light of the EU multiple crises.

---

[41] *MSS v Greece and Belgium*, no 30696/09, 21 January 2010; *AA v Greece*, no 12186/08, 22 July 2010. Most recently the new media reforms in Greece have raised concerns over state interference in the affairs of the free press and media industry. See S Michalopoulos,' New Media Law Sparks Intense Controversy in Athens', *EurActiv*, 26 January 2016, available from www.euractiv.com/section/digital/news/new-media-law-sparks-intense-controversy-in-athens/.

[42] See quote from S Burgess, in P McGrail et al, *Together for the Common Good: Towards a National Conversation* (London, SCM Press, 2015) 70.

B. Conceptions on What the Rule of Law is

i. Background to the 'Thin–Thick' Dichotomy

As mentioned briefly in Chapter 1, there are two basic types of rule-of-law conception—a 'thin' (formal) and 'thick' (substantive) one which have contributed to understanding the rule of law. They are often antagonistic categories which have been criticised for 'wrongly suggest[ing] an irreconcilable or inimical relation which does not in fact exist.'[43] Having said that, the 'thin–thick' dichotomy is indicative of the inclination to taxonomise the complex characteristics evident in the rule of law. It is also a distinction that has been applied in relation to the rule of law at the EU level. For instance, it has been noted by some commentators that 'thick' understandings of the rule of law in the EU 'tend to mirror the connections and interdependence between rule of law, democracy and human rights.'[44]

The formalist or 'thin' approach requires that laws must comply with certain formal rules so that they are valid. It does not take into account the content of the rule of law or the type of government, whether democracy, dictatorship or monarchy. Craig stresses that the formal rule of law addresses 'the manner in which the law was promulgated, the clarity of the ensuring norm, and its temporal dimension' without, however, providing a treatise or critique of the content of the law.[45] On the other hand, the substantive or 'thick' approach concerns the content as well as the form of 'law', requiring substantive rights to be recognised. The substantive aspect of the rule of law provides, again according to Craig, that the principles 'should embrace, in addition to its formal attributes, ideals of equality and rationality, proportionality and fairness, and [in particular] certain substantive rights.'[46] In this respect, both formal and substantive dimensions of the rule of law are part and parcel of EU law.[47]

Formal or 'thin' notions place emphasis on the procedures through which rules are formulated and, in terms of judicial reasoning, they advocate a logical deduction from existing legal rules by courts. According to Dicey, who allegedly adopted a positivist method (he detached constitutional law from constitutional morality/convention) in his attempt to codify the British unwritten Constitution, the law has three main properties: first, it is supreme and it protects from arbitrariness.

---

[43] S Douglas-Scott, *The Law After Modernity* (Oxford, Hart Publishing, 2013) 226.

[44] J Wouters and M Burnay, 'The International Rule of Law: European and Asian Perspectives' (2013) 2 *Revue belge de droit international* 299, 302.

[45] P Craig, 'Theory and Values in Public Law: A Response' in C Harlow, P Craig and R Rawlings (eds), *Law and Administration in Europe: Essays in honour of Carol Harlow* (Oxford, Oxford University Press, 2003) 30.

[46] ibid 31. See also the definition provided by MH Kramer, *Objectivity and the Rule of Law* (Cambridge, Cambridge University Press, 2007) 102.

[47] See FG Jacobs, *The Sovereignty of Law: The European Way* (Cambridge, Cambridge University Press, 2007) 7; See also FG Jacobs, 'The Lisbon Treaty, the Court of Justice and the Rule of Law' in N Nic Shuibhne and L Gormley (eds), *From Single Market to Economic Union: Essays in Memory of John A Usher* (Oxford, Oxford University Press, 2012) Ch 19.

The law should be certain and prospective and, in so many words, punishment should not be retrospective. Second, everyone should be subject to the law and nobody should try to put themselves above it. Equality before the law is reminiscent of what ancient Greeks called *isonomia*. Third, the rule of law should emanate not from any written constitution but from common law which consists substantially of judge-made law (the rule of the judicature).[48] Dicey's exposition of the law can be read either as a light attempt to highlight three rules of the rule of law or as a more thoughtful endeavour to engage in a discourse on general principles of law. The latter approach has been favoured by Walters, who having thoroughly examined Dicey's unpublished material argues that: '*Law of the Constitution* is really a book about general principles, not rules, and these principles gain their meaning through Dicey's narrative; any attempt to peel away literary form from legal substance is thus bound to fail.'[49]

Despite his normative proposition of law, it is noteworthy that Dicey's assertion that the common law is the bastion of the rule of law, ie that sovereignty flows from law and that the courts which are independent from the sovereign have the final word on the meaning of law, received strong support from those who opposed government bureaucracy.[50] This is because it contained 'rules and maxims of immutable truth and justice'—a 'perfection of reason' that should not be overshadowed by positive legislation.[51] Likewise, Hayek favoured the idea of an independent judiciary from the lawmakers. He explained that the common law is a construct of the efforts of the judges as servants of an existing order consisting of a multitude of norms, rules, customs and practices.[52]

Dicey's and Hayek's ideas of common-law adjudication as a kind of judicial decision-making were criticised as inconsistent with democracy (a precondition to the rule of law according to Habermas)[53] and with the principle of separation of powers. Bentham, in particular, criticised the common law due to its 'complexity, access, the public character of the law, and judicial usurpation.'[54] The criticism that the common law is undemocratic has been underplayed by both national and European courts. The UK's Supreme Court, for instance, has recently placed specific emphasis on the common law, as opposed, for instance to the Human Rights Act 1998 and the ECHR, as fundamental rights sources.[55] Likewise, the influential

---

[48] AV Dicey, *Introduction to the Study of the Law of the Constitution* (1885).

[49] M Walters, 'Dicey on Writing the Law of the Constitution' (2012) 32 (1) *Oxford Journal of Legal Studies* 21, 33.

[50] G Sartori, 'Nota sul rapporto tra Stato di diritto e Stato di giustizia' (1964) *Rivista Internazionale di Filosofia Del Diritto* 310.

[51] Tamanaha (n 1)14.

[52] LF Hayek, 'The Origins of the Rule of Law' in *The Constitution of Liberty* (Chicago, University of Chicago Press, 1960) 162.

[53] J Habermas, *The Postnational Constellation: Political Essays* (Cambridge MA, MIT Press, 2001).

[54] M Steilen, 'The Democratic Common Law' (2011) *The Journal of Jurisprudence* 437, 446.

[55] *Kennedy v The Charity Commission* [2014] UKSC 20. See also other recent examples: *R (HS2 Action Alliance Ltd) v Secretary of State for Transport* [2014] UKSC 3; *Osborn v Parole Board* [2013] UKSC 61.

preliminary rulings of the CJEU and expansion of judicial precedent are testaments of the contribution of the common law tradition to the development of EU law.[56]

During the second half of the twentieth century, the rule of law became synonymous with a constraint to discretionary power and along with it a more substantive or 'thicker' concept of the rule of law was developed. While formalists ignored the operation of legal rules in social settings, 'thick' definitions focused on the rule of law in its relationship with substantive outcomes, such as justice and democratic governance. At the defence of the 'thicker' conception of the rule of law were Dworkin and Habermas. Dworkinian 'interpretivism' and Habermasian interpretation of natural law from the point of view of modern social theory (legitimisation) placed the positive value of political and legal integrity and democratic participation at the heart of the rule of law.[57] They both advanced a non-instrumental approach to law (ie dismissed that law is an empty vessel subject to the ultimate will of the legislator) while they acknowledged the existence of the opposite view of law. Still, however, scholarship is still divided about whether the inclusion of justice in the definition of the rule of law advances or corrupts the concept and, therefore, impacts negatively on the discourse about legality and political authority.[58]

While the 'thin' rule-of-law school was challenged for not specifying the kinds of law a society must have, it continued to grow strong and find prominent supporters. In particular, Raz argued that the imposition of strict moral criteria to legality is problematic because, to use one of his arguments, the content of an authoritative directive must be identifiable outside the moral reasons that justify its existence.[59] To do otherwise would 'rob us of the potential benefits of subjection to the discretionary guidance of experts who can direct us to the realisation of substantively valuable ends.'[60] Raz articulated characteristics similar to those proposed earlier by Fuller and declared himself to be a legal positivist advocating the separation thesis. Yet his approach to legal-theoretical questions still differs to conventional positivist accounts. For instance, Raz does not seem convinced by the primacy of the idea of justified authority—he rather entertains the idea of moral properties of authority. This has little to do with the original positivist claim that the legal validity of a rule is to be distinguished from its morality.

Despite the occasional conceptional osmosis described in Raz's work above, some contemporary scholars have spoken of the predominance of the 'thin' rule

---

[56] T Tridimas, 'Precedent and the Court of Justice: A Jurisprudence of Doubt?' in J Dickson and P Eleftheriadis (eds), *Philosophical Foundations of EU Law* (Oxford, Oxford University Press, 2012) 307.

[57] See R Dworkin, *Law's Empire* (Oxford, Hart Publishing, 1998); See also TRS Allan, *Constitutional Justice: A Liberal Theory of the Rule of Law* (Oxford, Oxford University Press, 2001).

[58] P Craig, 'Formal and Substantive Conceptions of the Rule of Law: An Analytical Framework' (1997) *Public Law* 467.

[59] See J Raz, 'About Morality and the Nature of Law' (2003) 48 *American Journal of Jurisprudence* 1.

[60] J Raz, 'The Rule of Law and its Virtue' in the *The Authority of Law* (Oxford, Clarendon Press, 1979) 210.

of law conception over the 'thick' one. Tamanaha, for instance, has attributed this development to the gradual shift in legal consciousness towards an instrumental understanding of the law. Using the United States as a case study, he argues that the law can be *a means to an end* (a tool for obtaining certain desirable results) employed in the interests of a narrow group instead of the 'common good'.[61] As mentioned earlier, an instrumentalist understanding of legal interpretation is purpose-oriented, and akin to realists' ideas of pragmatic adjudication which holds that judges share law-making power with the legislature.[62] In terms of content, the instrumental approach resembles the formal rule of law notion in that it is vacant from content (eg built-in integrity) inclusive of any embedded restraints imposed by natural law, reason or custom.[63]

Tamanaha explains characteristically that within its instrumental setting, the law is an 'empty vessel'. He criticises 'the prospects for the rule of law if the law lacks any core integrity and is not tied to the service of the public good.'[64] Accordingly, both a core of what is right and the promotion of public good are interconnected and inseparable ideas about the law and its entitlement to obedience. Yet, placed in the current context, Tamanaha's critique of instrumentalism has been disapproved as slightly anachronistic. For instance, it has been argued that on the issue of legal interpretation, especially on his discussion about constraints on judicial discretion, his textual approach resembles Hartian positivism. Second, it has been claimed that 'modernity' is not adequately addressed in his work as a cause that has altered the ancient conception of the 'common good'.[65]

ii. The Thin–Thick Dichotomy Relevance to the EU Rule of Law

The EU system of judicial review includes both procedural and substantive elements and thus is probably best described as reflecting a version of the 'thick' understanding of the rule of law. Still, however, the thin–thick dichotomy can tell us little about the rule-of-law realisation. Krygier has openly rejected the formal–substantive taxonomy due to the fact that 'formal conceptions "are often too spare to amount to much", whereas substantive conceptions are "too rich to allow one to sustain any useful distinction between the rule of law and whatever else you would like to find in a society."'[66] Equally, Douglas-Scott poses an interesting question in this light:

> [I]s it possible to affirm the rule of law without remaining committed to a traditional account of rules and rule following? In other words, is it possible to embrace the rule

---

[61]   Tamanaha (n 1) 215.

[62]   R Posner, *Law, Pragmatism and Democracy* (Cambridge MA, Harvard University Press, 2004) 61.

[63]   See on distinction between formalism and instrumentalism: M Quevedo, 'Formalism and Instrumentalism (1985) 73 (1) *California Law Review* 119.

[64]   Tamanaha (n 1) 215.

[65]   O Raban, 'Real and Imagined Threats to the Rule of Law: On Brian Tamanaha's *Law as a Means to an End*' (2008) 15 *Virginia Journal of Social Policy and the Law* 478.

[66]   C Ling, 'Martin Krygier's Contribution to the Rule of Law' (2013) 4 *The Western Australian Jurist* 211, 249.

of law as a means to justice without either, on the one hand, turning to legal positivism or formalism based on a model of rules or, on the other, denigrating the rule of law in a postmodern critique of law as based on ideology or power? May the rule of law and the functions that it serves be reclaimed for law after modernity?[67]

Douglas-Scott examines a variety of different critiques of the rule of law to arrive at the conclusion that the rule-of-law objective will prevail in the end regardless of the quarrel between positivists and anti-positivists and the rule-of-law polemicism of postmodern jurisprudence which strays beyond the boundaries of conventional lawyering. It follows that by observing the values inherent in the rule of law (summarised in the prohibition of unrestrained power and freedom and equality) we can protect ourselves from the *Kafkaesque* tendencies inherent in the so-called 'state of exception' democracies—a term used by Agamben to describe an otherwise democratic state that can, at its whim, exercise sovereign violence, ceasing therefore to function as a democracy and temporarily circumventing the constraints imposed by the rule of law.[68] Similarly, Pech emphasises that the thin–thick dichotomy is a rather artificial construct—since 'even the narrowest understandings [of the rule of law] contain substantive demands'—and, therefore, this conceptual divide does not add much to our quest for the EU rule of law.[69]

Having said that, we may provide some guidance to the reader viz how the formal and substantive intertwined conceptions play out in the EU rule of law. The formal or 'thin' aspect of the rule of law can be attached to the legitimacy repositories at EU level, as well as principles such as consistency and legality; and the subjection of all public authorities' acts to judicial review. As noted, judicial review is central to the CJEU's interpretation of the rule of law at the EU level. Such interpretation dovetails neatly with the 'thick' or substantive aspect of the rule of law which places emphasis on the right to effective judicial protection of the individual. Conversely, this formulation is close to the commitment of the EU to the rule of law as expressly mentioned in the Treaty. In this respect, the EU rule of law forms part of a bundle of overlying principles together with democracy and human rights which place the individual at the forefront of EU integration. The CJEU has, for instance, interpreted the Treaty broadly in order to overcome its procedural limitations and enforce compliance with the rule of law by providing a litigation platform for individuals and ensuring effective judicial review viz fundamental rights protection. Aside substantive rights, the CJEU's interpretation has been pivotal for the EU narrative of transition from a purely economic to a union of rights. As put by Advocate General Cosmas in *Deutsche Telekom*:

[R]egardless of whether th[e] economic objective truly reflected the intentions of the historical Community legislature, it no longer corresponds to present-day thinking. In a

---

[67] Douglas-Scott (n 43) 248.

[68] According to Agamben, investigating the concept of the state of exception, the ability to declare a state of exception constitutes the ultimate expression of sovereignty. See G Agamben, *State of Exception* (Chicago: University of Chicago Press, 2005).

[69] L Pech, 'The Rule of Law as a Constitutional Principle of the European Union', Jean Monnet Working Paper 04/09, 28, 29 and 52.

community governed by the rule of law, which respects and safeguards human rights, the requirement of equal pay for men and women is founded mainly on the principles of human dignity and equality between men and women and on the precept of improving working conditions, not on objectives which are economic in the narrow sense ...[70]

Still, however, as mentioned, EU law may not always be disposed to (using Tamanaha's words) the 'service of the public good'. For instance, physical and social exclusion in the EU has become commonplace in some Member States as a reaction to the multi-crises in Europe. Despite political calls for intra-EU solidarity and a 'thick' sense of collective identity as found in the Member States, there is still some way to go, especially as concerns the establishment of 'a cohesive political community ("Europe") capable of self-rule through institutions "constituted" for that purpose.'[71] Not only there is a lack of a historical narrative but, perhaps most importantly, any efforts to stabilise the EU's socio-political foundations have been recently undermined by, inter alia, the questionable status of refugees under the EU asylum system, the unstable social dimension of EU economic governance and the contradictory CJEU's case law on welfare benefits to mention but a few areas of EU activity. Supranational action in those areas often raises issues that are borderline to EU competence and reveal that the EU institutions often lack the capacity to mobilise the Member States' resources.[72] Certain scholars have even argued that if the EU is not prepared to deal with its functional demands then a strategic retreat might be necessary.[73] Such a retreat would of course have an adverse impact upon the constitutional character of the EU project and the 'thick' (substantive) rule-of-law framework that the EU aspires to contribute through integration.

The above lead us to question whether the ongoing practice of conceptual 'stretching' of the rule-of-law concept has been met with success in the EU in terms of delivering justice to the individual. Douglas-Scott identifies several challenges facing the successful realisation of justice in the distinctive context of the EU.[74] She holds firm to the view that, given the kind of polity that the Union is, justice is a virtue which is crucial to it, and to which its constitutional arrangements must aspire. She argues that the most promising way forward in this regard is to recast and reinterpret rule-of-law requirements in terms of 'Critical Legal

---

[70] Case C-50/96 and Joined Cases C-234/96 and C-235/96 *Deutsche Telekom* [2000] ECR I-00743, para 80.

[71] P Lindseth, 'Equilibrium, Demoi-cracy, and Delegation in the Crisis of European Integration' (2014) 15 (4) *German Law Journal* 529.

[72] See for a comprehensive analysis of these issues: A Schrauwen, C Eckes et al, 'Inclusion and Exclusion in the European Union—Collected Papers' (6 September 2016) available at SSRN: http://ssrn.com/abstract=2835345.

[73] P Lindseth, 'Supranational Organizations', CEILA Key Note Series, Queen Mary University, London, 29 October 2015.

[74] S Douglas-Scott, 'The Problem of Justice in the European Union: Values, Pluralism and Critical Legal Justice' in J Dickson and P Eleftheriadis (eds), *Philosophical Foundations of EU Law* (Oxford, Oxford University Press, 2012).

Justice', a conception of justice which points to adherence to the underlying values which rule of law requirements aim to protect—such as opposition to unrestrained, despotic power, and an emphasis on the accountability of power, and on the freedom and equality which are enhanced by restraining it—and can thus be understood as aspiring to and attempting to realise the spirit of the rule of law rather than its formal letter.

III. THE RULE OF LAW, NOT THE RULE OF ONE STATE

In this section we will examine the way the rule of law has evolved beyond the state. We will look into the international rule of law as the rule of global standards, before we move on to discuss the EU rule of law taken to imply a rule of common values shared between Member States which has in time morphed into a unique reference point that contributes to global standards.

A. The International Rule of Law as the Rule of Global Standards

Globalisation has immensely affected national and international law. Recent efforts by international organisations, such as the UN and the EU, to deal with an increasing number of global and regional crises and improve the quality of laws around the world have given credence to the rule of law as a meaningful concept in international relations. In international law the concept of the rule of law is what we can call 'hereditary material'—it emanates from sovereign states acting together through international organisations and global regulatory networks.[75] The purpose of this community of states is the promotion of global legal standards legitimised through common institutional structures, a sentiment of communitarian or cosmopolitan solidarity and mechanisms of compliance that are sensitive to national diversity. The ultimate purpose is a democratic and equitable international legal order which promotes the economic and social welfare of citizens and resolves crises.

Political and legal commentators have stressed that it is possible for traditional concepts developed for the nation-state, such as democracy and the rule of law, to be transmitted to international institutions and laws. They tend to focus on the pre-requisites needed for a successful transplantation of concepts from the national to the supranational realm. These include, inter alia, solidarity, democratic accountability and the formation of a common consciousness in the form

---

[75] See A Watts, 'The International Rule of Law' (1993) *German Yearbook of International Law* 36; P Johnson, 'Laying Down the Law—Britain and America led the way in Establishing Legal Regimes based on Universal Principles' [1999] *Wall Street Journal* 22; S Beaulac,' The Rule of Law in International Law Today' in Palombella and Walker (n 34). On 204, Beaulac claims that 'there is no one formal norm-creating authority on the international level; states (not individuals) remain the principal legal actors and there is no enforcement mechanism (such as a police force).'

of a union of peoples.[76] Indeed, international organisations have 'ticked' most of these 'boxes' by seeing to a quantitative and qualitative increase of principles which enjoy wide application in the signatory states. A good example is Resolution 1594 (2007) of the Parliamentary Assembly of the Council of Europe on the principle of the rule of law which identifies a consensual definition of the rule of law.[77]

Still, however, there is a long history of prejudice against a globalised rule-of-law model which relates to the problematic nature of the mental construct that all international organisations are integrated and work together in harmony.[78] As such, any effort to turn the 'international rule of law' to a cultural norm is deemed to failure. The standard tendency is, therefore, to acknowledge the rule of law in international affairs but treat it as if it is different to the notion that manifests itself at the national level. Let us now explore the root causes of the above bias. First of all, the rule of law at the international level constitutes a legal import as far as the majority of states are concerned. Indeed state organs have often formulated a particular—almost Westphalian—understanding of the rule of law. Some of them have been reticent to accept the international rule of law because they conceive it at worst as a by-product of foreign authority and at best as part of a pseudo-narrative which aims to legitimise a transnational community driven by states that exercise hegemonic power. Second, and relevant to the previous point, the international rule of law becomes an empty vessel when it is based on the wrong cultural assumptions. Some commentators have rightly remarked on the incompatibility between the legitimate authority of international law and state sovereignty.[79] Hence, the mere existence of international norms does not produce the rule of law. Indifference or defiance by state practice can significantly undermine it as a normative ideal.

Third, there is a growing sentiment that international organisations often disseminate a rule-of-law paradigm to the world which does not tally with their actions, therefore defaulting in their own rule-of-law terms. For instance, despite the doctrine of implied powers we have witnessed at times a mission creep from the part of international organisations which together with a failure to develop a robust internal ultra vires review system threatens the rule of law. Hence, some commentators have entertained the characterisation of disobedience by states as a lawful countermeasure against international organisations.[80] What is more, despite

[76] See Eleftheriadis and Dickson (n 56) Ch 1, 'Introduction: The Puzzles of European Union Law'.
[77] Available at http://assembly.coe.int/nw/xml/XRef/Xref-XML2HTML-en.asp?fileid=17613&lang=en.
[78] B Tamanaha, 'What is International Law?', Presentation at Queen Mary University of London Law School, 25 May 2016.
[79] S Besson, 'Sovereignty, International Law and Democracy' (2011) 22 (2) *European Journal of International Law* 380.
[80] Tzanakopoulos has for instance addressed states' non-compliance with UN Security Council Resolutions viz their ability to legitimately disobey unlawful sanctions purportedly imposed by it pursuant to art 41 of the UN Charter. A Tzanakopoulos, *Disobeying the Security Council. Countermeasures against Wrongful Sanctions* (Oxford, Oxford University Press, 2013).

some positive steps, international organisations present greater diversity compared to states and are difficult to hold to the law of international responsibility in order to provide redress to aggrieved parties.[81] For instance, it can be argued that, aside from Article 24 (3) of the UN Charter, the UN Security Council lacks a system of accountability and scrutiny, often passing resolutions that are haphazardly enforced. This may lead one to conclude that states have fallen prey to their own creation since they remain the primary focus of responsibility for wrongful actions that flow from international organisations.

The above arguments aside, we cannot overlook the plurality of constitutional systems and examples of vertical interplay as points of influence for the rule of law as a foundation for administrative law. Certain international organisations have acted as promoters of a meaningful and normatively acceptable form of the 'rule of law' which gives precedence to democratic process of law-making and fundamental rights principles. For instance, the European Court of Human Rights (ECtHR) has engaged in norm-creation which dovetails with its 'mission towards more constitutional justice' and procedural rights.[82] 'European consensus' is often cited by the ECtHR as a means of justifying and legitimising its decisions.[83] More significantly, such international organisations have also held in check their counterparts where their protection in individual cases is manifestly deficient.

For instance, it is well-known that the ECtHR would carry out its external control over the EU in concrete human rights cases regarding the conformity of secondary EU legislation, such as the European Arrest Warrant Framework Decision, to fair trial guarantees.[84] The ECtHR application of the *Solange* method in *Bosphorus*, ie that the Strasbourg Court would not exercise its jurisdiction as long as the fundamental rights protection within the EU is ECHR compatible, is daring since there was no hint of such a proposition in the EU Treaties.[85] Likewise, when the CJEU decided its first cases there was no textual mention of fundamental rights in the EU Treaties. There has never been, however, an adverse ECtHR decision as

---

[81] International Law Commission, Draft articles on the responsibility of international organizations (2011) 2 (2) *Yearbook of the International Law.*

[82] N Croquet, 'The European Court of Human Rights' Norm-creation and Norm-limiting Processes: Resolving a Normative Tension' (2010) 17 *Columbia Journal of European Law* 307.

[83] See K Dzehtsiarou, *European Consensus and the Legitimacy of the European Court of Human Rights* (Cambridge, Cambridge University Press, 2015).

[84] See K Dzehtsiarou, T Konstadinides et al (eds), *Human Rights Law in Europe: The Influence, Overlaps and Contradictions of the EU and the ECHR* (London, Routledge, 2014).

[85] See for a summary on the 'Bosphorus presumption': T Lock, 'The Future of the European Union's Accession to the European Convention on Human Rights after Opinion 2/13: Is it Still Possible and is it Still Desirable?' (2015) 11 (2) *European Constitutional Law Review* 239, 267–68. Lock claims that future EU–ECHR accession would provide an opportunity for the ECtHR to revisit the *Bosphorus* presumption in that violations would be attributed straight to the EU instead of the Member States (in which case the EU would have to remedy the situation promptly). See for a more recent reflection on developments of European human rights jurisprudence: J Masing, 'Unity and Diversity of European Fundamental Rights Protection' (2016) 41 (4) *European Law Review* 490.

regards the EU–ECHR compatibility although the Strasbourg judges have fine-tuned the *Bosphorus* doctrine in more recent jurisprudence.[86]

Most notably, the CJEU is now complicit in the preservation of the fundamental rights 'global standards' status quo. More often than not Luxembourg judges are making occasional references to ECtHR case law, and thus confirming the commitment of the CJEU to an international rule-of-law conception which gravitates around the adequate protection of individuals.[87] Still, however, recent practice of the CJEU demonstrates that there are more 'selfish' reasons why the EU promotes 'global standards'. In the *Schrems* case, the CJEU invalidated the European Commission Decision approving the US Safe Harbor. The point of contention was pertaining to the legitimacy of the personal data transfer from Facebook Ireland to servers in the US—a jurisdiction that purportedly does not provide adequate protection. The CJEU used its own indicators to measure fundamental rights in the EU. An adequate level of protection was, therefore, deemed to be one that is 'adequate' in all the circumstances of the case, taking into account the factors listed in Article 25 of the Data Protection Directive.[88] Still, the outcome of *Schrems* may not be the best example of global standard setting from the part of the EU. This is because it is doubtful whether it will strengthen the protection of data privacy in the US. It carries, however, important ramifications for the regulatory competence of the EU over the US.

A better example perhaps of the EU's complicity to global rule-of-law protection is the well-documented outcome of *Kadi* viz the review of UN-imposed terrorist sanctions against individuals and legal entities.[89] Although for reasons of economy we will not delve into the details of the case, it is worth recalling that as well as improving the system of review of UN Security Council Resolutions, the CJEU also attempted to protect the integrity of its rule-of-law paradigm. It rejected the claim that international law should be given primacy 'as long as' it complies with fundamental EU legal norms. It rather excluded such automatic primacy over all primary EU law.[90] From a rule-of-law perspective, it is therefore open to discussion whether the approach of the CJEU in *Kadi* was driven by a judicial mindedness of setting global rule of law standards. Having said that, we shall

---

[86] *Michaud v France* (App no 12323/11) Judgment, Strasbourg, 6 December 2012, Final 06/03/2013.

[87] See G De Burca, 'After the EU Charter of Fundamental Rights: The Court of Justice as a Human Rights Adjudicator?' (2013) 20 (2) *Maastricht Journal of European and Comparative Law* 168. De Burca speaks of a figure of 81 judgments over a 9-year period where the CJEU referred to the ECHR. See 170.

[88] Case C-362/14 *Schrems v Data Protection Commissioner* [2015] ECLI:EU:C:2015:650. Similar to the *Bosphorus* presumption, the CJEU required the Commission to find that the US ensures through its domestic law or its international commitments, a level of protection of fundamental rights essentially equivalent to that guaranteed within the EU under the Directive read in the light of the EU Charter of Fundamental Rights. The CJEU contended that the Commission did not make such a finding.

[89] Joined Cases C-402/05 P and C-415/05 P, *Kadi and Al Barakaat* [2008] ECR I -06351.

[90] P Eeckhout, 'Kadi and Al Barakaat: Luxembourg is not Texas or Washington DC', Blog of the European Journal of International Law, 25.02.2009, 3. See also Case C-308/06 *Intertanko* [2008] 3 CMLR 9; Joined Cases C-120/06 P and C-121/06 P *FIAMM* [2008] OJ C 285/3; Case C-205/06 *Commission v Austria* [2008] OJ C 102/2; Case C-249/06, *Commission v Sweden* [2008] OJ C 102/2.

equally appreciate that the CJEU has in other cases allowed its internal standards to be compromised in disputes concerning the legality of certain EU international agreements.[91] In this respect, the EU-Canada Passenger Name Records Opinion of the CJEU[92] on the compatibility of the Agreement with Articles 7, 8 and 52 (1) of the EU Charter of Fundamental Rights as regards the right of individuals to protection of personal data will be interesting viz the possibilities for processing Passenger Name Records (PNR) data in the aftermath of recent human rights friendly decisions such as *Digital Rights Ireland*,[93] *Schrems* and *Tele2 Sverige AB.*[94]

B. The EU Rule of Law as the Rule of Common Values

While the EU is by no means the bellwether of international organisations when it comes to the rule of law, both EU legislation and judicial pronouncements are emphatic that the law is superior and binds everyone. Snyder adds that 'the constitutional principles of the EU as seen from a macro-sociological perspective are: regional integration, a divided-power system, the Member States as "Masters of the Treaty", the integrity of the EU and the rule of law.'[95] As it has been established, the notion of the rule of law originates in the constitutional traditions of the Member States. For instance, freedom under the law forms part of the common constitutional tradition reflected in Europe. What is more, in addition to specific provisions on the right to liberty and security, national constitutions require, in limitation clauses, that any fundamental rights restrictions need to be prescribed by law. We find the same restriction in the EU Charter of Fundamental Rights Article 52 (1) which provides that '[a]ny limitation on the exercise of the rights and freedoms recognised by this Charter must be provided for by law.'

But let us go back in time to explore the EU rule of law as a rule of common values. As early as 1979, in *Granaria* the CJEU made reference to the rule of law in the context of judicial review (annulment) of EU acts under what is now Article 263 Treaty on the Functioning of the European Union (TFEU). It claimed that the EU

[91] See Joined cases C-317/04 and C-318/04 *Parliament v Council* (PNR) [2006] ECR I-4721. Although the CJEU held in favour of the European Parliament (ie that the PNR Directive was adopted under the wrong legal basis) it failed to examine the Parliament's pleas on proportionality and breach of fundamental rights. What is more, following the PNR judgment a new agreement between the US and the EU on the use and transfer of Passenger Name Records to the United States Department of Homeland Security was signed on 8 December 2011. Available from: http://register.consilium.europa.eu/doc/srv?l=EN&f=ST%2017434%202011%20INIT.
[92] Opinion 1/15 (EU–Canada PNR Agreement). See Advocate General Opinion Mengozzi in the Request for an Opinion 1/15, 8 September 2016. The Advocate General argued that the Agreement cannot be entered into in its current form.
[93] Case C-293/12 *Digital Rights Ireland* [2014] ECLI:EU:C:2014:238.
[94] Case C-203/15 *Tele2 Sverige AB* [2016] ECLI:EU:C:2016:970.
[95] F Snyder, 'The Unfinished Constitution of the European Union: Principles, Processes and Culture' in JHH Weiler and M Wind (eds), *European Constitutionalism beyond the State* (Cambridge, Cambridge University Press, 2003) 61.

is based on the rule of law and as such the exercise of supranational public power is subject to the law.[96] Hence it was early established that since the EU is founded on the rule of law and respects fundamental rights as general principles of EU law, EU institutions and Member States (when they implement EU law) are subject to review of the conformity of their acts with the Treaties and the general principles of the law. Access to courts was perhaps the first common value that emerged from the CJEU's case law—a key element of a Union based on the rule of law, underpinning the EU legal order. Likewise, the right to an effective remedy before a court of competent jurisdiction was based on the constitutional traditions of the Member States as well as Articles 6 and 13 ECHR.

Despite the zealousness of European judges to bring the rule of law to the EU level through court practice, it was not until 13 years after *Granaria* that the EU textually articulated its support for the rule of law in the TEU through the Treaty of Maastricht. This support was further consolidated with the Treaty of Amsterdam which inserted into the body of the Treaties what is now Article 2 TEU. Still, however, it was in the context of the conduct of its foreign policy that the CJEU contextualised the rule of law as a basis for the then Community. In Opinion 1/91, the CJEU compared and contrasted the European Economic Area (EEA) with the former EEC (European Economic Community). It stressed that while the former entails no transfer of sovereign rights to its institutions 'the EEC Treaty, albeit concluded in the form of an international agreement, none the less constitutes the constitutional charter of a Community based on the rule of law.'[97] Such an early proclamation by the CJEU of the nature of the EU legal order paved the way for a better articulation later of the principles of primacy and direct effect that underpinned this new legal order.

With a small linguistic variation to the early CJEU's references to the rule of law, current Article 2 TEU emphasises that the EU is not merely *based* but rather *founded* on the rule of law. This is taken to mean that, almost like a federal entity, the EU is governed by law. As such, neither its institutions nor its Member States can avoid a review of compatibility of their actions with the Treaty. Against the symbolism that judicial commitment to the rule of law carries, it can be argued that the principle of the rule of law as enshrined in Article 2 TEU does not offer a means of judicial review. Nonetheless, there are other functions that the rule of law serves in the Treaty that have a practical bearing. It has in recent years become a benchmark and has influenced the accession process of prospective Member States to the EU. The so-called Copenhagen Criteria, which set the political and economic conditions of EU membership, expressly require, inter alia, that prospective entrants must maintain stable institutions that guarantee democracy and the rule of law.[98] What is more, the rule of law has a more obvious

---

[96] Case 101/78 *Granaria* [1979] ECR 623, para 5.
[97] Opinion 1/91 *EEA Agreement* [1991] ECR 6097, para 1.
[98] See C Hillion, 'The Copenhagen Criteria and their Progeny' in C Hillion (ed), *EU Enlargement. A Legal Approach* (Oxford, Hart Publishing, 2004).

exportable quality in the context of EU foreign policy. Both development and security and defence policies are driven by the EU's 'missionary principle' anchored in Article 3 (5) TEU which demonstrates the EU's tendency to promote its values not only within, but also outside of Europe. The exportation of the rule of law is, therefore, of utmost importance in the maturing of the EU to a normative power.[99] It also demonstrates the unity of Member States behind the EU as a global actor.

In light of a lack of definition or pointers by the Treaty drafter as to how common the rule of law is as a principle, we may look for answers in the semantic variations of the rule of law. We can, for instance, take the view that, as with the general principles of EU law, one can get close to a European definition by adopting a comparative detour, looking into the meaning of the rule of law in the Member States.[100] In that vein it is argued that the rule of law is the product of consensus between a host of divergent definitions. As such, the EU rule of law is as much the offspring of the *Rule of Law* as we know it in the UK as it is of *Rechtsstaatsprinzip, L'État de droit* and *Retsfaellesskab* emanating from Germany, France and the Scandinavian traditions respectively. Seen in this perspective, the fact that the terms *Etat de droit* and *Rechtsstaatlichkeit* feature in the French and German versions of Article 2 TEU suggest that each Member State has approached the rule of law according to its national understanding which is akin to statehood. In other words, EU law expressly upholds the rule of law but its meaning and content is left to the Member States to define according to their own versions of the principle enshrined in their Constitutions. The constitutionalisation of the rule of law in the Treaty of Lisbon as a common value is therefore perhaps one of the few tailor-made instances in the Treaty where Member States have been allowed the freedom to use a term familiar to them in order to describe a binding obligation under EU law.

Perhaps the commitment of the EU to a principle that Member States can directly relate to is a welcome development in terms of enhancing proximity between the EU and its component parts. Indeed some legal scholars have welcomed the close connection between the understanding of the rule of law in the Member States and the EU not only as a rule manifested in written provisions but also as a rule enshrined in a number of unwritten principles which promotes unity. Von Bogdandy has pointed out that the term 'rule of law' (*prééminence du droit* or *Herrschaft des Rechts*) is more accurate compared to 28 different terminologies linked to the state.[101] Others have stressed that 'in terms of legitimisation what is the main rule of recognition for a constitution is whether it can be perceived

---

[99] E Herlin-Karnell, 'EU Values and the Shaping of the International Legal Context' in F Amtenbrink and D Kochenov (eds), *European Union's Shaping of the International Legal Order* (Cambridge, Cambridge University Press, 2013) 3.

[100] See Pech (n 69).

[101] A Von Bogdandy, 'Founding Principles' in A Von Bogdandy and J Bast (eds), *Principles of European Constitutional Law* (Oxford, Hart Publishing, 2010) 28.

to be establishing a *Rechtsstaat* or a system under the [UK] Rule of Law.'[102] Still, however, some critics have expressed the view that—from a linguistic angle—the legitimacy of the EU cannot be measured by using the predominantly British concept of the 'rule of law', which lends much power to the courts, or indeed any other version of the rule of law which emanates across the Member States.[103]

It transpires, therefore, that a 'theory of relativity' would result if Member States were to measure the EU's adherence to the rule of law according to their own model. By contrast the ideal position would be one where each definition is viewed relative to that provided by other Member States. In this respect, the term *prééminence du droit* (which denotes the abstract superiority of the rule of law) is perhaps preferable to *etat de droit* mentioned (which is bound with the notion of the state in which the rule of law prevails) in the original Treaty of Maastricht. The former term occupies a key position in the Statute of the Council of Europe and the case law of the ECtHR. It forms an accepted principle of interpretation of the ECHR, a framework for the exercise of the ECtHR judicial powers and a means of consolidating a European public order in the field of human rights.[104] The Strasbourg judges have promoted the term *prééminence du droit* as a principle which highlights the substantive conception of the rule of law.[105] They have done so in cases such as *Lelièvre v Belgium* concerning failure of state judicial authorities to give serious consideration to the question of alternatives to preventive detention for individuals who have committed criminal offences.[106]

Likewise, *prééminence du droit* has been relevant in the establishment of the EU rule of law as drawn from universal values deriving from the common tradition of the Member States. To add to Ward's remark about the EU as a post-modern polity, the legitimacy of the 'new Europe' not only depends upon 'the resolution of its identity' per se but also on the identity of the rule of law that the EU aspires to.[107] This is obvious in the judgments of the CJEU where the term *etat de droit* has been adjusted to fit to the particularities of the EU as a supranational polity. Thus, instead of *etat de droit*, the expression *Communauté de droit* has been employed by

---

[102] P Birkinshaw and C Kombos, 'The UK Approach to the Emergence of European Constitutionalism Repositioning the Debate: Departure from Constitutional Ontology and the Introduction of the Typological Discussion', Report to the XVIIth International Congress of Comparative Law, July 2006, 9, available from www.ejcl.org/103/art103-2.pdf.

[103] H Koch, 'A Legal Mission: 'The Emergence of a European "Rationalized" Natural Law' in H Petersen et al (ed), Paradoxes of European Legal Integration (Hampshire, Ashgate, 2008) 46.

[104] Council of Europe, Parliamentary Assembly, Committee on Legal Affairs and Human Rights, 'The Principle of the Rule of Law', 6 July 2007, available from http://assembly.coe.int/nw/xml/XRef/X2H-Xref-ViewHTML.asp?FileID=11593.

[105] Council of Europe, Parliamentary Assembly, 2007 Ordinary Session, 1–5 October 2007, Vol VII. Having said that, the ECtHR uses also the term Etat de droit 'when reasoning on rule of law-founded articles.' See J Polakiewicz and J Sandvig, 'Council of Europe and the Rule of Law' in W Schroeder (ed), Strengthening the Rule of Law in Europe: From a Common Concept to Mechanism of Implementation (Oxford, Hart Publishing, 2016) 118.

[106] *Lelièvre v Belgium*, No 11287/03, ECtHR Judgment 8.11.2007, para 104.

[107] I Ward, *The Margins of European Law* (Basingstoke, Macmillan, 1996) 16, 161.

Luxembourg judges in order to refer to established EU constitutional principles. For instance, the CJEU has linked the EU's commitment to the principle of legality or certain general principles of EU law such as the right to an effective remedy to the establishment of the EU as a 'Union subject to the rule of law'.[108] But still there are certain grey areas related to the application of the rule of law in the EU which result from the conceptual stretching of *etat de droit*. Problems, for instance, can arise when Member States need to reach consensus within the Council in relation to sanctioning a Member State in the aftermath of a breach of the rule of law. This is because what may constitute a rule of law violation to one Member State, such as *en masse* deportation of refugees, may be considered as a strict stance to immigration by another and, therefore, an internal situation. Thus, it may be contended that the freedom Member States enjoy to phrase the rule of law in Article 2 TEU of their own linguistic version of the Treaty according to their domestic understanding may produce double standards across the Member States. Such double standards may in turn favour one rule-of-law interpretation over another and ultimately threaten the harmonious application of the principle of equality of Member States enshrined in Article 4 (2) TEU.

Of course, it can be argued that the vision of the Treaty drafters was exactly the opposite from creating a Community of double standards. The model they had in mind was probably very specific from the outset—ie to establish the EU as a *Communauté de droit* by transplanting into the EU legal framework the French notion of *etat de droit* which appears in the official version of the Treaty. If this is true, it is then a matter of historical accident how Member States ended up translating the notion of the rule of law into their own linguistic versions of the Treaty using domestic terminology. At the same time, however, we can appreciate that this was more of a serendipity because during the early steps of the EU, the association of the EU legal order with national expressions of the rule of law must have made it easier for EU policies to be accepted at the national level. Then, inevitably, in due course the EU rule of law was gradually stretched from its historical origins because, similar to the general principles of EU law, the CJEU was simply not under an obligation to interpret it in light of the constitutional traditions of the Member States. Such an exercise would have been at best impractical. Hence, nowadays, European judges are called to interpret the EU's version of the rule of law which contains new distinctive features but also inevitably entails all these values originating from the national legal orders. This is something emphasised by the Treaty of Lisbon which, while it has expanded the list of substantive translations to the abstract notion of the rule of law (pluralism, non-discrimination, tolerance, justice, solidarity, sex equality), still stresses that these values are *common to the Member States*. This is a reminder that the EU is as ever borrowing from the Member States that compose it—the European dimension of the rule of law is part of the national law.

---

[108] See Case 294/83 *Les Verts* [1986] ECR 1339, para 23. See also for a recent reference: Advocate General Wathelet in Case C-682/15, *Berlioz* [2017] ECLI:EU:C:2017:2, para 57.

At the same time, the EU rule of law is not merely concerned with imitating or replicating the values originating from the Member States. After all, the EU is a collective national construction which, compared to states, addresses different regional needs. Thus, for instance, the EU has found new roles for the rule of law stemming from its utility as an accession criterion in the context of EU enlargement to an exported norm in the conduct of its foreign policy.[109] These notions transcend the traditional idea about the rule of law and its features as manifested in the Member States.

IV. CONCLUSION

We will not attempt to summarise the entirety of the issues raised in this chapter. Suffice it to say that the preceding analysis confirms that the EU and its Member States are based on the principle of the rule of law and that the rule of law marks the relationship between them. We conceptualised the EU rule of law by discussing what the rule of law is not: first by revisiting the notion that the rule of law is not the rule of man (therefore looking into the history of the reduction of arbitrariness as its key objective and the relevance of thick and thin rule-of-law conceptions in this context) and second by affirming that the rule of law is not the law of one state (therefore opening up the debate for the international and European takes on the concept). The EU rule of law is the product of different Constitutions and judicial systems. Its historical roots are entrenched in a majoritarian take of national diverging trends emanating from the Member States.

The rationale for the protection of the rule of law at the EU level is connected to the claim that the EU forms an autonomous legal order distinct from other international organisations, and hence on this basis it must take responsibility and subject the actions of its institutions to judicial review. A lot of emphasis has been placed, in particular, on the constitutional guarantee of fundamental rights protection. As the CJEU has stressed:

> [T]he review by the Court of the validity of any [EU] measure in the light of fundamental rights must be considered to be the expression, in a community based on the rule of law, of a constitutional guarantee stemming from the ... Treaty as an autonomous legal system which is not to be prejudiced by an international agreement.[110]

Despite the EU's claim for autonomy by, inter alia, holding the Member States, the EU institutions and the individual to the rule of law, there is a further incentive behind the protection of the rule of law at the supranational level related to

---

[109] It has been noted, however, that 'the Union can be criticised in compromising to some extent its internal standards on the protection of fundamental rights and criminal law in order to achieve broader political objectives such as enlargement or good relations with its neighbours.' V Mitsilegas, *EU Criminal Law* (Oxford, Hart Publishing, 2011) 318.

[110] Joined Cases C-402/05P & C-415/05P *Kadi and Al Barakaat v Council* [2008] ECR I-6351, para 316.

the validation of the EU as a constitutional democracy. The role of the European courts is key in this regard. The CJEU is the highest authority on the interpretation of EU law—hence, as will be established in Chapter 4, it is essential that it is equipped to deal expeditiously with the cases it is called on to decide. European judges should interpret the law in order to advance the common good by interpreting the acts of the EU institutions as only secondary and contingent upon the requirements of the rule of law.

A final point is that the rule of law at the EU level helps to shape the fundamental values to which the EU aspires. Since the rule of law does not form a ground for review in itself, we may locate it within principles governing the relations between the EU and its Member States, and those governing the relations between the EU and the individual.[111] As we will discuss in the next chapter, the former includes, inter alia, principles of the order of competences and sincere cooperation between the supranational and national levels. The latter consists of the principle of protection of fundamental rights, democracy and solidarity. These principles have simultaneously boosted the autonomy and consistency of the EU legal order and its relationship with third parties.

---

[111] See for instance, W Van Gerven, *The European Union: A Polity of States and People* (California, Stanford University Press, 2005) 104. Van Gerven pointed out three formal features of the rule of law that are essential for any system of democratic governance, the EU inclusive: i) submission of all public authority to judicial review by an independent judge; ii) respect for human rights and fundamental freedoms; iii) the existence of a clear legal basis for the exercise of public authority and the need for high quality legislation.

3

Locating the EU Rule of Law

I. INTRODUCTION

IT HAS BEEN established that the EU constitutes a Union of values, inclusive of the rule of law which is part of Europe's legal heritage. According to the Commission, '[t]he conquest of these values is the result of our history. They are the hard core of the Union's identity and enable every citizen to identify with it.'[1] This chapter will provide a constitutional reading of the rule of law by focusing on how the concept manifests itself within the primary sources of EU law: the Treaty; the EU Charter of Fundamental Rights; and certain constitutional principles, inclusive of general principles of EU law, broadly defined as EU primary law. It will critique the sources that often describe vague goals and invite elaboration on the relations between the EU and its Member States and, likewise, between the EU and the individual.

The chapter will begin by locating and discussing the Treaty's primary provisions that make explicit reference to the rule of law as a common value among Member States. Apart from providing us with a reference point about the relevance of the rule of law at the EU level, these Treaty provisions have provided the basis for the development of a host of constitutional and administrative law principles grounded on the rule of law. As such, the discussion on primary Treaty provisions will be followed by an analysis of the less obvious contribution to the rule of law of principles enshrined both in the Treaty and the Court of Justice of the European Union (CJEU)'s jurisprudence. Some of these consist of the so-called general principles of EU law fervently debated in EU legal literature concerned with the CJEU's advances in European integration.[2] Describing how these principles play out in the development of the rule of law is relevant to understanding the contribution of the CJEU to the development of the EU rule of law viz the conduct of both the EU institutions and Member States in their respective exercise and review of their power.

---

[1] Communication from the Commission to the Council and the European Parliament of 15 October 2003 on Art 7 of the Treaty on European Union: Respect for and promotion of values on which the Union is based COM (2003) 606 final.

[2] T Tridimas, *The General Principles of EU law* (Oxford, Oxford University Press, 2016); U Bernitz et al, *General Principles of EU Law and European Private Law* (The Hague, Kluwer Law International, 2013); X Groussot, *General Principles of Community Law* (Groningen, Europa Law Publishing, 2006).

In particular, Article 19 Treaty on European Union (TEU) illustrates that the CJEU 'shall ensure that in the interpretation and application of the Treaties the law is observed.' This statement can be interpreted as setting the record of the CJEU's duties as a high-level judicial body bound by the rule of law. But what does exactly the Article 19 TEU reference to the 'law' entail in terms of sources and content according to the Treaty drafter? According to Nic Shuibhne:

> When the Treaty asks that 'the law is observed', the French, Italian, German, and Dutch versions all use the latter word, meaning any relevant rule of law, from whatever source, that is applicable in the circumstances ie including general principles of law, international law, and so on. The development of the general principles of EU law in this way is a good example of how the Court made significant 'new' EU law to develop its application and interpretation of the Treaties.[3]

It can also be argued that the understanding of the term 'law' in other languages includes enacted laws as well as broader ideas of justice. As such, an amendment of the English version of the Treaty so that it would state: 'the rule of law is observed' would be undesirable since, according to Jacobs, 'the rule of law is only part of what is right, or what is just; and its meaning should not be too far diluted.'[4] Having said that, the broad scope of Article 19 Treaty on the Functioning of the European Union (TFEU) means that the CJEU has often departed from the literal wording of the Treaty in order to give full effect to the intentions of the Treaty.[5] To appease any expansionist concerns, Wennerström notes that the term 'law' in Article 19 TEU is, however, not capable of embracing all the components of the EU rule of law such as the protection of fundamental rights.[6] Tridimas adds that the reference to the obligation encapsulated in Article 19 TEU that the law is observed, is weaker than the peremptory disposition of Article 220 EEC which provided that the law 'must be observed.'[7]

With regard to how EU law regulates discretionary power viz public liability, according to the Treaty, the review of the acts of the EU institutions under Article 263 (2) TFEU, examined in detail in Chapter 4, is not only available for Treaty breaches but also for 'any rule of law relating to its application'. Such a phrase may have been intended to simply connote compliance with secondary EU legislation but can also be interpreted to include rules developed in due course by the CJEU which are relevant to the application of the Treaty. According to Paul Craig, 'in any event, the very ambiguity in the phrase ['any rule of law'] provided the [CJEU] with a window through which to justify the imposition of administrative law principles as grounds of review.'[8]

---

[3] N Nic Shuibhne, *The Coherence of EU Free Movement Law: Constitutional Responsibility and the Court of Justice* (Oxford, Oxford University Press, 2013) 2.

[4] F Jacobs, *The Sovereignty of Law. The European Way* (Cambridge, Cambridge University Press, 2007) 37.

[5] ibid 44.

[6] EO Wennerström, *The Rule of Law and the European Union* (Uppsala, Iustus Förlag, 2007) 131.

[7] T Tridimas and P Nebbia (eds), *EU Law for the 20th Century: Rethinking the New Legal Order* (Oxford, Hart Publishing, 2004) 116.

[8] European Parliament DG for Internal Policies (authored by Paul Craig), 'EU Administrative Law: The Acquis', 2010, available from www.europarl.europa.eu/RegData/etudes/note/join/2010/432745/IPOL-JURI_NT(2010)432745_EN.pdf.

The shortlisting of these administrative law principles has been made in this chapter on the basis of the influence that they have exerted upon the application of the rule of law (interpretation and review of EU law) in the EU legal system irrespective of whether they are now codified (ie Treaty-based) or not.

The Treaty's express references to the rule of law discussed in the first part of this chapter emphasise the appropriateness of the EU's commitment through legislative recognition. Moreover, the constitutional and administrative principles discussed in the latter part of the chapter with reference to the EU's implied protection of the rule of law demonstrate the consequentiality of the EU's commitment through judicial activism. Beyond locating the rule of law in the primary (written and unwritten) sources of EU law, this chapter will also help the reader to reflect on the broader picture, namely the commonality underpinning the rule of law in the EU explored earlier and the readiness of the EU to deal with rule-of-law crises across Europe, discussed later in this book.

II. EXPRESS COMMITMENT TO THE RULE OF LAW IN EU PRIMARY LAW

This section will explore, through an analysis of the relevant provisions, how the Treaty caters for the rule of law. It is observed that the Treaty provides that the rule of law applies in three separate contexts: first, as a common value in EU internal policies and second as an exported norm in the context of EU external action (external dimension). Last but not least, the rule of law features in the EU Charter of Fundamental Rights as a common value shared between Member States. As such, there is direct correlation in EU law between the rule of law and the rights guaranteed under the Charter. The above textual references to the rule of law apply over the whole spectrum of the Treaty, we will hereafter consider them in turn.

A. The Internal Dimension of the EU Rule of Law: Self-proclamation

Already in the Preamble to the TEU it is made explicit that the EU rule of law is inspired by Europe's rich inheritance consisting of universal values. Hence, the rule of law constitutes an EU 'value' explained in universalistic rather than EU-specific terms. This is a symbolic and rather political statement which adds little substance to the ever so contentious institutional ethos and philosophy of the EU.[9] In the words of the Preamble, the Member States' Heads of State and Government are '[d]rawing inspiration from the cultural, religious and humanist inheritance of Europe, from which have developed the universal values of the inviolable and inalienable rights of the human person, freedom, democracy, equality and the rule of law'.

---

[9] A Williams, *The Ethos of Europe: Values, Law and Justice in the EU* (Cambridge, Cambridge University Press, 2010).

Such a reference to Europe's inheritance is at best parochial and, seen in practical terms, it overlooks the potential accession of countries like Turkey or Albania to what the Preamble proclaims to be a 'Christian club' with shared values.[10] A few sentences later the Preamble confirms the EU's abidance to the rule of law, ranking it rather dogmatically together with democracy and respect for fundamental rights but somewhat separate from them. The Heads of State and Government are, therefore '[c]onfirming their attachment to the principles of liberty, democracy and respect for human rights and fundamental freedoms and of the rule of law'.

Apart from the above declaratory reference to the rule of law in the Preamble to the TEU, the next textual reference in the Treaty on the rule of law appears in Article 2 TEU. This is perhaps the most formal reference to the rule of law in the Treaty of Lisbon within a provision which carefully lists the values upon which the EU is founded. Article 2 TEU uses the language of the Preamble to the TEU in that the rule of law constitutes a 'value' and adds that it is 'common' to Member States. The latter reference to commonality preempts any criticism about the EU attempting to forge a monolithic notion of the rule of law. According to Article 2 TEU:

The Union is founded on the values of respect for human dignity, freedom, democracy, equality, the rule of law and respect for human rights, including the rights of persons belonging to minorities. These values are common to the Member States in a society in which pluralism, non-discrimination, tolerance, justice, solidarity and equality between women and men prevail.

Despite symbolism, the formal reference to the rule of law in the Treaty as 'government' according to 'law' is significant because it applies to all EU areas of action and is applicable to both Member States and their citizens. Such attachment to the rule of law reinforces the axiom established in the early case law of the CJEU that EU law imposes obligations on individuals and confers upon them substantive rights which constitute an essential part of their legal heritage. Yet, the Treaty is silent about the features of the rule of law that the EU aspires to. As mentioned earlier, the CJEU's jurisprudence provides insight, although duly focused only in the specific context of judicial review of EU legislation. The standard declaration made by the CJEU is the following: '[T]he European Union is a union based on the rule of law in which the acts of its institutions are subject to review of their compatibility with, in particular, the Treaties, the general principles of law and fundamental rights.'[11]

Clarifying the adherence of the EU to the rule of law as a defining virtue of the EU polity is important because, apart from securing judicial review of the acts

---

[10] Of course the prospect of Turkey joining the EU in the near future has become unrealistic following recent reforms which undermine the rule of law (a criterion for EU accession) allowing, inter alia, politically inspired, criminal prosecutions of anti-government MPs. See S Tisdall, 'Erdoğan's draconian new law demolishes Turkey's EU ambitions', *The Guardian*, 8 June 2016, available from www.theguardian.com/world/2016/jun/08/erdogans-draconian-new-law-demolish-turkeys-eu-ambitions.
[11] See Case C-583/11P *Inuit* [2013] ECR I-0000, para 91; Case C-550/09 *E and F* [2010] ECR I-6213, para 44.

of EU institutions, it reinforces the legitimacy and legality of European integration including resort to the supranational exercise of power and protection of individuals at EU level. However, the symbolism behind the EU's commitment to the rule of law as an act of political self-definition is much more intricate to establish in the EU as opposed to the Member States. This is not least because, as discussed, the EU is endeavouring to adopt a notion whose precise content is indefinite amongst the 28 Member States. It may also be argued that legal attachments alone are unlikely to foster a sense of belongingness amongst the EU's citizens.

Most crucially, as it has been argued by certain legal scholars,[12] the EU lacks the sort of societal solidarity that creates a fertile ground for the rule of law to flourish as a binding value. The question is whether once transplanted and isolated from its traditional setting the rule of law can be repackaged and smoothly disseminated back to the Member States and other third parties.[13] Seen in this perspective there are limitations to the EU rule of law which is further constrained by the fact that the EU operates on the basis of conferred powers. As such, European and national judges are charged with the task of upholding the EU rule of law and ensuring the effective enforcement of EU law in a way which is compatible with the EU's limited powers. The judicial interpretation of the EU rule of law in chorus with the principle of attribution of powers is plausible, at least in theory. In practice, however, (once the CJEU is given a platform to adjudicate on a case) the robust enforcement of EU law may enhance EU competence and thus the EU's visibility as an autonomous legal order compared to its Member States or, indeed, other international organisations offering individuals (primarily EU citizens and their families) an extra layer of protection.[14]

B. The External Dimension of the Rule of Law: Value Promotion

The EU's internal and external policies must be coordinated and consistent if they are to be effective and credible. This is particularly important as, for example, the EU uses a broad range of policy instruments ranging from both the TEU and TFEU to achieve the somewhat abstract external objectives of the so-called Area

---

[12] JHH Weiler, 'Does Europe Need a Constitution? Demos, Telos and the German Maastricht Decision' (1995) 1 *European Law Journal* 219.

[13] Neil Walker refers to the absence of a 'strong pre-existing pan-European cultural substratum and sense of common society'. See N Walker, 'The Rule of Law and the EU: Necessity's Mixed Virtue' in N Walker and G Palombella (eds), *Relocating the Rule of Law* (Oxford, Hart Publishing, 2009) 119.

[14] The concept of autonomy of EU law has been contested by commentators. Kochenov, for instance, argues that 'for the sake of "autonomy", the appeals to a reality beyond the one presumed by the EU's *acquis* are pre-empted.' D Kochenov, 'EU Law without the Rule of Law' (2015) *Yearbook of European Law* 1, 20. See how the principle of autonomy stands in the EU external relations context: RA Wessel and S Blockmans (eds), *Between Autonomy and Dependence: The EU Legal Order under the Influence of International Organisations* (The Hague, TMC Asser Press/Springer, 2013).

of Freedom Security and Justice.[15] As such, having provided in the preamble to the TEU and Article 2 TEU that the rule of law constitutes a shared value in EU law, the next reference to it comes from Article 21 (1) TEU. This provision places the rule of law in a different context—that of EU foreign policy—and attributes to it an exportable quality. The logic behind this provision is that if the rule of law has inspired the creation of the EU as a democratic system of governance, then it can be legitimately exported to third parties. This is a unique function of the rule of law, which distinguishes it from the intrinsic notion operating within the bounds of the Member States' constitutional orders. In this respect, Article 21 (1) TEU boosts the extraterritorial claim of the EU as a value promoter alongside the UN and the Council of Europe. It provides:

> The Union's action on the international scene shall be guided by the principles which have inspired its own creation, development and enlargement, and which it seeks to advance in the wider world: democracy, the rule of law, the universality and indivisibility of human rights and fundamental freedoms, respect for human dignity, the principles of equality and solidarity, and respect for the principles of the United Nations Charter and international law.

When implementing Article 21 TEU, the EU applies the EU Charter of Fundamental Rights, as well as applicable UN and European Convention on Human Rights (ECHR) human rights standards. To that effect the EU produces annual reports on human rights and democracy about the enumeration of these values within the EU and outside the EU.[16] The external aspect of the rule of law is further elaborated in Article 21(2) (a) and (b) TEU which provides a mission statement vis-à-vis the aims of the EU's external action. Not only is the EU seen as an exporter of values but, most importantly, as an organisation which 'consolidates' and 'supports' the rule of law. Article 21 (2) (a) and (b) TEU also endorses the EU's initiation or partaking in rule of law missions in third countries and aspires to put it on the map as a normative power.

> The Union shall define and pursue common policies and actions, and shall work for a high degree of cooperation in all fields of international relations, in order to:
>
> (a) safeguard its values, fundamental interests, security, independence and integrity;
> (b) consolidate and support democracy, the rule of law, human rights and the principles of international law.

Finally, Article 49 TEU establishes that inter alia, respect to the rule of law constitutes a membership condition to the EU. Such conditionality is reminiscent of

---

[15] See RA Wessel et al, 'The External Dimension of EU's Area of Freedom, Security and Justice' in C Eckes and T Konstadinides (eds), *Crime within the Area of Freedom Security and Justice: A European Public Order* (Cambridge, Cambridge University Press, 2011); M Sossai, 'The Anti-terrorism Dimension of ESDP' in M Trybus and NG White, *European Security Law* (Oxford, Oxford University Press, 2007).

[16] See, for instance, Report from the Commission to the European Parliament, the Council, the European Economic and Social Committee and the Committee of the Regions of 30 March 2011–2010 Report on the Application of the EU Charter of Fundamental Rights COM (2011) 160 final.

the Copenhagen criteria which stress that, in order to be able to accede to the EU, a candidate state has to ensure the stability of institutions guaranteeing democracy and the rule of law.

> Any European State which respects the values referred to in Article 2 and is committed to promoting them may apply to become a member of the Union. The European Parliament and national Parliaments shall be notified of this application. The applicant State shall address its application to the Council, which shall act unanimously after consulting the Commission and after receiving the consent of the European Parliament, which shall act by a majority of its component members. The conditions of eligibility agreed upon by the European Council shall be taken into account.
>
> The conditions of admission and the adjustments to the Treaties on which the Union is founded, which such admission entails, shall be the subject of an agreement between the Member States and the applicant State. This agreement shall be submitted for ratification by all the contracting States in accordance with their respective constitutional requirements.

It shall be noted that the Copenhagen political criteria predate the provisions of Article 49 TEU. It is only since the Treaty of Amsterdam in 1999 that membership has been open to European states that respect the principles set out in Article 2 TEU including the rule of law. Article 49 TEU therefore 'epitomises, and partly "constitutionalises", the previously established Copenhagen political conditionality.'[17] The Copenhagen criteria and membership conditionality based on rule-of-law adherence are integral to the EU's claim for autonomy based on external delimitation and internal cohesion.

But certain scholars have contended that being autonomous is not enough to be recognised as an actor in international relations. Accordingly, the EU has to do more than merely exhibit its autonomy and independence—it has to work towards shaping and influencing world politics.[18] The EU has taken steps in this regard. For instance, not only has the EU employed the rule of law as a 'selling point' of its constitutional authority outside its territory, it has also used it as a yardstick of the legality of emerging EU–third country agreements, such as the EU–Turkey agreement on Syrian refugee resettlement in 2016.[19] In particular, adherence to the rule of law is important in the legal classification of Turkey as a 'safe third country' for refugees as well as the establishment of support structures in tackling the current migration crisis. Hence the rule of law may create constraints at substantive policy level.

---

[17] C Hillion, 'The Copenhagen Criteria and their Progeny' in C Hillion (ed), *EU Enlargement. A Legal Approach* (Oxford, Hart Publishing, 2004) 3; MV Feketija and A Lazowski, 'The Seventh EU Enlargement and Beyond: Pre-Accession Policy vis-à-vis the Western Balkans Revisited' (2014) 10 *Croatian Yearbook of European Law and Policy* 1.

[18] See C Bretherton and J Vogler, 'The European Union as a Global Actor' (London, Routledge, 2005).

[19] See EU–Turkey statement, 18 March 2016, available from www.consilium.europa.eu/en/press/press-releases/2016/03/18-eu-turkey-statement/; See also European Council conclusions, 17–18 March 2016, available from www.consilium.europa.eu/en/press/press-releases/2016/03/18-european-council-conclusions/.

To use another example, external policies, such as Common Foreign and Security Policy (CFSP), are also subject to the EU rule-of-law constraining and enabling framework.[20] This notion was expressed, amongst others, by Advocate General Trabucchi in 1976 in the context of the proposition that the Member States might enjoy competence in all cases where EU participation might prove uncomfortable for third country negotiating parties. The Advocate General opined that third country participants' objections to EU participation in negotiations 'could in no way affect the rule of law which, in the Community legal order, marks the relationship between the [EU] and its Member States.'[21] Most importantly perhaps, the Article 7 TEU procedure for rule-of-law breaches may also be applicable with regard to Member States' actions (or inaction) in the context of the CFSP. The fact that the CFSP enjoys no express judicial procedure in the Treaties for enforcement and penalties in case of breaches makes a strong case for Article 7 TEU to be utilised against recalcitrant Member States.[22]

Although the external dimension of the EU rule of law falls outside the scope of this book, it shall be noted that the rule of law has been important, inter alia, in boosting the EU's claim for an EU-specific identity as a tool to defuse the pressure exercised by the EU's international commitments. Indeed, the autonomy of EU law in the context of EU external relations has been the subject of increasing speculation. This is especially since, as Eckes supports, the participation of the EU in international relations has shaped its internal constitutional development.[23] One, however, can take a moderate stance pointing to the fact that whilst the scope of EU law has widened considerably in recent years, EU acts must always be interpreted and their scope delimited, to the extent possible, consistent with the relevant rules of international law. In particular, Article 3 (5) TEU provides that 'the EU shall uphold and promote ... the strict observance and the development of international law.' This translates for instance in the context of the EU–Turkey deal on Syrian refugees, as an EU guarantee of access to effective asylum procedures for all individuals in need of international protection. The EU institutions have to make sure that all returns are legal not only pursuant to EU law but also in accordance with the 1951 Refugee Convention which outlines the rights of the displaced and the legal obligations of signatory states to protect them.[24] Likewise, the EU

---

[20] G De Baere, 'European Integration and the Rule of Law in Foreign Policy' in J Dickson and P Eleftheriadis (eds), *Philosophical Foundations of European Union Law* (Oxford, Oxford University Press, 2012); M Cremona, 'Values in EU Foreign Policy' in P Koutrakos and M Shaw (eds), *Beyond the Established Orders Policy Interconnections between the EU and the Rest of the World* (Oxford, Hart Publishing 2011).

[21] Case 3, 4 and 6/76 *Kramer* [1976] ECR 1279 at 1317.

[22] Opinion of Advocate General Wahl in Case C-455/14 P *H v Council and Commission* [2016] ECLI:EU:C:2016:212, para 39.

[23] See C Eckes, 'Protecting Supremacy from External Influences: A Precondition for a European Constitutional Legal Order?' (2012) *European Law Journal* 230; C Eckes, 'Environmental Policy Outside-In?: How the EU's Engagement with International Environmental Law Curtails National Autonomy' (2012) *German Law Journal* 1151. See also Wessel and Blockmans (n 14).

[24] Available at www.unhcr.org/uk/3b66c2aa10.

has to respect the principle of non-refoulement including the (Dublin) system of processing asylum applications and returns of asylum seekers to non-EU states in line with the European Court of Human Rights (ECtHR) jurisprudence.[25]

The above EU engagement with international law in the context of the migration crisis is particularly important especially in light of the questionable capacity of Turkey to provide such protection. Yet, as we will see in this book, the EU express commitment to international law in the Treaty has at times been criticised. Initially, the criticism was directed towards the CJEU for attempting in the relevant litigation to establish a new hierarchical structure between EU and international law by diminishing the latter's effects within the EU legal order.[26] More recently, however, the criticism has shifted to address the 'failure' of the burden-sharing initiatives promoted by the EU political institutions and, thus, the EU's international responsibility.

C. The Human Rights Dimension of the Rule of Law: Polity Building

Apart from the Treaty of Lisbon, the Preamble to the EU Charter of Fundamental Rights contains an express provision on the rule of law as a common value shared between 'the peoples of Europe'. For some time, the Charter was an instrument of considerable inspiration to EU institutions and the Member States when they acted within the scope of EU law. As it is well known, since the Treaty of Lisbon came into force, Article 6 (1) TEU provides that the Charter has the same legal value as the EU Treaties, raising it to primary law status. With the entry into force of the Treaty of Lisbon, the Charter has become legally binding and under Article 51 (1) of the Charter the provisions of the Charter are addressed to the Member States when they are implementing EU law—ie when they are acting within the scope of EU law.[27]

It should be noted at this point, that during the last five years or so the scope of EU law has been broadly defined by the CJEU to allow for a wider application of the Charter than that originally anticipated by Member States.[28] The CJEU's creative interpretation of the areas of application of the Charter and its reluctance to give the green light for the EU accession to the ECHR have led to a substantial

---

[25] See the ruling of *MSS v Belgium and Greece*, No 30696/09, ECtHR, 21 January 2011.

[26] See special issue 'Beyond Pluralism? Co-Implication, Embeddedness and Interdependency between Public International Law and EU Law' (2016) 35 (1) *Yearbook of European Law* 513–32.

[27] See on the CJEU's observations regarding the scope of the Charter: Case C-617/10, *Åkerberg Fransson* [2013] ECLI:EU:C:2013:105, para 19; Case C-265/13, *Torralbo Marcos* [2014] EU:C:2014:187, paras 28 and 29, C-650/13, *Delvigne* [2015] EU:C:2015:648, paras 25 and 26. See also Case C-279/09, *DEB* [2010] with reference to the interpretation of Art 6 (1) (3) and Art 52 (7) of the EU Charter of Fundamental Rights.

[28] See F Fontanelli, 'Implementation of EU Law through Domestic Measures after Fransson: the Court of Justice Buys Time and "Non-preclusion" Troubles Loom Large' (2014) (5) *European Law Review* 682.

reinforcement of EU (human rights) law in the Member States. Indeed, national legislation would be 'governed' by EU law in so far as it triggers the application of the Charter. This of course does not mean that the EU has detached itself from the ECHR. On the contrary, the Charter reinforces the case law of the ECtHR. This is evident, for example, in cases regarding setting the limits on the length of detention of suspects in extradition cases.[29] All in all, Luxembourg judges are called to pinpoint the correct balance between the obligation which Member States are under to ensure the security of individuals within their territory and observance of the fundamental rights enshrined in the Charter.

Indeed, the Charter embodies in a single, coherent and legally-binding instrument the fundamental rights which are binding also upon both the EU institutions and bodies. For instance, the CJEU has gone as far as establishing that even within the framework of mechanisms such as the European Stability Mechanism (ESM) (under which Member States incur no liability before EU courts),[30] any Charter violations (eg signing a Memorandum of Understanding that is inconsistent with EU law—the Charter, in particular) can give rise to damages (non-contractual) liability under Article 340 TFEU against the EU institutions—in particular the Commission or the European Central Bank (ECB) who play an active part in the context of the adoption of Memoranda of Understanding adopted by the ESM.[31]

But what does the Charter say about the rule of law? Its Preamble sets the tone:

> The peoples of Europe, in creating an ever closer union among them, are resolved to share a peaceful future based on common values.

> Conscious of its spiritual and moral heritage, the Union is founded on the indivisible, universal values of human dignity, freedom, equality and solidarity; it is based on the principles of democracy and the rule of law. It places the individual at the heart of its activities, by establishing the citizenship of the Union and by creating an area of freedom, security and justice.

The Preamble to the Charter spells out the closest reference to the citizen one may come across in EU primary law in relation to the application of the rule of law. Yet, as with the Preamble to the TEU, or indeed Article 2 TEU, one can hardly draw any

---

[29] See Case C-237/15 PPU *Lanigan* [2015] ECLI:EU:C:2015:474.

[30] See Case C-370/12 *Pringle* [2012] ECLI:EU:C:2012:756 where the question was whether the establishment of the ESM is in breach of Art 47 of the Charter (right to effective judicial protection). The CJEU held that the Member States are not implementing EU law, within the meaning of Art 51(1) of the Charter, when they establish a stability mechanism such as the ESM (the Treaties do not confer any specific competence on the EU to establish such a mechanism). Hence, since the ESM Treaty is not part of the EU legal order, the application of the Charter is redundant.

[31] See Joined Cases C-8/15 P *Ledra Advertising v Commission*, 20 September 2016. The case concerned the liability of the Commission and the ECB in the negotiation and signing of the 2013 Memorandum of Understanding concluded between Cyprus and the ESM. See also Joined Cases C-105/15 P to C-109/15 P *Mallis*, 28 October 2016. The case concerned the liability of the Commission and the ECB for the annulment of the Eurogroup's 2013 statement viz the restructuring of the Cypriot banking sector. Both appeals to the CJEU were dismissed but these cases are important for the sake of future precedent.

practical significance from the claim made in the Preamble to the Charter about the EU's adherence to the rule of law. There is no justiciability in symbolism since one cannot infer any legally binding obligations or enforcement avenues to address rule of law violations. A similar conclusion can be reached with reference to the protection that the Charter affords to fundamental principles which underpin the rule of law in the EU. In particular, there is a stark contrast in the Charter between the classic civil and political rights and economic and social rights which seem to be aspirations or objectives common to Member States, or—in short—principles.[32]

The above distinction is important because while individual rights, also guaranteed by the ECHR, are justiciable, some of the economic and social rights found in the Solidarity Title (IV) of the Charter only provide incentives for national legislation and interpretative aids for courts—they are not enforceable rights as such. This is the case especially with the somewhat controversial right to strike found in Article 28 of the Charter. Not only is the right to strike not an absolute right under the Charter but also, and perhaps more significantly to Member States, it is subject to national restrictions. These restrictions, confirmed both by the CJEU and the ECtHR, are such that render the right to strike rather harmless to national sovereignty.

The non-justiciability of the right to strike is further reinforced in Article 1 (2) of the UK and Polish Protocol on the application of the Charter.[33] This declaration is an empty letter, considering that the right to strike appears to be an aspiration in the Charter.[34] Thus, both the UK and Poland seem to have gained a clarification through the Protocol that the Charter will not introduce new rights or new EU competences. This is only good in so far as 'political haggling' is concerned, especially with regard to the protection of rights, such as the right to data protection, not conferred by the ECHR.[35] But still, one can see the duplication in safeguards vis-a-vis the Charter's scope of application. For instance, Article 1 (1) of the Protocol repeats the line taken by the Charter drafters in the Preamble as well as Article 51 (2) of the Charter (scope and interpretation of rights and principles) and Article 6 (1) TEU with reference to the unlikelihood of EU rights competence enhancement post-Charter.

Similarly, as established by the CJEU in *NS*, the rights enshrined in the Charter are still applicable as general principles of EU law.[36] This is important because

---

[32] See J Kenner, 'Economic and Social Rights in the EU Legal Order: the Mirage of Indivisibility' in T Hervey and J Kenner (eds), *Economic and Social Rights under the EU Charter of Fundamental Rights* (Oxford, Hart Publishing, 2003).

[33] UK Parliament Select Committee on the EU, 10th Report, Session 2007–08, available at www.publications.parliament.uk/pa/ld200708/ldselect/ldeucom/62/6209.htm.

[34] C Barnard, 'The "Opt-Out" for the UK and Poland from the Charter of Fundamental Rights: Triumph of Rhetoric over Reality?' in S Griller and J Ziller, *The Lisbon Treaty: EU Constitutionalism without a Constitutional Treaty* (Wien/New York, Springer, 2008).

[35] See *R (AB) v Secretary of State for the Home Department* (2013) EWHC 3453 (Admin), para 12.

[36] Joined Cases C-411/10 and C-493/10 *NS and Others* [2011] ECR I-13905. See further: V Moreno-Lax, 'Dismantling the Dublin System: MSS v Belgium and Greece' (2012) 14 *European Journal of Migration and Law* 19.

first, the Protocol is silent on the matter and second, because Article 6 (3) TEU is explicit that fundamental rights remain general principles of EU law, and therefore binding upon all Member States. This being the case, it appears that Article 1 (2) of the Charter on the non-justiciability of the principles enshrined in the Solidarity Title (IV) of the Charter is on a par with Article 52 (5) of the Charter. Although, the Charter does not generally distinguish between rights and principles, Article 52 (5) of the Charter broadly identifies the circumstances under which principles guaranteed under the Charter may be justiciable (ie they do not give rise to direct claims for positive action).[37] It remains to be seen how 'the operating conditions of the "principles", and … the scope of their justiciability' will play out in future CJEU case law.[38]

Suffice to say for now that in cases where there is a direct link with EU law, the Charter would be reinforcing existing rights, such as those stemming from inter alia the ECHR (Article 52 (3) of the Charter) and the general principles common to the constitutional traditions of the Member States.[39] Indeed, there are provisions in the Charter whose meaning is identical with the rights guaranteed in the ECHR or the general principles of EU law as established by the CJEU prior to the Charter becoming legally binding. To use an example, the principle of effective judicial protection, which comprises a general principle of EU law[40] enshrined both in the ECHR (Articles 6 and 13) and the general constitutional principles of the Member States, finds expression in Article 47 of the Charter (the right to an effective remedy). As such, it could be said that the elevation of the Charter's status by the Treaty of Lisbon from declaratory to legally binding has little resonance in the European Courts' jurisprudence on effective judicial protection. This is because the Charter merely reiterates previous binding sources of EU law. For instance, Article 47 (1) of the Charter is unlikely to alter the system of judicial review as laid down by the Treaties, especially the provisions on admissibility for direct actions before European Courts.

Notwithstanding the above, it appears that the Charter has a much stronger presence in the CJEU's jurisprudence on the substantive dimension of the rule of law after the Treaty of Lisbon came into force. Despite the express limitation that the Charter will not alter the way EU competences are delimited, national judges have to recast questions referred to the CJEU concerning the principle of effective judicial protection so that they relate to the specific interpretation of, for instance, the right to be advised, defended and represented enshrined in Article 47 of the Charter. Although this development could have occurred as part of the CJEU's expanding jurisprudence on the general principles of EU law—and

[37] See for a detailed legal explanation of the EU Charter of Fundamental Rights at www.eucharter.org; S Peers et al, *The EU Charter of Fundamental Rights: A Commentary* (Oxford, Hart Publishing, 2014).
[38] See Opinion of Advocate General Cruz Villalon in Case C-176/12, *Association de médiation sociale* [2013] ECLI:EU:C:2013:491.
[39] See Case C-396/11 *Radu* [2013] ECLI:EU:C:2013:39.
[40] See Case 222/84 *Johnston* [1986] ECR 1651.

therefore in the absence of the Charter—one cannot overlook the potential of the Charter as a mechanism for providing new opportunities in EU fundamental rights protection.[41]

Already in 2001, in *Wouters*, Advocate General Léger mentioned—citing Article 47 of the Charter—that 'the importance of the role played by lawyers has prompted the European Union and its Member States to include among fundamental rights that of being advised, represented and defended by a legal adviser.'[42] A good case to illustrate the above argument following the 'legalisation' of the Charter is *DEB*. In its judgment the CJEU illustrated that in a state liability claim before a national court, a legal person can in accordance with the Charter rely on the principle of effective judicial protection so that legal aid granted pursuant to it covers dispensation from advance payment of court costs and legal assistance.[43] If we make a forceful case that such a decision would not have been reached without the Charter in place, then the 'legalisation' of the Charter is not merely a case of fundamental rights rebranding but one of constitutional significance.

The work of judges is therefore affected by the Charter because whenever it is applicable, its provisions take primacy over conflicting national legislation and all domestic courts are under an obligation to dis-apply such legislation. By granting the Charter legal status, therefore, the CJEU and national courts are both entitled and expected to rule on Charter violations. The Charter's scope, however, is determined by Article 51 (1). Accordingly, the Charter has 'teeth' only insofar as Member States implement EU law. As such, where a legal situation falls outside the scope of EU law, the CJEU would have no competence to rule on it and the Charter provisions relied upon by individuals cannot, of themselves, form the basis for such competence.[44]

At the time of writing, judicial recourse to the Charter constitutes a sound basis for judicial review to annul EU secondary legislation. For instance, Article 47 of the Charter has already been invoked successfully against the EU legislative institutions in cases regarding the operation of EU asylum procedures under an EU directive and judicial review of EU regulatory acts.[45] It has also been employed as a means for bringing an action for damages against the EU under Article 268 TFEU and Article 340 (2) TFEU on the grounds of failure of European Courts

---

[41] See T Lock and P Layden, 'Protection of Fundamental Rights Post-Lisbon: The Interaction between the EU Charter of Fundamental Rights, the European Convention on Human Rights (ECHR) and National Constitutions, FIDE National Report for the United Kingdom', 2011, available at https://ssrn.com/abstract=1940381.

[42] Opinion of Advocate General Philippe Léger in Case C-309/99 *Wouters* [2002] ECR I-1577, para 175.

[43] Case C-289/09 *DEB* [2010] ECR I-13849; See also Case C-265/13 *Marcos v Korota SA* [2014] ECLI:EU:C:2014:187.

[44] See Case C-617/10 *Åkerberg Fransson* [2013] ECLI:EU:C:2013:105; Joined Cases C-614/12 and C-10/13 *Dutka and Sajtos* [2014] ECLI:EU:C:2014:30; Case C-332/13 *Weigl* [2014] ECLI:EU:C:2014:31.

[45] See Case C-69-10 *Samba Diouf* [2011] ECLI:EU:C:2011:524 and Case C-583/11P *Inuit* [2013] ECLI:EU:C:2015:535.

to adjudicate within a reasonable time.[46] As such, it can be argued that the legal elevation of the Charter in the post-Lisbon dispensation reinforces the substantive notion of the rule of law viz securing the protection of specific fundamental rights. Of course, the EU is not the only organisation committed to spreading the rule of law in Europe. Suffice to say at this stage that the contribution of the Council of Europe as a human rights watchdog is going to be vital, regardless the fate of the accession of the EU to the ECHR.[47] For instance, competition and criminal law proceedings will raise particular interest vis-a-vis the rights to due process, to an effective remedy and to a fair trial provided for in the Charter and under the ECHR.[48]

III. IMPLIED COMMITMENT TO THE RULE OF LAW IN EU CONSTITUTIONAL PRINCIPLES

The express references to the rule of law aside, EU law contains numerous implied commitments to the rule of law manifested in the obligations stemming from a number of constitutional and administrative principles which underpin the EU legal order. These principles, aimed at consolidating the scope and application of EU law, can be broadly pigeonholed as 'general principles' of EU law and, according to the CJEU, common to the Member States. Hence, the EU rule of law is more than the sum of its parts (ie the general principles herein discussed). These general principles are of primary law status in that they bind all EU institutions in the exercise of their legislative and administrative competence.

It is also worth mentioning that other constitutional principles that impliedly give expression to the EU rule of law, such as that of sincere cooperation, have different intensity in their application to the EU institutions and the Member States. What is more, these principles do not always prevail in the everyday political life of the EU: in some situations the EU and its Member States overlook them, therefore opting for a more autonomous behaviour outside the contours of EU law. Of course, this development fuels criticism of 'double standards' and inconsistency in the application of the EU rule of law. In this section, we will attempt to conceptualise the EU rule of law by wrapping up the relevant constitutional principles that

---

[46] Case C-40/12 P *Gascogne Sack Deutschland v Commission* [2013] ECLI:EU:C:2013:768 concerned a claim for compensation for the damage caused by the failure by the General Court to adjudicate within a reasonable time (over five years) on a case concerning agreements in the plastic industrial bags sector about inter alia price-fixing and sales quotas in the Benelux states, Germany, Spain, and France.

[47] See on the technicalities of EU-ECHR accession P Craig, 'EU Accession to the ECHR: Competence, Procedure and Substance' (2013) 36 *Fordham International Law Journal* 1115.

[48] With regard to competition law, Lenaerts argues that 'the [CJEU] has consistently and correctly rejected arguments to the effect that the Commission's role as investigator and decision-maker, subject to a judicial review of its rulings by the [General Court], is incompatible with the safeguards required by Article 47 of the Charter.' K Lenaerts, 'Due Process in Competition Cases' (2013) 1 (5) *Neue Zeitschrift für Kartellrecht—NZKart* 1, 22–23.

support it. The list is not exhaustive—hence this section does not pretend to capture every single constitutional and meta-constitutional principle that impliedly contributes to the EU rule of law, but rather to provide an overview of a set of justiciable principles which uphold the rule of law in the EU.

A. The Principle of Sincere Cooperation and its Progeny

The principle of sincere cooperation or, in short, loyalty underpinned in Article 4 (3) TEU is inspired by the unwritten German constitutional principle of *Bundestreue*, that of good faith featuring in the UN Charter and the *pacta sunt servanda* principle in the Vienna Convention.[49] Contrary to its cousin principles in national and international law, loyalty has often been attributed a dual role by the CJEU. First, the CJEU has employed loyalty as a coercive norm, requesting Member States to act in a particular way so as to uphold communal will and to abstain from jeopardising their obligations under the Treaty. Second, the CJEU has employed loyalty as a means for legitimising an expansive interpretation of the Treaty.

For instance, in *Francovich*, the judges in Luxembourg used loyalty as an ingredient for establishing a universe of private enforcement in EU law which, was (and still is) absent in the Treaty.[50] Attributing the establishment of indirect effect of directives and state liability to the principle of loyalty was important for Luxembourg judges. A teleological reading of loyalty legitimised these developments which would otherwise look arbitrary. As such, loyalty mandates a best endeavours obligation from the part of the Member States to act in chorus with EU objectives as well as maintain an open mind about the contours of European integration.[51] This includes placing domestic courts under a duty to ensure the full effectiveness of EU law by, for instance, allowing individuals a platform for action in order to fight obstacles to free movement within the EU.[52] It also prompts Member States

---

[49] B de Witte, 'Institutional Principles in Judicial Development of the EU Legal Order' in F Snyder (ed), *The Europeanisation of Law: The Legal Effects of European Integration* (Oxford, Hart Publishing, 2000) 86, 87. It is worth saying that although loyalty will be used here for reasons of economy, the CJEU has never referred to the principle of sincere cooperation in that respect. See on *pacta sunt servanda* D Davison-Vecchione, 'Beyond the Forms of Faith: Pacta Sunt Servanda and Loyalty' (2015) 16 (5) *German Law Journal* 1163.

[50] Nonetheless, the CJEU has refrained from resorting to loyalty in private antitrust enforcement cases. For instance, in *Courage* the legal basis for reliance on a violation of Art 101 TFEU before national courts was the *effet utile* of Art 101 TFEU itself and the principles of equivalence and effectiveness. See Case C-453/99 *Courage v Crehan* [2001] ECR I-6297.

[51] See for a detailed study of the duty of loyalty: M Klamert, *The Principle of Loyalty in EU Law* (Oxford, Oxford University Press, 2014); also on the application of the principle in the field of external relations see G De Baere, 'O, Where is Faith: O, Where is Loyalty? Some Thoughts on the Duty of Loyal Cooperation and the Union's External Environmental Competences in the light of the PFOS Case' (2011) 36 (3) *European Law Review* 405.

[52] Case C-265/95 *Commission v France* (Spanish strawberries) [1997] ECR I-6959.

to trust EU institutions in their decisions and allow them a certain margin of discretion to develop the Treaty.

In short, when Member States are acting within the scope of EU law, loyalty preserves the axiom that the integrity of the EU legal order goes first while the protection of national regulatory autonomy follows. This idea, which reinforces the principle of primacy of EU law, seems to apply even against national countervailing principles—such as the rule of law—which at first glance appear to be uncompromisable.[53] At the same time, however, we need to accept that, as Jacobs explains, '[EU] law must necessarily prevail over national law. That was indeed inherent in the very idea of [an EU] based on the rule of law.'[54] Such a use of loyalty is counter-productive to Kumm's 'best fit' principle which advocates that national judges shall always look for the right conflict rule and apply it.[55] Finally, as far as effective judicial protection is concerned, Member States are under a positive obligation as a matter of loyalty to ensure the availability of effective remedies in their legal order so that both national and EU legislation can be reviewed under the Treaty. This aspect of loyalty pointing to the maintenance of essential procedural requirements will be discussed further in the next chapter.

The principle of loyalty is not only applicable to the conduct of Member States when they are acting within the scope of EU law. It also applies to EU action, ensuring that the EU institutions are under a corresponding duty to show equal respect to the Member States when exercising their powers under the Treaty. Such a duty has become manifest in the relevant literature dealing with national identity or EU external relations.[56] In this respect, loyalty carries another connotation—that of a mutual duty which is neither apparent from the wording of Article 4 (3) TEU nor its predecessors in the former EC Treaties. Loyalty, therefore, has a flip-side in that apart from Member States it also applies to EU institutions—it mandates sincere cooperation from their part and forbids the exercise of arbitrary power.[57] The CJEU has been explicit that since the EU is subject to the rule of law the relations between Member States and the EU institutions are governed according to

---

[53] See G Martinico, *The Tangled Complexity of the EU Constitutional Process: The Frustrating Knot of Europe* (London, Routledge, 2012) 34.

[54] Jacobs (n 4) 40.

[55] M Kumm, 'The Jurisprudence of Constitutional Conflict: Constitutional Supremacy in Europe before and after the Constitutional Treaty (2005) 11 *European Law Journal* 262. See for criticism of Kumm's approach: G Letsas, 'Harmonic Law: The Case Against Pluralism' in Dickson and Eleftheriadis (n 20).

[56] See for instance on the duty of loyalty viz respect to national identity: E Cloots, *National Identity in EU Law* (Oxford, Oxford University Press, 2015); C, Alcoberro Llivina (eds), *National Constitutional Identity and European Integration* (Cambridge, Intersentia, 2013). See also on the legal quality of obligations based on the principle of loyalty in the external relations context: C Hillion, 'Mixity and Coherence in EU External Relations: The Significance of the Duty of Cooperation' in C Hillion and P Koutrakos (eds), *Mixed Agreements Revisited—The European Union and its Member States in the World* (Oxford, Hart Publishing, 2010).

[57] K Mortelmans, 'The Principle of Loyalty to the Community and the Obligations of the Community Institutions' (1998) *Maastricht Journal of European and Comparative Law* 67.

Article 4 (3) TEU.[58] This is where, according to De Witte, the duty of loyalty 'becomes a true principle of law containing additional legal obligations beyond those found in the Treaty.'[59] For instance, the principles of consistency and conferral of powers find expression in the duty of loyalty.[60]

So when can the EU be 'disloyal'? A transgression of competence boundaries by the EU, a violation of the principle of conferral, or perhaps a blatant disregard for the principle of subsidiarity constitute instances where the EU is skirting the edges of the rule of law. It is worth noting that loyalty has become akin to principles that are binding upon EU institutions (eg subsidiarity) but may also be justiciable in an action against them. But justiciability in this regard is embedded in a theoretical context. There is only one case where the CJEU held that indeed the EU legislature breached the principle of conferral.[61] Conversely, there is no case at hand where the CJEU struck down a piece of EU legislation on the basis of subsidiarity violation.[62] So based on the above, one can deduct that either the EU institutions always act within their legal margins or that simply the CJEU insists on the importance of the intent of the EU legislature to harmonise national action and allows a wide discretion. The latter is more likely. The CJEU would only exercise its review powers when there is proof of a manifest error, misuse of powers or excess of discretion from the side of the EU legislator.

Critics have argued that 'the result is a light-touch standard of judicial review'.[63] Others have talked of the 'failure of subsidiarity as a judicial review principle' and its better fit as a legislative review principle.[64] For the purpose of our study it is important to establish how the above low level of scrutiny would play out in cases regarding the invocation of the rule of law as a ground of review. In particular, since there is no sign from the CJEU that subsidiarity (although justiciable in theory) would be treated differently as principles of judicial review of EU action in future cases, we can only assume that the rule of law would be as hard to pin down in terms of judicial application. Still, however, the rule of law is broader as a principle—it encompasses inter alia an obligation owed *erga omnes partes* to the EU, other Member States and the individual—creating, therefore, a legal interest for everyone involved in EU integration to seek enforcement against each other.[65]

---

[58] Case C-2/88 *Zwartveld* [1990] ECR I-3365, para 17.

[59] de Witte (n 49) 87.

[60] E Herlin-Karnell and T Konstadinides, 'The Rise and Expressions of Consistency in EU Law: Legal and Strategic Implications for European Integration' (2013) *Cambridge Yearbook of European Legal Studies* 139.

[61] Case C-376/98 *Germany v. European Parliament and Council* [2000] ECR 1-8419.

[62] See for an extensive review of the principle of subsidiarity: J Öberg, 'Subsidiarity as a Limit to the Exercise of EU Competences' (2017) *Yearbook of European Law* 1, published online on 25 November 2016, available from https://academic.oup.com/yel.

[63] See X Groussot and S Bogojevic, 'Subsidiarity as a Procedural Safeguard' in L Azoulai (ed), *The Question of Competence in the European Union* (Oxford, Oxford University Press, 2014) 244–45.

[64] GA Moens, 'The Principle of Subsidiarity in EU Judicial and Legislative Practice: Panacea or Placebo?' 41 (1) *Journal of Legislation* 65.

[65] R Baratta, 'Rule of Law "Dialogues" Within the EU: A Legal Assessment' (2016) *Hague Journal on the Rule of Law* 1.

Commentators are perhaps right to point out that 'the sovereignty of EU law establishes a rule of law, to which all public institutions within the Member States are subject, including national courts'.[66] As mentioned, most of the rule of law debate is predicated on Member States defaulting in different shapes or forms. Still, however, we shall not forget that EU institutions are equally bound by the same notion of the rule of law. This is even more so since, as discussed, the quality of judicial review of EU legislation on 'disloyalty grounds' is rather thin and judicial monitoring of the principles of conferral and subsidiarity needs improvement. We shall not fail to notice, however, the BVerfG's adamant position viz Germany's EU membership which does not exclude an ultra vires review of EU law in order to assess its conformity with the national constitutional framework concerning human rights and the rule of law, especially when they are deemed to be threatened.[67] The more recent jurisprudence of the Constitutional Court of Germany (BVerfG) has extended the BVerfG's scope of review of EU legislation to a supplementary intra vires assessment of EU acts which may impair the constitutional identity of the Basic Law.[68] According to the BVerfG, such an 'identity review' is inherent in the Treaty (Article 4 (2) TEU) and as such does not violate the principle of loyalty.[69]

This new kind of review remains so far a theoretical possibility and has not gained any express support by the Government or the Bundestag.[70] For instance, in its Outright Monetary Transactions (OMT) decision following a preliminary ruling by the CJEU the BVerfG confirmed that the OMT bond-buying programme does not 'manifestly' exceed the competences attributed to the European Central Bank (ECB) so as to trigger such a review. It, therefore, agreed with the CJEU that the OMT's effects on economic policy were only indirect and yielded to the primacy of EU law.[71] It further confirmed that the CJEU's decision that the OMT programme is within the bounds of EU competences and does not violate the prohibition of monetary financing of the budget remains within the mandate of the

---

[66] D Chalmers, *European Union Law: Cases and Materials* (Cambridge, Cambridge University Press, 2010) 203.

[67] *Brunner*, 2 BvR 687/85, 8 April 1987; *Lissabon-Urteil*, BVerfG, 2 BvE 2/08, 30 June 2009.

[68] *Gauweiler*, 2 BvR 2728/13, 14 January 2014.

[69] *Re: Extradition for the purpose of executing a sentence rendered in absence*, 2 BvR 2735/14, 15 December 2015.

[70] *Lisbon Urteil*, Judgment of 30 June 2009, BVerfG 2BvE 2/08, paras 211, 217; See also *Gauweiler (or OMT decision)*, Judgment of 14 Jan 2014, BVerfG, 2 BvR 2728/13, para 30 (cc). The BVerfG mentioned a number of cases decided by the Supreme Courts of Denmark, Estonia, Ireland; the Italian and Czech Constitutional Courts and the Polish and Spanish Constitutional Tribunals as well as the French Constitutional Council. According to the BVerfG these cases serve as examples of the protection of constitutional identity in other Member States. Still, however, in this respect, it is telling that the German Government did not seek the annulment of the OMT Programme by resorting to Art 263 TFEU. Neither did the Bundestag criticise the OMT Programme as a set of self-contained economic measures nor did it made any political pronouncements about its desirability. See T Konstadinides, 'Dealing with Parallel Universes: Antinomies of Sovereignty and the Protection of National Identity in European Judicial Discourse' (2015) 34 (1) *Yearbook of European Law* 127–69.

[71] Case C-62/14 *Gauweiler and Others* [2015] ECLI:EU:C:2015:400.

CJEU under Article 19 (1) sentence 2 TEU.[72] This provision can in turn be interpreted as setting the record of the CJEU's duties as a high-level judicial body bound by the rule of law.[73] Despite the OMT case outcome, the BVerfG reiterated (faintly) that when conducting its identity review, it looks into whether Article 79 (3) GG (Basic Law for the Federal Republic of Germany) has been affected by the Bundestag's transfer of powers to the EU. In particular, the Karlsruhe-based court emphasised its commitment to fundamental rights protection, especially human dignity under Article 1 GG as well as 'the fundamental principles that characterise the principles of democracy, of the rule of law, of the social state, and of the federal state within the meaning of Art 20 GG.'[74]

We shall also not forget that the principle of loyalty applies horizontally between the EU institutions encouraging inter-institutional dialogue and fostering institutional balance.[75] Additionally, it can be taken to imply respect between Member States when acting within the EU law spectrum. This idea takes the notion of equality before the law to the next level—ie the equal and concrete subjection of all actors of European integration (the Member States viz the EU institutions, the EU institutions viz the Member States, the EU institutions viz the EU institutions and the Member States viz their counterparts) to the principle of loyalty.[76] Such a notion of equality before the Treaties is underpinned by Article 4 (2) TEU with regard to the Member States. In particular, the CJEU has employed it to emphasise that the new Member States shall be treated on the basis of equality with the old Member States.[77]

Last, and in connection with the previous point, 'the solidarity principle creates an effect, via its procedural dimension (loyalty to the Union), of the Member States and the EU working together loyally.'[78] Indeed, Article 4 (3) has served as the basis of solidarity amongst Member States, initially acting as a barrier to the adoption of unilateral measures by the Member States in breach of the Treaties. In its early 'loyalty' jurisprudence, the CJEU stressed that the 'failure in the duty of solidarity accepted by Member States by the fact of their adherence to the Community strikes at the fundamental basis of the Community legal order.'[79] Solidarity was given a renewed emphasis in the Treaty of Lisbon.[80] Yet, in the context of

---

[72] Judgment of 21 June 2016–2 BvR 2728/13. See briefly: Press Release No 34/2016, 21 June 2016.

[73] Nic Shuibhne (n 3) 2.

[74] The Federal Constitutional Court, 'Constitutional Complaints and Organstreit Proceedings Against the OMT Programme of the European Central Bank Unsuccessful', Press Release No 34/2016 of 21 June 2016.

[75] Opinion of AG Tesauro in Case C-65/93 *Parliament v Council* [1995] ECR I-643, para 20.

[76] AV Dicey, *Introduction to the Study of the Law of the Constitution* 8th edn (Carmel, Liberty Fund Inc, 1982).

[77] Case C-336/09 *Poland v Commission* [2012] ECR I-0000.

[78] A Steinbach, 'The "Haircut" of Public Creditors under EU Law' (2016) 12 (2) *European Constitutional Law Review* 223, 322–23.

[79] Case 39–72 *Commission v Italy* (Slaughtered Cows) [1973] ECR 101, paras 24–25.

[80] Post-Lisbon, mutual solidarity appears in Art 67 (2) TFEU (framing a common policy on asylum, immigration and external border control), Art 122 TFEU (financial assistance in cases of severe

the multiple crises in Europe, one has to weigh the proliferation of mutual solidarity references in the Treaty against the hard reality of solidarity deficit in the EU. Hence when looking at the solidarity provisions in the Treaty, we come across a paradox that recent references to solidarity in the Treaty takes place in those areas where the legal framework is so intergovernmental that it cannot produce it. As such, the discussion of whether the EU can take a corrective approach to solidarity has to take place in the context of its competence to act. For instance, we need to note that any attempt for EU aid towards defaulting Member States has to take into account the spirit of the Treaty.[81]

B. The Principles of Consistency, Legitimate Expectations and Legal Certainty

The principle of consistency, also referred to as coherence, is important to the application of the rule of law in the EU. It embodies the idea that the law should make sense if considered as a whole by being rational and orderly.[82] As such, it constitutes a virtue by which a given legal system is to be judged. For the sake of clarity, in EU law, consistency can be divided into vertical consistency based on clear competence delimitation and conflict prevention/resolution between the EU and the Member States' legal orders, and horizontal consistency based on cooperation between the institutional actors involved in EU decision-making. We have discussed elsewhere the history and modern development of the principle of consistency.[83] Suffice to say here that the principle finds expression within a web of legal obligations in EU law. It is reflected in the notions of loyalty, discussed above, and primacy, as well as in the broader principles of good administration and governance related to openness, transparency and accountability. Loyalty, in particular, can be interpreted as the driving force to setting common principles and unified objectives in EU policies with the aim of eliminating contradiction.[84] Most importantly, under the Treaty of Lisbon the principle of consistency has become a justiciable principle under Article 7 TEU and Article 21 (3) TEU—hence

---

difficulties caused by natural disasters or exceptional occurrences), and Art 194 TFEU (Union policy on energy), Art 42 (7) TEU, the so-called 'mutual aid and assistance clause', and Art 222 TFEU, the so-called 'solidarity clause', re: express commitment of Member States to assist each other in the event of a terrorist attack or natural and manmade disaster.

[81] For instance, any attempt for EU temporary financial aid towards heavily debt-laden Member States has to take into account the spirit of the 'no-bailout' clause enshrined in Art 125 (1) TFEU.

[82] The search for a distinction between consistency and coherence often arises in the context of EU external relations: M Cremona, 'Coherence in EU Foreign Relations Law' in P Koutrakos (ed), *European Foreign Policy: Legal and Political Perspectives* (Cheltenham, Edward Elgar, 2011) 60 onwards; S Duke, Consistency as an issue in EU external activities, EIPA Working Paper 99/W/06, 3.

[83] See Herlin-Karnell and Konstadinides (n 60) 139.

[84] For a detailed discussion on how consistency links with loyalty, see Herlin-Karnell and Konstadinides, ibid.

EU institutions may be held accountable for undermining it. Having said that, the CJEU appears reluctant to enforce it against the EU institutions.[85]

Consistency is also relevant from the perspective of another synonymous principle—that of legal certainty, a general principle of EU law which requires that decisions are consistent with the framework of the existing legal system.[86] The CJEU embraces certainty in its jurisprudence claiming that the principles of legitimate expectations and legal certainty consist of part of the EU legal order.[87] In its original state context, legal certainty and legitimate expectations are interrelated because if the law is certain about its content and effect, citizens are in a position to set their expectations and rely on government policies. What is more, even when the law is certain, citizens shall be entitled to rely upon it as it has been presented by the public authority which knows the law. This relationship of trust between the governed and the governing is built upon the premise that administrators shall be held to their representations.

Likewise any changes in public policy shall balance the public interest and the expectations protected by the law. This is so that any modification to the law must be foreseeable so as to safeguard the expectations of the individual which may flow from such a modification. This is especially the case since such expectations may have given assurances which have been relied upon by the individual. It transpires that when the law is uncertain or misrepresented, citizens may be misled as to whether their conduct is right or wrong according to the law. The same occurs if the law applies to an act contrary to the principle of non-retroactivity, ie prior to that law being adopted. We shall also stress that in the event of an unlawful measure adopted by the state, its retroactive revocation has to take into account the extent to which the subjects of that measure have relied upon it. This protection of trust is vital to the preservation of the EU rule of law and constitutes a superior rule of the EU legal order for the protection of the individual.[88]

We shall note that the protection of legitimate expectations in EU law extends beyond procedural relief to include substantive judicial protection.[89] Early in its case law the CJEU established that the course of conduct followed by an administrative authority (eg the Council) may give rise to expectations which, even in the

---

[85] See Case T-512/12, *Front Populaire v Council* [2015] ECLI:EU:T:2015:953, para 153. With reference to the justiciability of Art 7 TFEU against the acts of the EU institutions, the General Court provided that: 'The various policies of the European Union derive from different provisions of the founding treaties and acts adopted pursuant to those provisions. The supposed "inconsistency" of an act with the policy of the European Union in a given area necessarily implies that the act concerned is contrary to a provision, a rule or a principle which governs that policy. That fact alone, if it were established, would be sufficient to lead to the annulment of the act concerned, without it being necessary to rely on Article 7 TEU.'

[86] See for an analysis on legal certainty: Lord Mance, 'Should the law be certain?' The Oxford Shrieval lecture, 11 October 2011, available at www.supremecourt.gov.uk/docs/speech_111011.pdf.

[87] Joined Cases 205-215/82 *Milchkontor GmbH v Germany* [1983] ECR 2633.

[88] See Opinion of Advocate General Trabucchi in Case 5/75 *Deuka* [1975] ECR 759.

[89] See for detail A Turk, *Judicial Review in EU Law* (Cheltenham, Edward Elgar, 2009) 129–33.

absence of a private law right, may be recognised in public law.[90] In this respect the CJEU has also stressed that the protection of legitimate expectations 'appears to be an expression, taking the form of a subjective right, of legal certainty.'[91] A sudden change of EU policy, for instance, which cannot be foreseen by the prudent trader and causes her unexpected financial consequences, may constitute a violation of the principle of legitimate expectation and therefore the rule of law. The CJEU has established the relevant conditions that must be satisfied in order for individuals to claim entitlement of the protection of the legitimate expectation.[92]

Despite the above judicial guarantees, there are expectations which are difficult to challenge before European Courts. In *Mugraby*, the appellant brought a case against the Council and of the Commission before the CJEU invoking the latter's obligations under the human rights clause written in the EU Association Agreement with Lebanon (Article 2) to take measures against Lebanon (eg suspension of economic aid under Article 86 (2) of the Agreement) on account of repeated human rights violations in the country.[93] In particular, Mugraby claimed that he had legitimate expectations that his fundamental rights would be protected by all EU institutions, including the European Courts. He also argued that those institutions were under a duty to hold the parties to the Agreement accountable to their obligations. The General Court dismissed his action for failure to act. Then Mugraby appealed to the CJEU claiming, inter alia, that the General Court's interpretation of the concept of 'broad margin of discretion' that the EU institutions enjoy in the conduct of EU external relations violates the concept of the rule of law. The CJEU dismissed the appeal confirming that there was no unlawful conduct from the part of the EU institutions which justified an award for damages. Furthermore, according to the CJEU, Mugraby did not establish how he could acquire a right from his expectations, especially since the Agreement in question did not give rights to individuals.

Turning now to legal certainty as a key requirement for the rule of law, it can be stressed that the principle that EU measures have to enable individuals to know the extent of the obligations imposed on them (so as to be aware of their rights and obligations and act accordingly) has a long tradition in the EU jurisprudence.[94] For the principle of legal certainty to be respected the publishing of the EU measure in question is essential—an EU regulation cannot take effect in law unless it has been published in the Official Journal. This allows individuals to ascertain whether the

---

[90] Case 81/72 *Commission v Council (Civil Service Salaries)* [1973] ECR 575; See: Case 74/74 *CNTA v Commission* (1975) ECR 533.

[91] C-177/99 *Ampafrance* [2000] ECR I-7013, para 67.

[92] See Case T-347/03 *Branco v Commission* (2005) ECR II-255, para 102.

[93] T-292/09 *Mugraby v Council and Commission* [2011] ECLI:EU:T:2011:418. The case was appealed to the CJEU. See Case C-581/11 *Mugraby v Council and Commission* [2012] ECLI:EU:C:2012:466.

[94] Joint cases 42/59 and 49/59 *SNUP A T v High Authority* ([1961] ECR 109; Case C-63/83 *R v Kirk* [1984] ECR 2689, para 21; Case C-331/88 *R v MAFF, ex parte Fedesa* [1990] ECR I-4023.

national rules comply with EU law.[95] Today it has been established that preserving legal certainty is an important task for EU institutions when legislating in sensitive areas, such as counter-terrorism. Advocate General Bot remarked in his Opinion in *European Parliament v Council* that the succinct delimitation of the spheres of application of Article 75 TFEU and Article 215 (2) TFEU shall not be based on the Council's abstract distinction between 'internal', 'external' and 'international' terrorists.[96] He posited that since terrorism is damaging to 'common values and the very foundations of the rule of law' it affects and concerns the international community at large. As such, according to Bot, the geographical scale of a terrorist threat at issue is irrelevant in determining the legal basis under which restrictive measures shall be adopted. The Advocate General concluded that 'in so far as it generates legal uncertainty, the distinction advocated by the Council runs counter to the need for an effective fight against terrorism.'[97]

Legal certainty has to be balanced against other fundamental principles of EU law. For instance, on the one hand the CJEU has been explicit that national rules which confer finality on judicial decisions or arbitration awards contribute to legal certainty. On the other hand, however, Advocate General Mazak stressed in *Agenzia delle Entrate* that domestic courts are under a duty 'to defend the rule of law in the [EU]—which is liable to be affected by a domestic rule … which seeks to lay down the principle of *res judicata*, in so far as that rule makes it impossible for national courts to apply an [EU] rule correctly.'[98] It follows that although EU law does not generally require Member States to amend their rules of procedure conferring finality on a decision, such rules (establishing legal certainty) have to be reconciled to give effect to the principles of legality, EU law primacy and effectiveness in order to remedy a breach of EU law. The obligation to preclude the principle of *res judicata* by obliging a Member State to review and reopen a decision also flows from the principle of sincere cooperation. If any conclusion can be drawn, at this stage, it is that at times the uniform and effective application of EU law would prevail over legal certainty guaranteed by domestic rules of procedure. This is not only diminishing Member States' procedural autonomy but renders the application of the EU rule of law rather unpredictable and subject to a unilateral assessment by the EU institutions.

---

[95] C-345/06 *Heinrich* [2009] ECR I-1659. See comment by M Bobek, 'Case C-345/06, *Gottfried Heinrich*, Judgment of the Court of Justice (Grand Chamber) of 10 March 2009' (2009) 46 (6) *Common Market Law Review* 2077–94.

[96] Opinion of AG Bot in Case C-130/10 *European Parliament v Council* [2012] ECLI:EU:C:2012:472, para 75. The case concerned a challenge by the European Parliament against the adoption of restrictive measures under Art 215 (2) TFEU against natural or legal persons and groups or non-state entities associated with terrorist activities. Under this legal basis, the European Parliament was excluded from the legislative process. The European Parliament insisted that the measure ought to have been taken on the basis of Art 75 TFEU, which ensured a greater degree of parliamentary participation through the ordinary legislative procedure.

[97] ibid.

[98] Opinion of Advocate General Mazak, Case C-2/08 *Amministrazione dell'economia e delle Finanze and Agenzia delle Entrate* [2009] ECLI:EU:C:2009:180, para 43.

C. The Principle of Legality

The core aspect of the rule of law is the idea of government or public authority only through and according to law. Since EU membership has established that the state is no longer the only source of legality, the status of legality as a constitutional principle is central in our understanding of the EU rule of law:

> The rule-of-law principle is very well established at the EU level. Moreover, as a result of the juridification of the global legal order, a global rule of law has emerged as a principle in this order. The idea behind an administrative legitimacy based on the rule of law is that the rule of law at the levels beyond the state absorbs some of the functions of the democratic principle transforming it into a meta-principle. This meta-principle plays not only the role of safeguarding legality but also the role of compensating for the lack of a global democracy. Especially at the levels beyond the state the distinction between the formal and the substantive elements of the rule of law acquires a vital role.[99]

Although legality constitutes a general principle of EU law, some critics have expressed doubts over the CJEU's presumption that legality is a common principle across the Member States. For instance, the UK differs from other Member States in that legality is not a derivative of popular sovereignty but rather emanates from the idea of liberty as regulated by common law endorsing, therefore, judicial activism and law-making.[100] This is important because, although the EU largely reflects the civil law doctrine, common law also constitutes a significant part of the European legal tradition that informs EU law. Furthermore, an abstract commitment to legality is no guarantee that the EU is consistent with the protection of procedural fairness, justiciable rights, due process and prevention of abuse of powers.

The above is particularly important in the context of EU enlargement since, contrary to the other constitutional principles explored previously, legality constitutes a condition for EU membership. As stressed by a commentator, the 'legality' aspect of EU accession 'is not only meant to guide CEE applicants but also reassure reluctant Member States that any disruption risks emanating from enlargement would be minimal'.[101] It therefore transpires that a vague notion of the principle of legality in the context of EU enlargement can be detrimental inter alia to the internal coherence of the EU rule of law and the EU's extra-territorial claim as a value promoter alongside the Council of Europe. A strong emphasis on legality as an EU accession criterion is particularly important if we take into account the current early stages of post-accession rule-of-law checks. For instance, we have

---

[99] E Chiti and BG Mattarella (eds), *Global Administrative Law and EU Administrative Law: Legal Issues and Comparison* (Berlin, Springer, 2011) 403.

[100] LFM Besselink et al, 'Introduction: Legality in Multiple Legal Orders' in LFM Besselink et al, *The Eclipse of the Legality Principle in the European Union* (The Hague, Kluwer Law International, 2011) 5.

[101] D Tamvaki, 'The Copenhagen Criteria and the Evolution of Popular Consent to EU law: From Legality to Normative Justifiability in Poland and the Czech Republic' in W Sadurski et al, *Spreading Democracy and the Rule of Law? The Impact of EU Enlargemente for the Rule of Law, Democracy and Constitutionalism in Post-Communist Legal Orders* (Berlin, Springer, 2006) 155.

witnessed in relation to developments in Romania, Hungary and Poland that once the safeguard clauses based on the Accession Treaties expire, the EU enforcement kit is weak, by comparison, to tackle any rule-of-law deficiencies arising in the Member States promptly and efficiently.

With regard to EU internal coherence, legality as a general principle of EU law is particularly important in the context of EU criminal law. It is codified in Article 49 of the EU Charter of Fundamental Rights, which apart from the public international law 'no crime without law' motif (*nullem crimen, nulla poena sine lege*),[102] sets out another two principles associated with the rule of law. These are the principles of non-retroactivity (mentioned above), and proportionality (analysed below) stemming from the common constitutional traditions of the Member States and the CJEU's established case law. These principles, as well as equality and non-discrimination, are at the epicentre of EU criminal law.[103] Whether as a general principle of EU law or as a codified principle of EU criminal law, legality serves a dual purpose. It constitutes a legitimacy factor which applies to the exercise of the EU legislature's criminal law competence as well as the national authorities' legislative power and control over the application of EU legislation.

Despite EU law's emphasis on legality, there have been criticisms regarding the relevant Treaty provisions establishing EU competence in criminal matters which turn legality on its head. The argument is twofold: first, there is the classic argument that the EU lacks the democratic mandate to impose criminal offences and sanctions. Second, it has been argued that the EU's newly-fangled criminal law competence in the TFEU lacks precision.[104] In relation to the first argument, given the shared nature of EU criminal law competence under the TFEU, EU institutions may introduce criminal offences in the form of directives while Member States need to implement the minimum rules set by those directives via their domestic law. In their endeavour to do so, however, national authorities may often find themselves constrained by the wording of the relevant directive adopted under Article 83 (2) TFEU which often determines the kind of behaviour that Member States should regard as criminal.[105] Hence Member States are at times portrayed as having lost an important competence to EU institutions that do not enjoy democratic mandate. Against this argument, it can be claimed that prior to the Lisbon Treaty matters were probably worse in respect of legality. As it may be recalled,

---

[102] S Lamb, 'Nullum crimen, nulla poena sine lege in International Criminal Law' in A Cassese et al (eds), *The Rome Statute of the International Criminal Court: A Commentary* Vol 1 (Oxford, Oxford University Press, 2002) 733.

[103] See Case C-303/05 *Advocaten voor de Wereld VZW v Leden van de Ministerraad* [2007] ECR I-3633, para 45. In this case, the CJEU upheld the legality of the structure of the mutual recognition system established by the Framework Decision.

[104] See H Labayle, 'EU Competence in Criminal Matters' in V Mitsilegas et al, *Research Handbook on EU Criminal Law* (Cheltenham, Edward Elgar, 2016) 74–75.

[105] See for an analysis of the competence and enforcement aspects of Art 83 (2) TFEU; E Baker, 'A Case of "Nested Enforcement": Article 83(2) TFEU, Compliance and the Area of Freedom, Security and Justice post-Lisbon' in S Drake and M Smith (eds), New Directions in Effective Enforcement of EU Law (Cheltenham, Edward Elgar, 2016).

criminal law was tucked away under the former Third Pillar (Police and Judicial Cooperation in Criminal Matters—PJCCM). But still, the EU legislature made attempts to adopt a unified approach under the former First 'Community' Pillar against crimes such as money laundering and terrorism by using an internal market legal basis (Article 114 TFEU). While it was successful in adopting measures whose centre of gravity did not concern the functioning of the internal market but public safety and crime prevention, the EU legislature did not enjoy at the time the (criminal law) competence to either provide a definite list of offences or create a threshold for criminal activity.[106] It can therefore be contended that it was the lack of EU criminal competence that undermined legality prior to Lisbon because although EU law was often occupied with the facilitation of national action in the field of criminal law, it was not sufficiently precise for a potential offender to know whether s/he will fall under the scope of criminal law or not. The CJEU was sometimes called on to define the boundary between measures coming under the former Community pillar and those related to criminal matters, which had to be adopted under the then Third Pillar.[107]

Two criticisms can be made with reference to the claim about competence imprecision in the field of criminal law and how it affects the legality principle in the post-Lisbon dispensation. The first relates to the way criminal law competence is shared in EU law. In constitutional terms, national implementation legislation is a domestic act which is separate from a given directive. In essence, therefore, a domestic act is not directly dependent upon the directive it purports to implement when it comes to a question about the domestic act's validity. On the other hand, however, the annulment of a Directive (eg on Data Retention) may carry substantial implications for the domestic implementing act, especially when there is pending criminal litigation under that domestic act. In this case, domestic law will have to fill the void by stipulating the conditions in which the right in question (eg privacy) could or could not be limited, providing protection against arbitrary interference. The CJEU has been instructive in this matter. By exercising a repatriated competence, the national legislature in question would have to act in a spirit of loyal cooperation and act in a way which is compatible to EU law—the Charter in particular. This may include the undertaking of an obligation that any limitations upon individual rights imposed by national legislation will be subject to judicial scrutiny.[108]

The second competence imprecision criticism relates to the modalities of Article 83 (2) TFEU. This provision enables the EU legislature to adopt measures

---

[106] See in the context of the 1991 and 2001 Money Laundering: E Herlin-Karnell, 'Is Administrative Law still Relevant? How the Battle of Sanctions has shaped EU Criminal Law' in Mitsilegas et al (n 104) 240; see also T Konstadinides, 'Wavering between Centres of Gravity: Comment on Ireland v Parliament and Council' (2010) 35 (1) *European Law Review* 88.

[107] With the Lisbon Treaty judicial co-operation in the fight against serious crime became a fully-fledged EU policy. The ordinary legislative procedure applies and the CJEU's jurisdiction has been extended in former Third Pillar areas, albeit subject to certain limits defined in Protocol 36 annexed to the Treaty.

[108] See C-203/15 *Tele2 Sverige AB* [2016] ECLI:EU:C:2016:970.

in criminal matters in order to ensure the effective implementation of EU policies. To the critical eye perhaps, it can be read as an open challenge to the *ultima ratio* principle—ie enabling the EU to adopt a wide array of measures in order to combat criminal behaviour resorting to excessive overregulation.[109] Of course this is a weak claim if we bear in mind that the exercise of powers provided in Article 83 (2) TFEU requires clear rules governing, for example, the extent of interference to fundamental rights allowed under Article 49 of the EU Charter of Fundamental Rights which shall also be in compliance with the principle of proportionality viz the necessity of the goal set by the EU legislature.[110]

D. The Principle of Proportionality

The principle of proportionality is linked to the 'emergence of the social state under the rule of law.'[111] It plays a key role in constitutional review of public acts and, in the context of the EU, it emphasises that the EU must be limited to what is necessary to achieve the objectives of the Treaties.[112] The principle applies to both legislative and administrative measures adopted by EU institutions as well as national measures falling within the scope of EU law.[113] In recent years the CJEU has used the proportionality principle as a means of weighing EU fundamental freedoms against national legislation that protects domestic interests (whether intimate to national competence or not).[114] The full content of proportionality

---

[109]   See E Herlin-Karnell, 'The Lisbon Treaty, a Critical Analysis of its Impact on EU Criminal Law' (2010) *The European Criminal Law Association's Forum* 59.

[110]   See M Miglieti, 'The New Criminal Law Competence in Action' IES Working Paper 5/2013, available from www.ies.be/files/Working%20Paper%20Miglietti.pdf.

[111]   W Sauter, 'Proportionality in EU Law: A Balancing Act?', TILEC Discussion Paper No 2013-003, 4. Available at SSRN: https://ssrn.com/abstract=2208467.

[112]   See for an extensive coverage of the principle of proportionality: E Ellis, *The Principle of Proportionality in the Laws of Europe* (Oxford, Hart Publishing, 1999).

[113]   In *R (Lumsdon) v Legal Services Board* [2015] UKSC 41 (paras 36, 37) the UK Supreme Court provided a useful summary of the principle of proportionality. As such, 'proportionality as a ground of review of EU measures is concerned with the balancing of private interests adversely affected by such measures against the public interests which the measures are intended to promote; proportionality functions in that context as a check on the exercise of public power of a kind traditionally found in public law. Proportionality as a ground of review of national measures, on the other hand, has been applied most frequently to measures interfering with the fundamental freedoms guaranteed by the EU Treaties. Although private interests may be engaged, the court is there concerned first and foremost with the question whether a Member State can justify an interference with a freedom guaranteed in the interests of promoting the integration of the internal market, and the related social values, which lie at the heart of the EU project.' See Case Comment 'R *(on the application of Lumsdon) v Legal Services Board*: Legal representation—Quality Assurance Scheme for Advocates—guidance' (2015) 11 *Criminal Law Review* 894.

[114]   This includes controversial cases where EU citizenship rights have been turned against an individual's own Member State of nationality. See Case C-135/08, *Rottmann* [2010] ECR I-1449, para 42. What is more, in recent years third country nationals have sought to rely on the principles of proportionality and other EU law concepts such as non-discrimination, to obtain EU citizenship-related rights. The CJEU has abstained from applying proportionality insofar as EU law has no competence in the level of social assistance to be paid to the 'Zambrano' carer. See Case C-34/09 *Zambrano* [2011] ECR I-01177.

has derived from the CJEU's jurisprudence as it has been applied over time. With reference to EU action the CJEU has established that 'the lawfulness of the prohibition of an economic activity is subject to the condition that the prohibitory measures are appropriate and necessary in order to achieve the objectives legitimately pursued by the legislation in question.'[115] Conversely, when it comes to assessing Member States' acts, they must not be applied in a discriminatory manner; they must be justified by imperative requirements in the general interest; and they must be suitable for securing the attainment of the objective which it pursues as well as necessary in order to attain it.[116]

The CJEU has decided that Member States enjoy certain discretion to decide on the degree of protection to be achieved with reference to legitimate interests underpinning national regulatory structures such as the protection of public health. This is because the level of public health protection may, for instance, vary from one state to the next. While, however, Member States are afforded a certain margin of discretion to achieve different legitimate objectives, the rule of law mandates that the law which pursues them shall be singular and coherent according to the Treaty. The reference to consistency in Article 7 TFEU *qua* sincere cooperation under Article 4 (3) TEU (which applies as much to Member States as to the EU itself) is reminiscent of the EU's obligation to set up common principles and unified objectives in EU policies whose aim is to eliminate contradiction. A similar logic seems to be applying in the way the CJEU is assessing objective justification defences. It follows that national provisions restricting fundamental freedoms under the Treaty to pursue legitimate objectives will only be appropriate if the competent domestic authorities use their discretionary powers according to transparent and objective criteria attaining, in a coherent and systematic manner, the objective pursued.[117] By contrast, Member States will not be afforded a margin of appreciation where the above basic requirements are not fulfilled, especially when other less restrictive means are available to protect their legitimate interests.[118]

But what is the position when Member States put forward singularities that do not consist of legitimate objectives or when they attempt to recalibrate legitimate objectives into constitutional values which are (according to their constitutional courts) unamenable to alteration? Take for example the increasing claims made by the Member States under Article 4 (2) TEU invoking national or constitutional identity as a means of derogating from their EU law obligations.[119] Indeed, rules on packaging and selling of goods or geographical and demographic restrictions related to the performance of a particular service in the internal market can hardly be invoked as aspects of national identity in the same way as, for instance, respect

---

[115] See Case C-331/88 *Fedesa* [1990] ECR-I4023, para 13.
[116] Case C-55/94 *Gebhard* [1995] ECR I-4165.
[117] See Case C-539/11 *Ottica* [2013] ECLI:EU:C:2013:591, paras 44–45.
[118] Case C-265/06 *Commission v Portugal* [2008] ECR I-2245.
[119] See Konstadinides (n 71) 127.

to a Member State's high regard for autonomous collective bargaining.[120] With regard to the latter cases, the CJEU may follow its jurisprudence on fundamental rights. The CJEU has established that apart from diminishing Member States' actions under an EU law derogation, fundamental rights may be solely relied upon as an EU law derogation themselves. The CJEU has, likewise, adapted the principle of proportionality to formulate a new approach to the relationship between EU market freedoms and fundamental rights as protected in national Constitutions.[121]

We may recall here the CJEU's landmark judgments in *Schmidberger* and *Omega* which managed pragmatically the conflict between fundamental rights and fundamental market freedoms.[122] The CJEU established that since both the EU and the Member States are required to respect fundamental rights, their protection is a legitimate interest which justifies restrictions upon EU law obligations (ie compliance with free movement law).[123] Indeed, the protection of fundamental rights as an attribute of constitutional identity runs like a leitmotif in the majority of post-Lisbon case law on Article 4 (2) TEU.[124] National identity has therefore been broadly construed to include constitutional autonomy and national self-determination, as well as concerns over the protection of fundamental constitutional rights or, in pre-Lisbon terms, legitimate interests. Like in *Schmidberger*, such interests are weighed by the CJEU taking into account all circumstances of the case at hand in order to strike the right balance between them. The purpose of proportionality is therefore to make sure that the restriction in question is suitable for ensuring the attainment of the legitimate objective pursued and does not go beyond what is necessary to achieve it.

Next to suitability and necessity the CJEU has added another limb to its proportionality test, namely proportionality *stricto sensu* which asks the question whether the burden imposed by the measure is disproportionate to the benefits secured.[125] This development implies that proportionality may be employed as an explicit balance of interests. This is important since the CJEU's proportionality test based on suitability and necessity seems somewhat outdated in the post-Lisbon dispensation. This is because EU law derogations on legitimate interests

---

[120] Having said that, one may still argue that Member States could resort to national identity to defend internal market restrictions.

[121] Case C-438/05 *Viking* [2007] ECR I-10779; Case C-341/05 *Laval* [2007] ECR I-11767.

[122] Case C-112/00 *Schmidberger* [2003] ECR I-5659; Case C-36/02 *Omega Spielhallen* [2004] ECR I-9609.

[123] We refer here to the examples provided by former Advocate General Maduro in Case C-213/07 *Michaniki* [2008] ECR I-9999, later recast in Case C-208/09 *Sayn-Wittgenstein* [2010] ECR I-13693 as early manifestations of national identity. Characteristically, Maduro commented in para 32 of Michaniki that, 'the preservation of national constitutional identity can ... enable a Member State to develop, within certain limits, its own definition of a legitimate interest.'

[124] For an extensive study see: Cloots (n 56); Alcoberro Llivina (n 56).

[125] The *proportionality stricto sensu* approach has been supported by CJEU's case law. See, for instance, Case C-283/11 *Sky Österreich* [2013] ECR I-0000. See also SA de Vries, 'Balancing Fundamental Rights with Economic Freedoms According to the European Court of Justice' (2013) 9 (1) *Utrecht Law Review* 169–92.

no longer concern solely the resolution of conflicts arising between economic and non-economic values and objectives. In recent years, Member States have invoked fundamental rights enshrined in their Constitutions as a means of derogating from EU law. At times, they have resorted to Article 4 (2) TEU as an express EU law derogation over the preservation of their constitutional identity.

Yet, although the introduction of Article 4 (2) TEU may have encouraged Member States to be more vocal about their claim of selfhood, it has coincided with the EU's renewed commitment to fundamental rights. Article 6 TEU has inter alia made the EU Charter of Fundamental Rights binding and applicable in all cases where Member States are acting within the scope of EU law.[126] This development has profoundly minimised national claims for differentiation. EU obligations to respect national identities are now subordinate to the common values and principles listed in Articles 2 and 3 TEU—the components of a workable European identity to which Member States have adhered.[127] The CJEU, thus, envisages a form of constitutionalism where although the state has an absolute monopoly over the definition of constitutional identity (the 'what'), the power to determine the compatibility of legitimate interests with EU obligations (the 'how') is vested in the CJEU.

IV. CONCLUSION

This chapter examined the origins, rise, legal geography and different expressions of the rule of law in the EU legal order. It located the manifestations of the rule of law in EU primary law and a number of constitutional principles which either emanate from the Treaty, the Charter or feature in the CJEU's case law as common to the Member States. The purpose of this chapter has been to illustrate that although somewhat cryptic and far from fostering a common European understanding, the express commitment to the rule of law in EU primary law confirms its multiple function in EU internal policies as a common value and the backbone for the legal protection of fundamental rights in Europe. The above functions demonstrate that the adaptation of the rule of law to the supranational level is a work in progress, although, as one may argue, in the form of patchwork rather than within a set of clear guidelines that would determine the scope of the EU constitutional project.

Often, the morphology of the rule of law is subject to a balancing exercise between field pre-emption by EU law (ie displacement of national law in the field

---

[126] Case C-617/10 *Åkerberg Fransson* [2013] ECLI:EU:C:2013:105.
[127] See L Gormley, 'Reflections on the Architecture of the European Union after the Treaty of Amsterdam' in D O'Keeffe and P Twomey, Legal Issues of the Amsterdam Treaty (Oxford, Hart Publishing, 1999) 60; T Konstadinides, 'Constitutional Identity as a Shield and as a Sword: The European Legal Order within the Framework of National Constitutional Settlement' (2011) 13 *Cambridge Yearbook of European Legal Studies* 195.

concerned), the application of general principles of EU law or other less established constitutional principles and the adaptation of national procedural autonomy to goalpost alteration by EU law. There, the danger is not so much in the crash impact between the EU rule of law and national countervailing principles but in the concern that adherence to the rule of law may become a justification to expand EU law in constitutionally illegitimate ways. Such an occurrence would shake the foundations of the EU–Member States relationship based on the caveat that each is supreme on their own terms.

If any conclusions could be drawn at this stage it would be that first, the EU's express commitment to the rule of law in the Treaty is relatively recent, second, that the EU rule of law is not entirely dependent upon national features and third, that in order to comprehend it, we need to conceptualise it within its constitutive values. It is, therefore, argued that the EU rule of law cannot be theorised on its own because it neither forms a self-containing constitutional principle, nor does it comprise a justiciable notion utilised in cases before European or national courts. It is rather an umbrella value under which a number of written and unwritten justiciable constitutional principles find shelter. As such, this chapter looked at both the Treaty references to the EU rule of law as well as examined the above-mentioned constitutional principles that underpin it in order for the reader to contextualise it and understand it better. These principles, such as the principle of sincere cooperation and legal certainty are as important for the Member States as they are for the EU institutions themselves to maintain constitutional order by limiting their ability to pursue policies that would compromise common goals. Neither can avoid a review of their actions vis-à-vis their conformity with those principles, most of them entrenched in the EU's basic constitutional charter, the Treaty.

Part II

Enforcement

4

Holding EU Institutions to the Rule of Law

I. INTRODUCTION

THIS CHAPTER WILL discuss whether the EU institutions account for their behaviour in accordance with rule of law standards. Let us begin by asking a simple question: when does the EU contravene the rule of law? As discussed earlier in the book, a transgression of the boundaries mandated by the principle of sincere cooperation, conferral, or perhaps a blatant disregard for the principle of subsidiarity constitute instances where the EU institutions are skirting the edges of the rule of law by going beyond the letter of the Treaty to achieve their policies. Such a misbehaviour may have an adverse effect upon the common good and brings to mind what Tamahana calls creeping or pervasive instrumentalism.[1] There are also instances where the quality of EU legislation is poorly justified on formal or substantive grounds or it is incompatible with fundamental rights creating, therefore, grounds for challenge against the decisions adopted by the EU institutions.[2]

This chapter focuses on a central idea to the rule of law—that administration should be procedurally and substantively accountable before the courts. The idea is that since democratic control is minimal at the adoption of an EU act then the EU—as a community based on the rule of law—can compensate the individual by providing her with ample opportunity to obtain effective judicial review of that act if it adversely affects her position. The chapter is therefore taking a rights-based approach to judicial review of EU acts. It begins with the premise that judicial review of the exercise of EU public authority is constitutive for the rule of law since absence or shortage of remedies for the wrongful acts of EU institutions would not only undermine the substantive rights conferred on individuals by

---

[1] See B Tamanaha, 'The Perils of Pervasive Legal Instrumentalism' Vol 1 (Montesquieu Lecture Series, Tilburg University, 2005).

[2] See C Murphy, *EU Counter-Terrorism Law: Pre-Emption and the Rule of Law* (Oxford, Hart Publishing, 2012). See in particular: 'Epilogue: EU Counter-Terrorism in a post-"War on Terror"'; Murphy's concerns are reflected in the more recent proposal for a new Counter-Terrorism Directive to be adopted in 2017 and replacing Council Framework Decision 2002/475/JHA on combating terrorism. See for criticism: Human Rights Watch, 'EU Counter-Terrorism Directive Seriously Flawed', 30 November 2016, available from www.hrw.org/news/2016/11/30/eu-counterterrorism-directive-seriously-flawed.

EU law. It would also jeopardise the character of the precepts of EU administrative law concerning procedural and substantive review.

Subsequently, the chapter examines the Court of Justice of the European Union (CJEU)'s and national courts' ability to stand by their role as protectors of individual rights through their respective power of judicial review of EU acts and preliminary rulings requests. Indeed, one of the main features of the EU as a polity based on the rule of law is encapsulated in the CJEU's function to ensure that the measures adopted by the EU institutions and the Member States are in line with the founding Treaties and the constitutional principles developed over time by the CJEU explored in previous chapters. In short, this chapter will discuss the substantive aspects of the rule of law by looking at how individuals can enforce their entitlement under EU law before EU and national courts.

Admittedly, the CJEU has been provided with a wide jurisdiction which can be summarised in guaranteeing the effectiveness of the EU Treaties and the observance of the rule of law. The original Article 6 Treaty on European Union (TEU) inserted by the Treaty of Maastricht provided that the CJEU shall ensure that in the interpretation and application of this Treaty, the law is observed. This statement is still reinforced in Article 19 TEU which suggests that the CJEU's compulsory jurisdiction is key in the development of the rule of law at EU level. More specifically, the CJEU 'shall ensure that in the interpretation and application of the Treaties the law is observed.' As it is eminent, early in its judgments, the CJEU made pronouncements about the character of the Treaty as a constitutional charter, albeit concluded in the form of an international agreement.[3] Most importantly, perhaps, for the purpose of this chapter, the CJEU has been explicit from the outset about its duty to ensure that the rule of law is enforced through judicial (including constitutional) review. According to the CJEU:

> [T]he European Union is a union based on the rule of law in which the acts of its institutions are subject to review of their compatibility with, in particular, the Treaties, the general principles of law and fundamental rights. To that end, the FEU Treaty has established, by Articles 263 and 277, on the one hand, and Article 267, on the other, a complete system of legal remedies and procedures designed to ensure judicial review of the legality of European Union acts, and has entrusted such review to the Courts of the European Union.[4]

In the absence of a rule-of-law specific provision (similar to Article 7 TEU) to target deviant EU institutions, we will consider two of the abovementioned provisions, Articles 263 and 267 Treaty on the Functioning of the European Union (TFEU), in turn discussing their contribution as direct and indirect means of

---

[3] See Opinion 1/91 [1991] ECR I-6079, para 21.
[4] Recently illustrated in Case C-583/11 P *Inuit* [2013] ECLI:EU:C:2013:625, paras 91, 92. The CJEU has also been willing to review measures adopted by other (less mainstream) bodies and agencies such as the European Investment Bank. It is interesting, for the purpose of our discussion, that the CJEU makes a connection there with the application of the rule of law. See Case C-15/00 *Commission v EIB* [2003] ECR I-7281, para 75.

contesting the legality of EU acts. Of course there are other actions that can be brought directly before the CJEU which, for reasons of economy, are not covered here.[5] The study of direct actions against the EU institutions and the preliminary reference procedure as a means of challenging EU decisions is relevant for the purpose of this book because, as stressed by the European Parliament's Directorate-General for Internal Policies, 'the imperative to use Articles 263 and 267 TFEU to develop principles of EU Administrative law was fuelled by the background precept of the rule of law, which is now recognised in Article 2 TEU.'[6]

II. JUDICIAL REVIEW OF EU ACTS AS A MEANS OF INDIVIDUAL PROTECTION

Judicial review is essential in tempering the power of the EU institutions and, as it is well documented, Member States have often taken action against the EU institutions claiming violation of one of the four legitimate grounds listed in Article 263 TFEU (lack of competence; infringement of an essential procedure; infringement of the Treaties or any rule of law; misuse of powers) or the principle of proportionality.[7] Still, however, judicial review at the EU level sometimes fails to protect individual rights. The history of the EU teaches us that it shall not be taken for granted that Member States will take action on every occasion to defend the procedural or substantive rights of their citizens who may be affected negatively by EU legislation. The reality is that since Member States act collectively through the EU, the majority of national representatives in the Council may have voted in favour of a controversial act regardless of its adverse legal implications at home for a category of citizens in their capacity as traders, internet service providers, environmental activists or cross-border migrants.

---

[5] Art 265 TFEU provides for actions against the EU institutions for failure to act. Although it can be pleaded as an alternative course of action, it is closely related to Art 263 TFEU which is considered in detail in this chapter. In fact the CJEU has described the two provisions as 'one and the same method of recourse' (Case 15/70 *Chevally v Commission* [1970] ECR 975). On a different note, a plea of illegality under Art 277 TFEU is a direct action but it is not independent from an action for annulment under Art 263 TFEU. Last Art 340 TFEU is an independent course of action. Individuals may bring an action for damages against the EU for damages caused by its officials but only in cases where the rule infringed confers rights on individuals, the breach is sufficiently serious and there is a direct causal link between the breach and the damage. This is reminiscent of state liability rules under *Brasserie* (See Case C-352/98 P *Bergaderm v Commission* [2000] ECR I-5291; Cases C-46/93 and C-48/93 *Brasserie du Pêcheur v Germany, & The Queen v Secretary of State for Transport ex parte Factortame* [1996] ECR I-1029). However, it must be noted that, due to the level of discretion left to Member States in the implementation of EU law (especially EU Directives) and considering the *Brasserie* criterion of 'sufficiently serious breach', the CJEU will rarely hold the EU responsible under Art 340 TFEU.

[6] European Parliament, DG for Internal Policies, 'EU Administrative Law: The Acquis', 2010, available from www.europarl.europa.eu/RegData/etudes/note/join/2010/432745/IPOL-JURI_NT(2010) 432745_EN.pdf.

[7] See on formal and substantive grounds of review: R Schütze, *An Introduction to European Law* (Cambridge, Cambridge University Press, 2012) Ch 8.

Even when Member States decide to take action under Article 263 TFEU by using the EU as a medium it may be out of self-interest. To provide an example, some years ago all national representatives in the Council of the EU apart from Ireland and the Czech Republic voted in favour of the (now annulled) Data Retention Directive (2006/24/EC), which introduced a blanket and indiscriminate surveillance for the purpose of the prevention, investigation and prosecution of serious criminal offences, including terrorism. In particular, the Directive required telephone and internet service providers to retain details of internet and call data for not less than six months and not more than two years, in order to ensure that the data is available for countering serious criminal offences. Ireland decided to challenge the Directive on the grounds that it was founded on an inappropriate legal basis (Article 114 TFEU)—one that relates predominantly to the functioning of the internal market rather than the facilitation of Police and Judicial Co-operation in Criminal Matters (PJCCM).[8] Yet, the motive of the Irish Government for bringing the challenge was far from highlighting any possible infringement by the Directive of fundamental rights resulting from interference with the exercise of the right to privacy.[9] Instead, Ireland wished to retain its own more pervasive national legislation rather than compelling the EU to protect the right to privacy under Articles 7 and 8 of the EU Charter of Fundamental Rights.

The lesson from this case is that even when a Member State decides to challenge EU legislation, there is no guarantee that such a challenge would be driven by the desire to defend individual rights.[10] Still, the individual may subsequently benefit from the outcome of Article 263 TFEU litigation, as was the case in the *Digital Rights Ireland* judgment where in a challenge against the same piece of legislation by a lobbying and advocacy non-governmental organisation (NGO) the CJEU declared the Data Retention Directive to be invalid.[11] However, the CJEU did not depart from its earlier findings regarding the gist of the Directive. It supported that the retention of data for the purpose of their possible transmission to the competent national authorities genuinely satisfies an objective of general interest, namely the fight against serious crime and, ultimately, public security. The Luxembourg Court did not delve into a debate about EU competence and the necessity to adopt the contested Directive under Article 114 TFEU (internal market legal basis) due to the fact that its provisions were allegedly limited to the activities of service providers

---

[8] In the so-called *PNR* case the CJEU held that the internal market measure of Art 114 TFEU could not justify EU competence to conclude an agreement with the United States on data processing for law enforcement purposes. Joined cases C-317/04 and C-318/04, *European Parliament v Council and Commission* [2006] ECR I-04721.

[9] Case C-301/06, *Ireland v European Parliament and European Council* [2009] ECR I-593. See for further analysis T Konstadinides, 'Wavering between Centres of Gravity: Comment on *Ireland v Parliament and Council*' (2010) 35 *European Law Review* 88; E Herlin-Karnell, 'Annotation of *Ireland v Parliament and Council*' (2009) 46 *Common Market Law Review* 1667.

[10] It was only Slovakia (which supported Ireland in its claim and the only other Member State that voted against the adoption of the Directive) that alleged an impairment of the right to privacy but Ireland's action related solely to the choice of legal basis.

[11] Case C-293/12 *Digital Rights Ireland* [2014] ECLI:EU:C:2014:238.

and thus did not govern access to data or the use thereof by the police or judicial authorities of the Member States. The CJEU's judgment was limited in this respect by only stressing that the Data Retention Directive exceeded the limits imposed by compliance with the principle of proportionality. Likewise, in more recent jurisprudence it has been established that a general obligation to retain data may be compatible with EU law. Yet, according to the CJEU, action by Member States against the possibility of imposing such an obligation shall be subject to satisfying strict procedural and substantive requirements including respect for private life and data enshrined in the EU Charter of Fundamental Rights.[12]

Despite confirming the appropriateness of a system of data retention, in the end, the CJEU afforded more protection to the individual than prior to the judgment. We would agree that in situations like the above, the regulation of the relationship between the administration and the aggrieved individual (in the case of the Data Retention Directive, for instance, almost everyone could claim that they are directly and personally concerned by the contested act) needs to be supported by justiciable EU law principles and the availability of redress mechanisms upholding the rule of law. In this respect, one could entertain the scope of the action for annulment under Article 263 TFEU as a kind of popular action (*actio popularis*). As it will be discussed, the EU is still to acclimatise itself in this direction and eliminate the majority of obstacles for individuals to bring proceedings en masse against the EU institutions under Article 263 TFEU. In the words of the CJEU 'the requirement that the applicant must be directly concerned therefore serves ... to rule out the *actio popularis*'.[13] Hence, the general perception is that it is increasingly up to the Member States to provide appropriate remedies.[14] To give an example, since the CJEU has highlighted the role of national courts viz Article 19 (1) TEU, some commentators have suggested that

the interpretation of Article 263 (4) TFEU (which allows private litigants to challenge EU Regulations even where they are legislative acts within the meaning of Article 289 (3) TFEU) and Article 19 (1) TEU in conjunction allocates jurisdiction to that end between national and EU courts.[15]

[12] See Advocate General Advocate General Saugmandsgaard Øe Opinion in Joined Cases C-203/15, C-698/15 *Tele2 Sverige*, 19 July 2016; also Case C-203/15 *Tele2 Sverige AB* [2016] ECLI:EU:C:2016:970.

[13] Opinion of Advocate General Kokott in Case C-274/12 P *Telefónica SA v European Commission*, 21.03.2013, para 61.

[14] A Korzenov, 'Locus Standi of Private Parties in Actions for Annulment: has the Gap been Closed?' (2014) 73 (1) *Cambridge Law Journal* 25.

[15] S Peers and M Costa, 'Judicial Review of EU acts after the Treaty of Lisbon' (2012) 8(1) *European Constitutional Law Review* 82, 100. The authors claim that 'In order to ensure that, as the Court of Justice claims, the EU legal order contains a *complete* system for the review of acts of the EU institutions, Article 19(1) TEU must therefore be interpreted to provide for a general right to challenge EU measures before national courts, even in the absence of direct concern or national implementing measures, subject to the general principles of equality and effectiveness, interpreted by analogy with the case-law on national remedies for enforcement of EU law.' See also S Balthasar, 'Locus Standi Rules for Challenges to Regulatory Acts by Private Applicants: the New Art 263(4) TFEU' (2010) 35(4) *European Law Review* 542.

The discussion about a platform where individuals can challenge EU law is crucial to the rule of law. The right to effective judicial protection needs to be considered against the availability of 'European' routes to challenge EU acts, inclusive of the preliminary reference procedure under Article 267 TFEU which operates following disputes that arise under EU law before national courts. Article 267 TFEU is not a free pass to litigation. It presupposes that there are court proceedings in a Member State aimed at a preliminary reference request on the validity of the EU measure. Once this happens, one can count on the contribution of the CJEU in unpacking the constitutional and human rights implications of EU legislation. To better illustrate the role of the CJEU in this respect, we should come back to our earlier example and point to the reader that the resolution of the legal dispute concerning the Data Retention Directive (2006/24/EC) emerged from a private challenge lodged by the civil rights advocacy group Digital Rights Ireland (DRI) against the Irish Minister for Communications. The Irish High Court decided to request a preliminary ruling from the CJEU on the EU institutions' alleged violation against the right to privacy. In light of the CJEU's previous jurisprudence, the Data Retention Directive was weighed against its alleged impact on privacy, and its overall design regarding its necessity and proportionality.[16] As such, the CJEU ruled in favour of DRI and annulled the Directive on the basis of its violation of Articles 7 and 8 European Convention on Human Rights (ECHR).[17] The decision carries implications for the CJEU's protection of the principle of effective judicial protection. Let us explore next what kind of obligations this principle intends to impose on both Member States and EU institutions.

It is well-known that the principle of effective judicial protection is a general principle of EU law stemming from the constitutional traditions of the Member States and supported by Articles 6 and 13 ECHR and Article 47 Charter of Fundamental Rights of the European Union (CFR). It embodies the obligation common to every polity that rights must be enforced. As such it is an essential element of the rule of law within the EU or, perhaps, the most discernible embodiment of the EU rule of law according to the CJEU. As mentioned, according to the CJEU, the principle of sincere cooperation or loyalty encompasses the need for Member States to provide a solid platform for the smooth implementation of EU law rights and provide for remedies to address breaches. In other words, it is for EU law to provide the rights and for national law to establish a system of legal remedies and procedures in a manner which guarantees the right to effective judicial protection of an individual's rights under EU law.[18] To this end, the Treaty states that it is the task of national judiciaries to provide effective means of enforcing the rights

---

[16] Joined Cases C-92/09 and C-93/09 *Schecke GbR* [2010] OJ C 13/6.

[17] Joined Cases C-293/12 and C-594/12 *Digital Rights Ireland & Seitlinger*, 8 April 2014, nyr.

[18] The CJEU case law is vast in this field. See indicatively: Case 106/77 *Simmenthal* [1978] ECR 629, paras 21 and 22; Case C-294/83 *Les Verts v European Parliament* ECR [1986] 1339; Case 222/84 *Johnston v Chief Constable of the Royal Ulster Constabulary* [1986] ECR 1651; Case C-213/89 *Factortame* [1990] ECR I-2433, para 19. See also more recently: Case C-279/09 *DEB* [2010] EU:C:2010:811; Case C-330/15 P, *Tomana & Others* (2016) ECLI:EU:C:2016:601, para 61.

stemming from EU law. Article 19 (1) TEU explicitly stresses that 'Member States shall provide remedies sufficient to ensure effective legal protection in the fields covered by Union law.'

Effective law enforcement, including judicial protection and enforcement of rights and sufficient remedies, is strengthening the notion of the rule of law. Effective judicial protection ensures that all national procedural rules maintain a basic threshold of judicial protection which is of acceptable standard within the EU. This idea is reminiscent of Zuckerman's remark that 'in a society governed by the rule of law we all have an interest in rights being respected and in wrongs being remedied. For in the absence of redress for wrong there is no value to rights and no reason to behave according to the law.'[19] Yet, the right to effective judicial protection needs to be considered against the existing *locus standi* rules on challenges to EU acts. Whilst the CJEU has put Member States under considerable pressure to demonstrate readiness to interpret national rules on standing and access to court in such a way that ensures the correct application of EU law, it has not followed the same stance with regard to challenges of the legality of EU action. It is in this respect that the right to effective judicial protection has been criticised as not featuring prominently in the case law of the CJEU.[20] As it will be stressed, most criticism about ensuring the highest standard of effective judicial protection in the EU judicial system has focused on the merits of the infamous *Plaumann* test[21] vis-a-vis the *locus standi* of private parties to challenge EU legislation under Article 263 (4) TFEU.[22]

III. JUDICIAL PROTECTION BEFORE EU COURTS

A. Background

The aim of this section is to locate the rule of law in the mechanisms available in the EU legal order that ensure effective judicial protection. To this purpose we will

---

[19] A Zuckerman, 'Comment on: The Principle of Effective Judicial Protection in EU Law by A Arnull', University of Birmingham, 18 June 2010, available at http://ukael.org/past_events_24_3656132649.pdf.

[20] P Craig, *EU Administrative Law* (Oxford, Oxford University Press, 2012) 310.

[21] See Case 25/62 *Plaumann* [1963] ECR 95 (recently reiterated in Case C-274/12 P *Telefonica* [2013] ECR I-0000, para 46).

[22] As already mentioned the CJEU has considered other avenues, such as the preliminary ruling system as a means of delivering effective judicial protection of EU citizens' rights. This has been confirmed by the European Parliament's DG for Internal Policies attempt to map out the framework of EU administrative law: 'The imperative to use Articles 263 and 267 TFEU to develop principles of EU Administrative law was fuelled by the background precept of the rule of law, which is now recognised in Article 2 TEU ... The idea that administration should be procedurally and substantively accountable before the courts has been central to the rule of law. The EU judiciary therefore perceived its task as one of developing analogous principles within the EU legal order, so as to enhance the legitimacy of the EU and ensure that it too was governed by precepts of the rule of law.' DG for Internal Policies (author Paul Craig), 'EU Administrative Law: The Acquis' (2010) PE 432.745, 6, available from www.europarl. europa.eu/RegData/etudes/note/join/2010/432745/IPOL-JURI_NT(2010)432745_EN.pdf.

be examining the relevant case law of the CJEU on judicial review with a focus on the liability of EU institutions and the process of challenging the lawfulness of their decisions under Article 263 TFEU. An insight into the system of review of EU acts under Article 263 (4) TFEU is relevant because, as mentioned earlier in the book, judicial review of public authority constitutes a key tenet of every legal system operating under the rule of law. Hence, the willingness of the CJEU to alter its long-standing interpretation of the notion of 'individual concern' in Article 263 TFEU will form a benchmark by which lawyers and prospective litigants are able to ascertain whether the EU system of judicial protection effectively affords adequate guarantees that the rule of law is observed. This is indeed a major challenge for the CJEU and its credibility as an institution.

In the case of the EU, there is no better expression of a Union based on the rule of law than through a legal framework in place which allows individuals to directly challenge the validity of EU acts, inter alia, in light of fundamental rights. This is not only because the right of access to the judicial process and an effective remedy constitute themselves fundamental rights under the EU Charter of Fundamental Rights and, therefore, their protection boosts the profile of the EU as a Union based on the rule of law. Most crucially, the CJEU has established a link between the rule of law and fundamental rights by extending the scope of review of EU acts to include fundamental rights protection. The CJEU has been explicit that since the EU is based on the rule of law, its institutions are subject to judicial review of the compatibility of their acts with the Treaty and with the general principles of law, including the fundamental rights to effective judicial protection and access to court.[23]

As it has been established in the CJEU's recent jurisprudence, the review of the validity of EU measures (especially in the light of fundamental rights) constitutes the expression, in a Union based on the rule of law, of a constitutional guarantee stemming from the Treaty. Such a guarantee enhances both the threshold of fundamental rights review in connection with the rule of law and the role of the EU as an autonomous legal system which is not to be prejudiced by international agreements stipulating a different level of protection.[24] The latter has created a catalyst in shaping EU law, especially with reference to EU external relations, and has attracted considerable academic criticism about the EU as a legal order which indulges in barricading itself from the norm-setting power of international organisations.[25]

Following the analysis of the access by individuals to judicial review of acts of the EU institutions, it emerges that the case law on individual standing has been affected by the Treaty of Lisbon alteration of the ingredients of Article 263 (4) TFEU.[26]

---

[23] See F Jacobs, *The Sovereignty of Law: The European Way* (Cambridge, Cambridge University Press, 2006) 50.

[24] Joined Cases C-402/05 P and C-415/05 P *Kadi* [2008] ECR, I-6351, para 316.

[25] G De Búrca, 'The EU, the European Court of Justice and the International Legal Order after *Kadi*' (2009) 51 (1) *Harvard International Law Journal* 1.

[26] On the post-Lisbon alteration of judicial control in EU law and the current role of the action for annulment under Art 263 TFEU see A Albors-Llorens, 'Remedies against the EU Institutions after Lisbon: An Era of Opportunity' (2012) 71 (3) *Cambridge Law Journal* 507.

This is evident, in particular, with reference to the interpretation of the notions of implementing measures and regulatory acts which have seemingly opened a small window of opportunity to individuals to bring (successful) actions for annulment against EU acts.

Notwithstanding the Treaty of Lisbon reforms, over the years one can identify a general tendency from the part of the CJEU to push litigation towards preliminary rulings and therefore change the route by which individual claims find themselves before the CJEU. This approach is effective in dealing with the kind of backlog problems similar to those that the European Court of Human Rights (ECtHR) is currently facing with regard to cases that are clearly inadmissible.[27] Yet, it contradicts the CJEU's earlier findings that a preliminary reference calling into question the validity of an EU measure would be inadmissible if the applicant in question had failed to avail of the opportunity to bring an action under Article 263 TFEU within the two-month time limit.[28] By increasingly handing matters to national courts to filter claims which may raise EU law points and then choose to refer them or not to Luxembourg, the CJEU is passing discretion to a plethora of domestic courts with different institutional agendas and ideas about what constitutes a 'European' and what a purely domestic dispute. At the same time, due to the limitations caused by standing requirements the CJEU is almost tactlessly blocking access to Article 263 (4) TFEU—a whole channel of judicial review which inter alia allows individuals to bring direct challenges against EU acts before the EU's supreme constitutional court.

Anticipating the gravity of the limited individual access to European courts, we will attempt to entertain the CJEU's statement that the Treaty maintains a 'complete system of legal remedies and procedures' designed to permit the CJEU to review the legality of measures adopted by the EU legislature in every case. We will also discuss the changes introduced by the Treaty of Lisbon to Article 263 TFEU and comment upon their utility vis-à-vis improving the *locus standi* of individuals before the CJEU. While the chapter agrees that the system of remedies is indeed complete due to the relationship of synergy and tolerance that exists between European and national courts, it critiques the procedures in place that give access to the EU judicial system.

B. Direct Challenges

i. *Review of Legality of EU Acts and Access to Justice*

The Treaty of Lisbon makes express reference to a system of review available in EU law. Article 19 (3) TEU provides the CJEU with competence to review EU acts

---

[27] See press release ECHR 312 (2013) 24.10.2013, available at http://hudoc.echr.coe.int/webservices/content/pdf/003-4546937-5490138.

[28] Case C-188/92 *TWD* [1994] ECR I-833.

and Article 263 TFEU sets out the basic requirements of reviewability, *locus standi* as well as the main grounds of review. This section will look specifically into Article 263 TFEU, in particular with regard to access of individuals to the CJEU and the nebulous notions of implementing measures and regulatory acts. The latter has only recently become relevant in opening out access to justice and potentially softening the *locus standi* of individuals before the CJEU. This analysis is, therefore, pertinent because access to justice is one of the constitutive elements of a Union based on the rule of law. Put differently, it is of utmost importance that the individual adversely affected by a rule is able to seek annulment of that rule on the basis that it is unlawful. In *Les Verts*, the CJEU highlighted that:

> The European Economic Community is a Community based on the rule of law inasmuch as neither its Member States nor its institutions can avoid a review of the question whether the measures adopted by them are in conformity with the basic constitutional charter, the Treaty.[29]

As established, the CJEU's commitment to the rule of law as subjection of all EU actors' conduct (both EU institutions and Member States) to judicial review is tantamount to the principle of effective judicial protection inherent in the system of remedies established by the Treaty. This aspect of the rule of law found favour with former Advocate General Jacobs who argued, almost a decade ago, that 'the key to the notion of the rule of law is ... the reviewability by independent courts of decisions of public authorities.'[30] It is noteworthy that the Treaty and, in particular, the requirements laid out by Article 263 TFEU, do not seem to limit the discretion of the CJEU vis-a-vis the manner in which it should be exercising its reviewing powers. For instance, as it is known, in *Les Verts* the *locus standi* rules under Article 263 TFEU regarding non-privileged applicants were modified by the CJEU so that the French Green Party could challenge the European Parliament (EP) for acting beyond its powers. This was the case despite the fact that originally Article 263 TFEU did not mention the EP as a possible defendant. The CJEU was therefore operating in its capacity as a law-making constitutional court filling a *lacuna* where the law was 'silent' about the position of the EP as a semi-privileged applicant.[31]

Notwithstanding the criticism or enthusiasm that the *Les Verts* judgment generated vis-a-vis the CJEU's discretion under Article 263 TFEU, the Luxembourg judges never implied that the provision constitutes an *actio popularis* with reference to non-privileged applicants. What is more, in the Treaty of Lisbon, judicial review was scarce outside the former first 'Community' pillar. Perhaps this partly explains why the law of the former second and third pillars were until lately

---

[29]   Case 294/83 *Les Verts* [1986] ECR 1339, para 23.

[30]   F Jacobs, 'The State of International Economic Law: Rethinking Sovereignty in Europe' (2008) 11 (1) *Journal of International Economic Law* 5.

[31]   D O'Keeffe and A Bavasso (eds), *Judicial Review in European Union Law, Liber Amicorum in honour of Lord Slynn of Hadley* (The Hague, Kluwer Law International, 2000) 76; T Tridimas, 'The Court of Justice and Judicial Activism' (1996) 21(3) *European Law Review* 199, 207–09.

uncharted territory in legal scholarship.[32] The position has now improved with regard to Common Foreign and Security Policy (CFSP) provisions which pre-Lisbon formed the EU's so-called Second Pillar. Post-Lisbon, under Article 24 (1) TEU, the CJEU has jurisdiction to monitor compliance with Article 40 TEU (non-affectation clause) and to review under Article 263 (4) TFEU the legality of certain decisions as provided for by Article 275 (2) TFEU (restrictive measures against natural or legal persons).[33]

Policing the boundaries between CFSP and other EU policies as well as reviewing the legality of decisions providing for restrictive measures against individuals adopted by the Council under Chapter 2, Title V TEU is a welcome development from the perspective of the rule of law, consistency in EU external action and the protection of fundamental rights.[34] For the first time the CJEU can review directly the legality of a CFSP measure and not merely the regulation adopted following a CFSP act. This is a positive change because, as seen in the *Kadi I* case, prior to the Treaty of Lisbon, the review of an EU measure implementing a CFSP act did not, at least in theory, stop the latter from being implemented in the Member States. Also, given that a challenge to a regulation only has limited effect, this new development is a good addition to the current system of remedies.[35]

Access to justice has also improved with regard to the former third pillar, which following the ratification of the Treaty of Lisbon subsumed the Treaty's criminal law *acquis* of PJCCM within the Area of Freedom, Security and Justice (AFSJ) and, therefore, within the Treaty proper. As a result, judicial co-operation in the fight against serious crime has become a fully-fledged EU policy. Post-Lisbon, therefore, the ordinary legislative procedure applies and the CJEU's jurisdiction has been extended to cover the former so-called Third Pillar areas, despite its initial subjection (until 2014) to certain limits defined in Protocol 36 annexed to the Treaty. It follows that contrary to the selective judicial review of CFSP acts, the Treaty of Lisbon brings within the ambit of Article 263 TFEU the totality of provisions formerly tucked away in the intergovernmental domain of the former Third Pillar. Under current Title V of the TFEU, measures in the area of PJCCM have already been altered and taken the form of regulations and directives. All these measures

---

[32] This applies, in particular, to the specific areas of Common Security and Defence Policy and EU Criminal Law. See P Koutrakos, *Common Security and Defence Policy* (Oxford, Oxford University Press, 2013); V Mitsilegas, *EU Criminal Law* (Oxford, Hart Publishing, 2011).

[33] A Dashwood, 'Article 47 and the Relationship between First and Second Pillar Competences' in A Dashwood and M Maresceau (eds), *Law and Practice of EU External Relations* (Cambridge, Cambridge University Press, 2008) 99.

[34] See G De Baere, 'European Integration and the Rule of Law in Foreign Policy' in J Dickson and P Eleftheriadis (eds), *Philosophical Foundations of EU Law* (Oxford, Oxford University Press, 2012) 354, 369.

[35] Joined Cases C-402/05 P and C-415/05 P *Kadi* [2008] ECR I-6351; Joined Cases C-584/10 P, C-593/10 P and C-595/10 P *Kadi II* [2013] ECLI:EU:C:2013:518. Of course national courts could have always chosen the narrow path of challenging the constitutionality of CFSP acts against the requirement of consistency in EU external action and contest *a la BVerfG* the compatibility of the national implementing legislation with domestic law.

now fall within the scope of the application of the Treaties and are therefore subject to judicial review.

The above developments aside, it needs to be stressed that any direct action brought by an individual against EU criminal law measures is still subject to the strict *locus standi* requirements under Article 263 (4) TFEU. Even with reference to the former First 'Community' Pillar, the CJEU has been careful not to open the litigation floodgates when it comes to its interpretation of direct and individual concern. It has also provided a veil of protection against individual challenges over the legality of EU legislative acts. The legacy of its infamous judgment in *Plaumann*[36] as confirmed in *UPA* has elucidated the position with reference to the habitual ineffectiveness of the otherwise 'effective' judicial protection in EU law when it comes to challenging EU legislative acts before the European Courts.[37] This is especially the case insofar as the *locus standi* requirements set out in Article 263 (4) TFEU may sometimes constitute a serious obstacle to individual applicants to establish direct and individual concern to challenge EU acts that were not addressed to them.

In *UPA*, AG Jacobs proposed (in vain) that the EU should enlarge individual standing before European Courts, therefore ensuring access to justice for individuals seeking redress. This proposal was partly embraced by the Treaty of Lisbon which in theory liberalised the standing requirements under Article 263 (4) TFEU. This is the case, in particular, with regard to the misty notion of 'regulatory acts'. Indeed, the final limb of the fourth paragraph of Article 263 TFEU allows

> any natural or legal person … [to] institute proceedings against an act addressed to that person or which is of direct and individual concern to them, and against a regulatory act which is of direct concern to them and does not entail implementing measures.

The innovation of the Treaty of Lisbon relaxation of *locus standi* rules lies in doing away with the obligation to prove individual concern when seeking annulment of a regulatory act not entailing implementing measures. This modification is in tune with the General Court's decision in *Jego Quere* and Advocate General Jacobs' Opinion in *UPA* which had no resonance in the original cases before the CJEU.[38]

ii. Challenging Regulatory Acts and Direct Access to European Courts

Challenges against the so-called regulatory acts have gained prominence following the Treaty of Lisbon reforms that allegedly liberalised individuals' standing requirements—making, therefore, litigation against EU legislation easier and more accessible to its addressees. But what is a regulatory act? In the absence of a textual definition in the Treaty as to what constitutes a 'regulatory act', the General

---

[36] Case 25/62 *Plaumann v Commission* [1963] ECR 25.

[37] Case C-50/00 *UPA* [2002] ECR I-6677, para 40.

[38] Case T-177/01 *Jego Quere v Commission* [2002] ECR II-2365; Case C-263/02 P *Commission v Jego Quere* [2004] ECR I-3425.

Court provided guidance in the context of an Article 263 (4) TFEU challenge from an association representing seal product manufacturers and traders against Regulation 1007/2009 which restricted the marketing of such products to those resulting from traditional hunts. The Regulation was adopted by the European Parliament and the Council under the ordinary legislative procedure.

In its judgment in *Inuit Tapiriit Kanatami*, the General Court established that regulatory acts include all acts of general application such as delegated acts under Article 290 TFEU and implementing acts under Article 291 TFEU.[39] By contrast, legislative acts under Article 289 (1) and (3) TFEU adopted under the Article 294 TFEU procedure fall outside the definition of regulatory acts.[40] The General Court, therefore, dismissed the action. Upon appeal to the CJEU, the Luxembourg judges confirmed the General Court's interpretation of regulatory acts—ie that since the challenged regulation had been adopted under the ordinary legislative procedure, it was a legislative act, not a regulatory act. As such, the regulation in question could be challenged only once the applicants proved direct and individual concern. The CJEU went on to apply the old *Plaumann* test: it subsequently held that the applicants were not individually concerned and dismissed the appeal in its entirety.[41]

The *Inuit* decision could be reviewed under the prism of the EU's ECHR delayed accession and the post-Lisbon binding status of the EU Charter of Fundamental Rights. It should be noted that the CJEU found no violation of Articles 6 and 13 of ECHR as a result of its restrictive interpretation of the standing conditions in Article 263 (4) TFEU. Additionally, the CJEU applied the same reasoning with reference to Article 47 of the Charter which protects the right to an effective remedy. It did not raise the principle of effective judicial protection in *Inuit* as a method of further softening (on top of the revision of Article 263 (4) TFEU) the *locus standi* rules for individuals before the CJEU. Instead it highlighted that the conditions laid down in the Treaty cannot be altered by the Charter. This attitude is illustrative of the CJEU's insistence to maintain the *Plaumann* test despite calls for relaxation of standing rules to comply with

---

[39] The basic rule is that delegated acts and implementing acts are mutually exclusive categories of non-legislative acts. A delegated act (ie an act aiming to achieve the adoption of rules coming within the regulatory framework of the legislative act) is adopted under Art 290 (1) TFEU by the Commission acting on its own. An implementing act (ie an act which provides further details with regard to the content of a legislative act so as to ensure that the latter is uniformly interpreted all across the Member States) is adopted under Art 291 (2) TFEU by the Commission acting together with a committee of representatives of the Member States. See Case C-427/12 *Commission v Parliament and Council* [2014] ECLI:EU:C:2014:170 concerning an inter-institutional dispute about an implementing act based on Art 291(2) TFEU. The CJEU held that generally the EU legislature has discretion to decide whether a power conferred on the Commission should be delegated or implementing. Accordingly, the CJEU will only exercise its scrutiny in the event of a manifest error.

[40] Case T-18/10 *Inuit Tapiriit Kanatami v Parliament and Council* [2011] ECR I-00164; See also Case T-262/10 *Microban v Commission* [2011] ECLI:EU:T:2011:623.

[41] Case C-583/11 P *Inuit Tapiriit Kanatami v Parliament and Council* [2013] ECLI:EU:C:2013:625.

the principle of effective judicial protection enshrined both within the general principles of EU law and the EU Charter of Fundamental Rights (both of which enjoy primary law status).[42]

As such, *Inuit* stresses that in cases involving challenges against legislative acts, the CJEU will remain faithful to its old jurisprudence which does not involve the language of fundamental rights protection in the assessment of the rules on admissibility of direct actions against the EU institutions. Thus, even if an individual applicant established direct concern to challenge an implementing act, this would not imply that s/he can go as far as challenging a legislative act (eg an EU regulation) if s/he cannot prove individual concern. Despite the negative outcome of the case, the CJEU emphasised that the EU is based on the rule of law, pointing, therefore, to a complete system of remedies established by the Treaties vis-a-vis the reviewability of supranational executive and administrative action by the European Courts. Although the CJEU's express commitment to provide a complete system of remedies is hardly comforting for individual litigants whose case has been declared inadmissible, at least it leaves some scope for admissibility and potential annulment of future challenged EU acts. For instance, the old restrictive approach in relation to actions by individuals against legislative acts is no more applicable with reference to the meaning of 'direct concern' and the lack of 'implementing measures' vis-a-vis regulatory acts. Evidence drawn from post-Lisbon case law shows that the direct access of individuals before the European Courts has been somewhat facilitated as a result of the modifications introduced to standing rules under Article 263 (4) TFEU.

In *Microban*, the contested act was a Commission Decision prohibiting the marketing of triclosan from the list of authorised additives which may be used in the manufacture of articles intended to come into contact with foodstuffs.[43] Since the Decision had been adopted under implementing powers delegated to the Commission, it did not constitute a legislative act. The Decision also applied to an open category of persons, namely the potential users of the product for the specified purpose. It, therefore, qualified as a 'regulatory act' which did not require any implementing measures. As such, the applicants only had to prove direct concern. It is notable that the General Court held that post-Lisbon the notion of direct concern could not be subject to a more restrictive interpretation than that established in the pre-Lisbon case law. Hence, the application for annulment in *Microban* was admissible and the General Court annulled the contested Decision. Future case law will tell whether this approach is sustainable in the long run to increase the possibilities of individuals challenging EU acts. For now the CJEU has been keen on showing the boundaries of 'regulatory acts'.

---

[42] See for more detail: A Kornezov, 'Shaping the New Architecture of the EU System of Judicial Remedies: Comment on Inuit' (2014) 39 (2) *European Law Review* 251; CF Bergstrom, 'Defending Restricted Standing for Individuals to bring Direct Actions against "Legislative" Measures' (2014) 10(3) *European Constitutional Law Review* 481.

[43] Case T-262/10 *Microban v Commission* [2011] ECLI:EU:T:2011:623.

Clearly, the CJEU has been cautious not to open the litigation floodgates to individuals challenging EU legislation. Once again, it considered the scope of 'implementing measures' in *Telefónica*, a case which concerned legislation adopted by the Member States within the definition of regulatory acts. In previous CJEU case law it was established that implementing measures include both measures taken by the Member States and those taken by the EU itself.[44] The question in *Telefónica*, however, was whether state aid decisions entailed implementing measures within the meaning of Article 263 (4) TFEU.[45] The CJEU rejected the proposition that an applicant (a state aid recipient company in this case) is individually concerned by virtue of being the beneficiary of an aid scheme.[46] It stressed that, in order to be individually concerned, an applicant must also be obliged to repay the aid in question or, at least, be exposed to the risk of having to repay it. This was not the case here since first, Telefónica did not have to repay the aid and second, the contested decision was not addressed to Telefónica as it entailed implementing measures. By ruling that there was no breach and by taking a stringent approach vis-à-vis the circumstances that individual concern can be satisfied the CJEU minimised the scope of Article 263 (4) TFEU.

The most recent attempt of the CJEU to explain the scope of the extension of the admissibility criteria in Article 263 (4) TFEU was in *T & L Sugars Ltd and Sidul Açúcares*—an appealed case from the General Court.[47] The case concerned a challenge by two European refiners of imported sugar against Regulation (EU) No 222/2011 and implementing regulations adopted in the same year that introduced an import tariff quota for sugar with the aim of addressing shortages in the EU. The CJEU dismissed the claimants' argument that the regulations were discriminatory and incapable of eliminating the import deficit. Most importantly, the CJEU disagreed with Advocate General Cruz Villalón who opined that the contested measures were regulatory acts that did not entail implementing measures within the meaning of Article 263 (4) TFEU. While the CJEU acknowledged that Article 263 (4) TFEU must be interpreted in the light of the fundamental right to effective judicial protection (enshrined in Article 47 of the EU Charter of Fundamental Rights), such an interpretation cannot have the effect of setting aside the conditions listed under the Treaty. As such, the CJEU established that the contested regulations produced legal effects vis-à-vis the claimants because the national authorities were involved in implementation by taking decisions about whether or not to grant certificates. According to the CJEU, such decisions constituted implementing measures in accordance with Article 263 (4) TFEU. The CJEU innovated here in that it established that any requirement for an implementing measure is sufficient to exclude standing under Article 263 (4) TFEU.

---

[44] Case T-16/04 *Arcelor v European Parliament and Council* [2010] ECLI:EU:T:2010:54, para 123.
[45] Case C-274/12 P *Telefonica* [2013] ECLI:EU:C:2013:852.
[46] ibid, para 42.
[47] Case C-456/13 *T & L Sugars Ltd & Sidul Açúcares v Commission* [2015] ECLI:EU:C:2015:284.

The outcome of the case is important for individual litigants because it clarifies that implementing measures can be adopted by both the EU institutions and the Member States themselves. The latter can be minor or ancillary and can even consist of measures such as EU tariffs and quotas that can be executed mechanically by the Member States. The CJEU's focus here was to prevent cases where claimants would have to break the law in order to bring a legal challenge against an act under national law. The CJEU thus emphasised that Member States should have in place a system of legal remedies and procedures which ensures respect for the fundamental right to effective judicial protection. It also stressed the importance of the preliminary reference procedure in cases concerning measures that Member States have adopted at the national level in order to implement EU rules. In this regard it reaffirmed the status quo that, as it springs out of Article 19 (1) TEU, judicial review is ensured not only by the CJEU but also by the courts and tribunals of the Member States. By doing so, the Luxembourg Court preserved the strict interpretation of the standing criteria for actions pursuant to Article 263 (4) TFEU.

C. Indirect Challenges

i. *Effectiveness and the Substitutive Reliance on Requests for a Preliminary Ruling*

Having become familiar with the Treaty of Lisbon reforms about the standing rules in place with regard to direct actions against the EU institutions we should pose the following question: how far are individuals protected against the application to them of general measures which they cannot contest directly before the CJEU by reason of the admissibility conditions laid down in Article 263 (4) TFEU? The CJEU's past case law on annulment actions, which save for the Treaty of Lisbon modifications is still relevant today, was predicated on points which broadly relate to the principle of effectiveness. The principle of effectiveness, a creation of the CJEU's jurisprudence,[48] is now enshrined in the second paragraph of Article 19 (1) TEU, which provides that 'Member States shall provide remedies sufficient to ensure effective legal protection in the fields covered by Union law'. This obligation encourages individual access to national courts in which applicants can raise both the invalidity of EU legislation and national implementing measures.

Effectiveness in the context of enforcement actions thus implies that national procedures must not make it 'practically impossible or excessively difficult' for individuals to exercise the rights conferred on them by EU law. Member States should be acting in compliance with their obligations under Article 19 (1) TEU and provide for effective judicial protection in a spirit of sincere cooperation. Having said that, it has been noted that the principle of effectiveness needs to take into account other principles of EU law, such as the principles of constitutional identity, procedural

---

[48] See indicatively: Case C-437/13 *Unitrading Ltd* [2014] ECLI:EU:C:2014:2318, 26–28.

autonomy and subsidiarity. This is particularly important when it comes to applying effectiveness to judge national constitutional review procedures.[49]

The principle of effective judicial protection features highly in EU law despite the limitations of Article 263 TFEU regarding the way a judicial review claim can be made against the legality of acts of the EU institutions. The EU's commitment to effective judicial protection is guaranteed in the following ways: first, as noted by the CJEU in the cases examined above, where implementation of EU law is a matter for the Member States, the validity of legislative acts of general application can be challenged by individuals indirectly before national courts. Second, following such a plea for invalidity, private applicants can be granted effective judicial protection at the EU level since any national court may then resort to the preliminary reference procedure in order to question the validity of EU law. Key to the idea that Member States are to make available effective procedures and remedies for enforcing EU law is the possibility for domestic courts to indirectly challenge EU legislation through the preliminary reference procedure under Article 267 TFEU. The role played by national courts in the EU system of judicial remedies, and especially the possibility for those courts to make references for preliminary rulings pursuant to Article 267 TFEU is central in the preservation of the EU rule of law. As Weiler has remarked:

> The secret of the principle of the 'rule of law' in the legal order of the Union is that genius process of preliminary references and preliminary rulings. The compliance pull of law in liberal Western democracies does not rest on the gun and coercion. It rests on a political culture which internalises, especially public authorities, obedience to the law rather than expediency. Not a perfect, but one good measure of the 'rule of law' is the extent to which public authorities in a country obey the decisions, even uncomfortable ones, of their own courts.[50]

The preliminary reference procedure is also a reminder that there is a chain of command when it comes to reviewability of EU law. According to the *Foto-Frost* precedent, national courts may consider the validity of EU acts but do not have jurisdiction to declare their invalidity.[51] Especially those courts against which no appeal lies must always refer the case at hand to the CJEU (Article 267 (3) TFEU). This is all the more crucial since it is only the CJEU that has jurisdiction both to declare an EU act void or invalid. Yet, it is noteworthy that the decision of whether or not to make a reference to the CJEU lies with the national judge, not the litigants to a case. In this respect, national courts have a gatekeeping role.

---

[49] M Bossuyt and W Verrijdt, 'The Full Effect of EU Law and of Constitutional Review in Belgium and France after the Melki Judgment' (2011) 7(3) *European Constitutional Law Review* 355.
[50] JHH Weiler, 'Europe in Crisis-On Political Messianism, Legitimacy and the Rule of Law' (2012) *Singapore Journal of Legal Studies* 248, 265.
[51] Case 314/85 *Foto-Frost* [1987] ECR 4199. See also Case C-143/88 *Zuckerfabrik* [1991] I-415, where the CJEU established that it was open to a national court to grant interim relief suspending the enforcement of a measure as long as it also made a preliminary reference to the CJEU. We shall note that the CJEU has been acting against the *Foto-Frost* principle when it comes to its own assessment of international law (See the CJEU's decision in *Kadi*).

To use an example, Harvey argues indicatively that 'the crucial part of any litigation involving the free movement of patients based on rights in Article 49 EC [current Article 56 TFEU], that is, the question of justification, is, technically at least, a question of fact for the national court.'[52] This approach is different, for instance, to the ECHR mechanism under which individual claims can be made directly to the ECtHR once domestic avenues have been exhausted. In the EU legal order, the only national courts which are bound to make a preliminary reference are those of final appeal, but also lower courts may make a reference in case they have ascertained that the challenged EU act may be invalid.[53] The latter has, in recent years, turned out to be an enforceable obligation: inaction of national judges to refer a case to their counterparts in Luxembourg may pass liability to the state under *Köbler*.[54] Despite *Köbler* liability, however, it is only on rare occasions that some national constitutional courts would choose to refer cases to the CJEU.[55]

Indeed, a remedial take on the principle of effectiveness may have been well intended as a means of fostering a decentralised enforcement of EU law. Nonetheless, one cannot easily overlook that the 'best efforts approach' (in relation to the availability of remedies) promoted by the CJEU in cases such as *UPA* has shifted dramatically the burden of responsibility to the Member States to ensure the effectiveness of EU law.[56] Accordingly, Member States are found in breach of their EU law obligations (especially the principle of loyalty laid out in Article 4 (3) TEU) in case they fail to make available effective procedures before domestic courts for challenging EU acts. As it is eminent, the approach taken by the CJEU in judicial review cases with reference to access to justice was met with criticism in Advocate General Jacobs' Opinion in *UPA* delivered in the context of an appeal from the ruling of the General Court. In what was to become one of the most cited Opinions, Jacobs criticised the fact that the onus is on Member States, which are under a positive duty to provide effective procedures in their legal system in order to ensure that EU acts can be effectively reviewed under EU law. He further noticed that the preliminary reference procedure has a number of disadvantages, namely serious delays and problems for applicants in obtaining interim relief.[57] As such,

---

[52]   T Harvey, 'The European Union and the Governance of Health Care' in G De Búrca and J Scott (eds), *New Governance in the EU and the US* (Oxford, Hart Publishing, 2006) 184.

[53]   Case C-210/06 *Cartesio* [2008] ECR I-9641.

[54]   Case C-224/01 *Köbler* [2003] ECR I-10239.

[55]   For example it is only recently that the very first references by such courts took place. See Case C-399/11 *Melloni* (re: the Spanish Tribunal Constitucional) [2013] CLI:EU:C:2013:107, Case C-168/13 PPU *Jeremy F* (re: the French Conseil Constitutionnel) [2013] ECLI:EU:C:2013:358 and Case C-62/14 *Gauweiler* (re: the German Bundesverfassungsgericht) [2015] ECLI:EU:C:2015:400.

[56]   T Corhaut, *EU Ordre Public* (The Hague, Kluwer Law International, 2012) 279. The author argues that the CJEU's decision have generated an 'obligation of result' approach (and not merely one of 'best efforts' as highlighted in *UPA*). This approach justifies the CJEU's 'optimism' in *Gestoras* (Case C-354/04 P, [2007] ECR I-1579) and *Segi* (Case C-355/04 P, [2007] ECR I-1657) vis-a-vis judicial protection in the field of criminal law.

[57]   AG Jacobs Opinion in Case C-50/00, *UPA* [2002] ECR I-6677, paras 35, 56. Of course we need to take into account the urgent preliminary ruling procedure or PPU which enables the CJEU to deal far more quickly with sensitive cases related to PJCCM. See C Barnard, 'The *PPU*: Is it Worth the Candle? An Early Assessment' (2009) 34 *European Law Review* 281.

he dismissed the adequacy of the CJEU leaving the challenge of normative acts to the national courts.[58]

On the same note, Gormley located three variables that led Jacobs to argue that proceedings before national courts may not provide effective judicial protection of individual applicants.[59] First, national courts do not have the competence to declare EU law measures invalid. Second, there is no such a thing as a right of access to the CJEU for a remedy under the preliminary reference procedure of Article 267 TFEU. It is rather the national courts that have discretion whether or not they should make a preliminary reference to the CJEU. At times they may exercise their discretion to refer erroneously. Having said that, we shall not forget that a decision of a national court not to refer a question for a preliminary ruling can arguably constitute a breach of Article 6 ECHR.[60] Third, it is impossible to challenge EU measures where they do not require implementing acts. Likewise it is impossible to challenge domestic acts where they are not based on an EU framework. When push comes to shove an individual may try a little diversion in order to challenge EU acts. She may violate directly applicable EU legislation and face civil or criminal consequences only to compel her national court to use the preliminary reference procedure. According to Gormley, this procedural malaise 'does not encourage respect for the rule of law'.[61]

Notwithstanding the AG Jacobs' Opinion, and Gormley's endorsement of it, there are two arguments to the CJEU's defence. First, it can be contended that the principle of procedural autonomy mandates that national courts shall constitute the first port of call for private parties to bring a challenge against EU acts. Second, this role of national courts is further enhanced by the umbrella principle of effectiveness, part of which dictates that Member States shall, in their best efforts, provide individuals with effective procedures and remedies for enforcing EU law before domestic courts.[62] These arguments do not, however, take into account the likelihood of rule of law deficiencies or absence of national remedies currently witnessed in certain Member States. Although this is not a matter for the EU to

---

[58] Case C-50/00 P *Unión de Pequeños Agricultores v Council* [2002] ECR I-6677 (Opinion delivered on March 21, 2002). The opinion cites various judicial Opinions, extra-judicial writing, and academic literature criticising the Court of Justice's traditional approach.

[59] LW Gormley, 'Judicial Review in EC and EU Law: Some Architectural Malfunctions and Design Improvements?' (2001) 4 *Cambridge Yearbook of European Legal Studies* 167.

[60] Broberg and Fenger claim that '[w]hile the existing case law of the ECtHR does not allow us to determine more precisely the requirements as to the content, precision and level of detail of the reasons that a national court must give when refusing to make a preliminary reference, it still appears safe to conclude that if, in a decision not to make such reference, a national court gives an account of the circumstances of the case which, in its view, are reasons for not making the reference and makes a detailed review of the Court of Justice's case law that is relevant to the case there will be no human rights problems.' See M Broberg and N Fenger, 'Preliminary references to the Court of Justice of the European Union and the right to a fair trial under Article 6 ECHR' (2016) 41(4) *European Law Review* 599, 607.

[61] ibid 179.

[62] Cases 33/76 *Rewe* [1976] ECR 1989, 106/77 *Simmenthal* [1978] ECR 629, paras 21 and 22; Case C-213/89 *Factortame* [1990] ECR I-2433, para 19; and Case C-312/93 *Peterbroeck* [1995] ECR I-4599, para 12.

remedy for there may be cases where it does not have the *Kompetenz Kompetenz* to interfere in domestic procedural law, where there is a direct correlation with the current EU efforts to prevent the emergence of systemic threats to the rule of law discussed in detail in Chapter 5.

Penultimately, from a workload perspective, the fact of the positive duty of Member States to provide individuals with effective remedies implies an unequal distribution of labour between the EU and its Member States. It also reveals a paradox in expectations and reality: the EU expects from Member States to secure a high standard of judicial protection in accordance with EU standards but such a standard is not apparent in its own practice when one considers the limited access of individuals to EU courts when they seek redress. Accordingly, one could argue that the EU's decentralised approach to remedies may contradict the high level of consistency and uniformity generally required by EU law in the transposition and application of EU legislation.[63] The idea that remedies shall be provided at the national level gives prevalence to the diversity of interpretations of the concept of the rule of law as it appears in the Member States' Constitutions and their official translations of the EU Treaty. It can also be perceived as a sign of a decentralised and rather state-centric approach to rights and remedies.

IV. JUDICIAL PROTECTION BEFORE NATIONAL COURTS

A. Background

As discussed so far, national courts are the main fora for private litigants to challenge EU acts. As such, Member States have a crucial role to play in shaping the remedial aspects of the EU rule of law. The ECHR also recognised the vital role of national courts in the EU legal system by explaining that 'it is essentially through the national courts that the [EU] system provides a remedy to individuals against a Member State or another individual for a breach of [EU] law.'[64] As discussed, historically, national courts have been responsible for making available effective procedures and remedies for enforcing EU law, including the possibility for domestic courts to indirectly challenge EU legislation through the preliminary reference procedure under Article 267 TFEU.

Indeed as also pointed by the CJEU,

> the national courts have the most extensive powers, or even the obligation, to make a reference to the Court if they consider that a case pending before them raises issues

---

[63] The CJEU held in *Impact* [Case C-268/06, [2008] ECR I-2483], for instance, that national judges must apply directly effective provisions of EU law even where national law does not expressly provide them with jurisdiction to hear and adjudicate on actions based on EU law. According to the CJEU, a failure to do so is liable to undermine the principle of effective judicial protection.

[64] *Bosphorus v Ireland*, App No 45036/98 (ECHR 30 June 2005), para 164.

involving an ... assessment of the validity of the provisions of European Union law and requiring a decision by them ...[65]

Hence, if we accept that national courts have indeed a critical role to play in the enforcement of EU law, then clearly certain conditions must be met for the enforcement of EU law rights (including the right of individuals to question the validity of EU legal acts) before national courts in order for these rights to have any practical utility. Zuckerman has pointed to three conditions which would have to be met in order to ensure effective judicial protection in EU law:

i.   There must be a judicial process capable of determining the true facts and applying the relevant EU legislation to them.
ii. Judicial decisions must be obtainable within a reasonable time; for delay may rob the judgment of its ability to remedy the wrong; and
iii. Enforcement must be obtainable at proportionate cost because disproportionate cost will have a chilling effect on access to court enforcement.[66]

Zuckerman stresses that whilst the CJEU shows concern for the first condition, its jurisprudence demonstrates certain agnosticism with regard to the second and third conditions, ie that procedures in the Member States are timely and not prohibitively expensive. This is the case in both actions against the Member States or the EU institutions. Especially in private actions against the Member States the CJEU seems to be satisfied in so far as the principle of effective judicial protection is complied with. In other words, whether individuals challenge domestic or EU law, Member States only need to provide evidence that they maintain a judicial process which applies the relevant EU legislation in a case before them. Not only has the CJEU held that it is for national courts to assess whether domestic procedure would lead to undesirable results,[67] it has also described national courts as 'ordinary courts within the European Union legal order', whose task is to 'implement European Union law.'[68]

The above inclusive attitude of the CJEU, which respects the principle of procedural autonomy, has been criticised in view of the fact that certain Member States neither maintain direct avenues to challenge legislative acts nor do they have in place indirect means of judicial review.[69] Other Member States, like the UK for instance, have traditionally expressed reticence towards serving damages awards to individuals as a form of redress against the unlawful acts of public authorities.[70] The customary argument against the current decentralised system of EU law enforcement is, therefore, that it jeopardises the uniformity of the rule of law because it both tolerates and endorses disparate and sometimes ineffective domestic procedural rules. As such, the argument goes, the EU's decentralised approach

---

[65] Opinion 1/09 (European Patents Court) [2011] ECR-0000, para 83.
[66] Zuckerman (n 19).
[67] Case C-268/06 *Impact v Minister for Agriculture and Food* [2008] 2 CMLR 47.
[68] Opinion 1/09 (EU-wide Patent Court) [2011] ECLI:EU:C:2011:123, para 80.
[69] A Turk, *Judicial Review in EU Law* (Cheltenham, Edward Elgar, 2010) 169.
[70] P Craig, *Administrative Law* (London, Sweet and Maxwell, 2016). See especially Pt 3 Remedies.

to judicial review sits somewhat uncomfortably within the profile of the EU legal system which is largely based upon a centralised system of approximation of national substantive laws and comprehensive remedies. We will hereafter consider briefly Zuckerman's three conditions to ensure effective judicial protection in EU law.

i. A Judicial Process Capable of Applying the Relevant EU Legislation

The requirement for a judicial process capable of applying the relevant EU legislation implies that the detailed rules for implementing EU law fall within the scope of the internal legal order of the Member States by virtue of the principle of their procedural autonomy and subject to the principles of equivalence and effectiveness[71] as well as proportionality[72] and dissuasiveness.[73] Despite the EU's decentralised approach to judicial review, the CJEU has regularly scrutinised domestic rules of procedure for compliance with those principles.[74] Equally, there are ways under which the EU can monitor or punish Member States for the incapacity of their national courts to apply the relevant EU legislation and provide an effective avenue for individuals to enforce their rights under EU law (even if this means litigating against the EU institutions). As we know, the Commission can instigate the procedure under Article 258 TFEU if a Member State fails to provide individuals with a remedy. In the context of a public enforcement action against a Member State, it makes little or no difference to the Commission whether the failure of a Member State to apply EU law and provide effective remedies concerns a systemic deficit (ie lack of domestic procedures available) or derives from the denial or omission of a national court to request a preliminary ruling from the CJEU.[75] All that matters is whether the obstacles in question have a detrimental effect upon the uniform application of EU law.

Likewise, the Commission's decision to take action against a Member State would not be influenced by considerations as to whether the latter maintains the appropriate infrastructure to provide any domestic remedies under public law in internal situations. The CJEU will only be looking for parity between EU and domestic remedies in so far as damages awards are concerned. There, in accordance with the principle of equivalence, Member States would have to remedy a

---

[71] See *Student Transport Scheme Ltd v Minister for Education and Skills* [2015] IECA 303 (CA (Irl)) where the Irish Court of Appeal considered the question of public procurement measures breaching the EU principle of equivalence.

[72] See C-360/09 *Pfleiderer* AG [2011] ECLI:EU:C:2011:389.

[73] See KE Sørensen, 'Member States' Implementation of Penalties to Enforce EU Law: Balancing the Avoidance of Enforcement Deficits and the Protection of Individuals' (2015) *European Law Review* 811, 818.

[74] See for examples of cases: Case 68/88 *Commission v Greece* (Greek Maize) [1989] ECR 2965; Case C-231/96 *Edis* [1998] ECR I-4951; Case C-147/01 *Weber's Wine World* [2003] ECR I-11365; Cases C-295-298/04 *Manfrini* [2006] ECR I-6619; Case C-69/09 *Visciano* [2009] ECR I-6741.

[75] Case C-129/00 *Commission v Italy* [2003] ECR I-14637, para 32.

breach of EU law in the same manner they would have had, had the breach concerned domestic legislation.[76] In this regard, we should remind the reader that a functioning and independent judiciary does not only constitute a pre-condition for the effective implementation of EU law but represents one of the main accession conditions—the Copenhagen political criterion of the 'rule of law'.[77]

Given the above observations, can we argue with confidence that the principle of equivalence is respected in new Member States, ie that procedural rules in respect of actions based on EU law are not less favourable than those governing similar domestic actions? The principle of equivalence aside, the application of EU law on effective judicial protection seems to promote a model of double standards. This goes against the ultimate purpose of the principle of effectiveness which is in essence to ensure 'uniform effectiveness'.[78] As mentioned, national courts are obliged to provide remedies for EU law breaches, therefore protecting the integrity of EU law, but such obligation does not extend to domestic law breaches.[79] Nonetheless, the role of the Commission to ensure the uniform application of EU law is crucial, because if individuals fail to contest EU acts before the CJEU by reason of the admissibility conditions laid down in Article 263 (4) TFEU, there are no other direct avenues available to challenge the validity of EU acts before the CJEU. The only alternative route to private parties is to invoke a right before a national court which may then trigger the Article 267 TFEU procedure as a means of indirectly challenging an EU act.

The ECHR carries the potential of providing individuals with an alternative means of redress under Article 6 ECHR in cases where there are no remedies in a Member State.[80] Two fairly recent ECtHR judgments, *Dhahbi* in particular,[81] have set the tone in this respect and have paved the way for more case law in the event of national courts' failure to make a preliminary reference to the CJEU.[82] There the

---

[76] See for instance Joined Cases C-397/98 and C-410/ 98 *Metallgesellschaft* [2001] ECR I-1727.

[77] The 1999 Helsinki European Council confirmed that all Eastern European candidates that had at that point applied for EU membership had met the 'rule of law' criterion. Still, however, there are significant problems as regards the functioning of their judiciaries. For instance, Baker warned about 'the overburdening of the judicial system in the applicant countries because of lack of staff, huge backlogs of cases, inefficient procedures and the unavailability in several applicant countries of alternative methods of dispute settlement (such as arbitration, mediation and reconciliation).' E Baker, 'Criminal Jurisdiction, The Public Dimension to "Effective Protection"' (2001) 4 *Cambridge Yearbook of European Legal Studies* 25, 33.

[78] See M Accetto and S Zleptnig, 'The Principle of Effectiveness: Rethinking Its Role in Community Law' (2005) 11 *European Public Law* 375.

[79] F Jacobs, *The Sovereignty of Law*, Hemlyn Lectures (Cambridge, Cambridge University Press, 2007) 65.

[80] See again Broberg and Fenger (n 60) 599.

[81] *Ullens de Schooten and Rezaabek v Belgium*, App no 3989/07 and 38353/07, ECtHR, 20 September 2011.The ECtHR found no violation here but it is important that the Strasbourg Court noted that the right of access to a court is not absolute under Art 6 ECHR but can, nonetheless, be violated if the failure to submit a preliminary reference is arbitrary. See also *Dhahbi v Italy*, App no 17120/09, ECtHR, 8 April 2014. This is the first case where the ECtHR found a violation of Art 6 ECHR by a national court of last instance for its refusal to make a preliminary reference to the CJEU.

[82] *Schipani v Italy*, App no 38369/09, ECtHR, 21 July 2015. In this case the Italian Court of Cassation refused to refer a question to the CJEU relating to Italy's alleged failure to implement two Directives within the time limits; *Chylinski and Others v the Netherlands*, App no 38044/12, ECtHR, 21 April 2015.

ECtHR seems to be acting as the CJEU's enforcer, ie making sure that EU Member States do not get away with refusing to refer a case to the EU courts.[83] In both *Dhahbi* and *Schipani*, the ECtHR found violations of Article 6 ECHR (right to fair trial) against the Italian Court of Cassation which refused to consider a request for a reference to the CJEU. While referring to the principles set out in *Vergauwen v Belgium*[84] the ECtHR emphasised in *Dhahbi* that:

> [F]rom the angle of Article 6 [ECHR], national courts whose decisions were not open to appeal under domestic law were required to give reasons, based on the applicable law and the exceptions laid down in ECJ case-law, for their refusal to refer a preliminary question on the interpretation of EU law. They should set out their reasons for considering that the question was not relevant, that the provision had already been interpreted by the CJEU, or that the correct application of EU law was so obvious as to leave no scope for reasonable doubt.[85]

The availability of a remedy under the ECHR in this regard is a welcome development in terms of the preliminary reference procedure becoming a pathway towards judicial remedies for individuals. The ECtHR established that in order for Member States to escape liability for violating Article 6 ECHR it suffices that their national courts have considered a preliminary question and have given reasons for refusing to make a reference to the CJEU. However trivial this may sound, it is important to state that such a duty to give reasons is neither required by EU law nor the case law of the CJEU. To be more precise, the ECtHR seems to extend the duty so far attributed to highest national courts of their choice not to refer a case under the 'acte clair' rules established in *CILFIT* to all courts regardless of their rank.[86] Of course, it is not the ECtHR that calls all the shots in this respect. In theory, there is a remedy under EU law for failure to refer. Yet, in practice things are rather complicated. A claimant would have to go back to the same domestic court that refused to make a reference in the first place and ask it to order the national government to pay damages for that court's failure to make a reference. This is the case, for instance, if the failure to refer has involved a manifest error—ie there is no doubt that a reference should have been made in the first place.

---

[83] *Dhahbi v Italy*, App no 17120/09, ECtHR, 8 April 2014. Mr Dhahbi, a Tunisian national—resident in Italy—applied for and was refused a household allowance on grounds of nationality. He relied upon an entitlement to this allowance in the association agreement between the EU and Tunisia (Euro-Mediterranean Agreement). The Italian court, however, refused his application to have the case determined by the CJEU. Strasbourg decided that there had been a violation Art 6 (1) ECHR (right to a fair trial) and Art 14 ECHR (prohibition of discrimination) in conjunction with Art 8 ECHR (right to respect for private and family life) and held that that Italy was to pay Mr Dhahbi 9,416.05 euros (EUR) in respect of pecuniary damage and EUR 10,000 in respect of non-pecuniary damage.

[84] *Vergauwen v Belgium*, App no 4832/04, ECtHR, 10 April 2012, paras 89–90.

[85] See Press Release issued by the Registrar of the ECtHR, 'An immigrant worker of Tunisian origin should not have been deprived of a household allowance on the sole ground of nationality', ECHR 098 (2014), 08.04.2014.

[86] Case 283/81 *CILFIT* [1982] ECR 3415; See also Case C-160/14, *Ferreira da Silva e Brito* [2015] ECLI:EU:C:2015:565.

So far there is no case in which damages have been ordered as a result of an Article 6 ECHR violation. This perhaps owes to the peculiar facts of the relevant cases. For instance, *Dhahbi* is an unusual case in that the applicant complained to the ECtHR both about the nationality discrimination he suffered (contrary to the ECHR), and about the Italian court's failure to make a reference (possibly required by EU law). Most applicants would have merely invoked their ECHR rights in Strasbourg, and not go into the additional effort of complaining about the failure of the national court to enforce EU law.[87] Having said that, recent case law confirms that the ECtHR's task in defining common minimum standards which are effectively observed by all High Contracting Parties will be present regardless of whether or not an individual has submitted a request to a national court for a preliminary reference to the CJEU. Such a request may concern, for instance, the risk of divergences in judicial decisions related to EU law.[88] This trend in the case law of the ECtHR is likely to increase the tension between the EU and ECHR legal orders viz who possesses the powers or responsibilities for securing the protection of the right to an effective remedy within the EU.

Prior to the ECtHR's *Dhahbi* jurisprudence, the position was that unless an individual succeeded in bringing her case before a national court and the national judge made a preliminary reference to the CJEU, the Luxembourg Court had virtually no role to play in ensuring that Member States offered effective remedies. This procedural dead end is still problematic from a rule of law point of view since the CJEU appears to be abdicating its responsibility under the Treaty to ensure that 'the law is observed'. Once, however, a case is admissible before a national court and the national judge decides to resort to a preliminary reference request, the CJEU would have jurisdiction to apply the EU Charter of Fundamental Rights whenever it is appropriate. Then, of course, the question is whether the scope of application of the Charter expands beyond the spectrum of EU law implementation per se. We will, therefore, need to consider whether the application of the Charter may cover cases where Member States fail to provide remedies sufficient to ensure effective legal protection in the fields covered by EU law and, therefore, act in breach of their Treaty obligations under Article 19 (1) TEU and the principle of loyalty under Article 4 (3) TEU.

It is apparent that the failure of Member States to provide effective procedures and remedies or even access to EU courts as such, does not involve the implementation of EU law *stricto sensu* but rather concerns the obligation of Member States under the Treaty to provide a functioning system of remedies whenever private parties seek to challenge EU acts or domestic measures implementing them. As such, the default position is that, in the absence of EU law implementation, the EU Charter of Fundamental Rights would be inapplicable in cases where an

---

[87] See for further reflection: M Broberg, 'National Courts of Last Instance Failing to make a Preliminary Reference: the (Possible) Consequences Flowing Therefrom' (2016) 22(2) *European Public Law* 243.

[88] See *Avotiņš v Latvia* App no 17502/07, ECtHR, 23 May 2016.

individual relies on the right to effective judicial protection to merely challenge a domestic systemic deficit which impinges upon his/her opportunity to challenge EU acts or domestic implementation measures. To put it differently, an individual cannot rely on the Charter in the abstract without there being a right that she can invoke before a national court. There are cases which illustrate this point.[89] The CJEU has emphasised that effective judicial protection relates to specific rights, such as, for example, the right to be advised, defended and represented enshrined in Article 47 of the Charter. Accordingly, in a state liability claim before a national court any person can in accordance with the Charter rely on the principle of effective judicial protection in order to receive free legal aid.[90]

The CJEU seems to have envisaged a wide interpretation of the term 'implementation' bringing almost every case that relates to EU law within the scope of the Charter's application and therefore under the wing of the CJEU which acts as the ultimate interpretive authority on EU fundamental rights protection.[91] Since *Internationale Handelsgesellschaft*, the CJEU has posited that the level of protection of fundamental rights in the Member States shall not undermine the unity, primacy and effectiveness of EU law.[92] Not only does this commitment go beyond the textual obligations of Member States under the Treaty but it also establishes a rather generic and abstract test to determine the scope of EU law. As seen in *Åkerberg Fransson*, 'implementation' was taken to encompass all situations where EU law applies allowing significant space for CJEU manoeuvring.[93] This all-encompassing approach from the part of the CJEU was not favoured by the BVerfG which remarked that the *Åkerberg Fransson* dicta shall constitute the exception and not the rule.[94] As a follow-up, and perhaps fearing further national reaction, the CJEU attempted in *Siragusa* to qualify its previous jurisprudence and create a catalogue of sorts containing concrete criteria for adjudicating future fundamental rights cases.[95]

As discussed in Chapter 3, the habitual conflict between national law and EU law has undergone an upgrade which now includes two possible scenarios of discord between the EU and the Member States. The first scenario involves the

---

[89] See F Fontanelli, 'National Measures and the Application of the EU Charter of Fundamental Rights—Does curia.eu Know iura.eu?' (2014) 14 (2) *Human Rights Law Review* 231.

[90] Case C-289/09 *DEB* [2010] ECR I-13849.

[91] See Case C-617/10 *Åkerberg Fransson* [2013] ECLI:EU:C:2013:105; Case C-236/09 *Test-Achats* [2011] ECLI:EU:C:2011:100; Case C-411/10 *NS* [2011] ECLI:EU:C:2011:865; Case 300/11 *ZZ* [2013] ECLI:EU:C:2013:363.

[92] Case C-11/70 *Internationale Handelsgesellschaft* [1974] ECR 1125.

[93] See M Szwarc, 'Application of the Charter of Fundamental Rights in the Context of Sanctions Imposed by Member States for Infringements of EU Law: Comment on Fransson Case' 20(2) *European Public Law* (2014) 229. See also E Frantziou, 'Case C-176/12 Association de mediation sociale: Some Reflections on the Horizontal Effect of the Charter and the Reach of Fundamental Employment Rights in the European Union' (2014) 10 (2) *European Constitutional Law Review* 332.

[94] BVerfG Judgment of 24 April 2013—1 BvR 1215/07, Press Release of Judgment accessible at www.bundesverfassungsgericht.de/pressemitteilungen/bvg13-031en.html.

[95] C-206/13 *Siragusa* [2014] ECLI:EU:C:2014:126.

classic national fundamental rights against EU fundamental freedoms clash. The second scenario is about a more intricate national fundamental rights against EU fundamental rights confrontation. With reference to the second scenario, not only has the Charter's increased relevance as a benchmark for the validity of EU acts helped the CJEU erode the boundary between fundamental freedoms and fundamental rights. It has also given the CJEU a platform to balance constitutional singularities, which may be related to fundamental rights protection in a Member State, with fundamental rights as protected in the EU legal order. This is, however, easier said than done. Since fundamental rights protection at both EU and national level also involve adherence to the ECHR, both CJEU and national judges are confronted with a barrage of hierarchy issues. These issues emanate from the overlapping application of national Constitutions, the Charter and the ECHR.

Given that the above balancing exercise is influenced by the principles of sincere cooperation and primacy, it will in most cases conclude in favour of the EU. As commented, this is the case even when EU law applies remotely to a domestic situation and even where the threshold of fundamental rights protection is higher in the Constitution of a Member State as opposed to the Charter itself.[96] Thus, it has accurately been pointed out by certain commentators that 'state-specific constitutional guarantees [even dressed-up as aspects of national identity] stand no chance of survival when they collide with the standards set by the Charter'.[97] What really matters for the CJEU is whether the national provision in question would lead to a result which is contrary to the application of EU law.

Conversely, the CJEU has made it explicit that national peculiarities endowed with constitutional status will not qualify as exceptions from the application of EU law if they fall below the fundamental rights threshold set by EU law. This is a route that can provide inspiration for adjudicating on future cases that may involve Article 2 TEU violations by national governments. The Roma repatriation crisis in France in 2010;[98] the constitutional crisis in Hungary in 2011;[99] the political crisis in Romania in 2012;[100] and Poland's rejection of EU rule-of-law interference in 2016 demonstrate that EU disciplinary procedures are rarely triggered when politics are so divisive. Although national identity was not expressly mentioned in any of these cases, future reliance on the identity clause could allegedly assist certain Member States to unilaterally escape the all-inclusive character of European

---

[96] See Case C-399/11 *Melloni* [2013] ECLI:EU:C:2013:107.

[97] See Fontanelli (n 89) 263.

[98] D Castle and K Bennhold, 'Dispute Grows Over France's Removal of Roma Camps' *The New York Times* (16 September 2010) available at: www.nytimes.com/2010/09/17/world/europe/17union. html?_r=0; 'EU may take legal action against France over Roma' *BBC* (14 September 2010) available at www.bbc.co.uk/news/world-europe-11301307.

[99] 'Hungary's new constitution "puts democracy at risk"' *BBC* (20 June 2011) available at www.bbc. co.uk/news/world-europe-13843400.

[100] 'EU warns Romania PM Victor Ponta over political crisis' *BBC* (12 July 2012) available at: www. bbc.co.uk/news/world-europe-18822790.

integration with all the consequences that such conduct may generate.[101] It is expected that where the invoked aspect of national identity falls below the EU's standard of fundamental right protection, the CJEU should be more explicit that national identity shall be broadly construed in conformity with the traditional democratic values underpinned in Article 2 TEU such as respect for democracy, fundamental rights and the rule of law. This approach implies that anything falling below such a minimum level of protection would jeopardise the EU's constitutional integrity or, dare we say, EU identity.

ii. *Judicial Proceedings shall be Fair, Equitable, Timely and not Prohibitively Expensive*

We will now turn to consider the last two limbs of Zuckerman's conditions necessary to ensure effective judicial protection in the EU (ie that judicial decisions need to be obtainable within reasonable time and at proportionate cost). As with the first requirement discussed above, ie that there must be a judicial process in place, these conditions are important whether an individual is bringing an action against the EU institutions or Member States.

The CJEU has considered infringements of the reasonable time requirement but not in relation to challenges against the EU institutions' decisions. For example, in competition cases, the CJEU has rejected cartel appeals but has allowed claims regarding infringements of the reasonable time requirement.[102] Indeed, the CJEU has borrowed from Article 13 ECHR which guarantees the availability at national level of a remedy to enforce the substance of the ECHR rights. According to the ECtHR, the effect of Article 13 ECHR is to require the provision of a domestic remedy to deal with the substance of an 'arguable complaint' under the ECHR and to grant appropriate relief.[103] By the same token and in line with the EU Charter of Fundamental Rights, the CJEU would be willing to clarify procedural issues arising in the Member States regarding decisions which are not obtained within a reasonable time. Most importantly, in line with Article 47 of the Charter, the CJEU can make an argument that there needs to be an effective remedy in case of a failure to adjudicate within a reasonable time. Whether the CJEU would compel national courts to do so in cases concerning challenges against EU legislation is, however, open to debate.

The CJEU has also established, especially in the context of environmental law, that litigation shall not be 'prohibitively expensive'. To give an example, in *Edwards and Pallikaropoulos* the CJEU drew from EU secondary legislation (in particular Directive 85/337 and Directive 96/61) and the Aarhus Convention (as implemented

---

[101] See V Reding, 'The EU and the Rule of Law—What next?' Speech: The EU and the Rule of Law—What next? European Commission—SPEECH/13/677, 04/09/2013.

[102] See A Keidel, 'Gascogne Sack Deutschland, Groupe Gascogne, and Kendrion: Excessive Length of Cartel Proceedings' (2014) 5(3) *Journal of European Competition Law and Practice* 142.

[103] *Kudla v Poland*, App no 30210/96, ECtHR, 26 October 2000, para 157.

by these Directives) and established that Member States shall ensure that litigation in environmental matters should not be 'prohibitively expensive'.[104] This implies generally that individual litigants should not be prevented from pursuing a claim by reason of the financial burden that they may incur. Having said that, the guidance provided by the CJEU on the test of what is 'prohibitively expensive' has been characterised as 'somewhat Delphic' and thus impossible to provide an autonomous and uniform interpretation throughout the EU.[105] Besides, as Advocate General Kokkott noted in her Opinion '[c]onsequently, the Member States' rules must actually prevent in each individual case the judicial proceedings covered from being prohibitively expensive.'[106]

National courts have not been particularly helpful either in this regard. Accordingly, the UK Supreme Court interpreted the guidance issued by the CJEU in such a way that it inferred that the cost of proceedings must also not 'appear to be objectively unreasonable'. Like the CJEU, the Supreme Court also failed to give clear guidance as to how to assess unreasonableness in this context.[107] The above approaches regarding the public right to bring challenges and have access to procedures that are not prohibitively expensive in light of a Member State's EU obligations (as well as their interpretative lacunae) would also be relevant in cases raised before national courts challenging EU legislation. In spite of this facilitation, however, individuals and NGOs would still have to rely on their own resources if they wished to challenge supranational decisions. Litigation in this respect can be lengthy and expensive. Conversely, when it comes to challenging national decisions, it is noteworthy that the Commission may step in and refer cases to the CJEU, removing therefore the burden from the individual.[108] This position points to two 'rule-of-law' enforcement mechanisms: one for the Member States and another for the EU and its institutions.

V. REVIEW OF EU LAW BY NATIONAL COURTS

As noted previously, some national courts have alluded to a future in which they may have jurisdiction to review legislation for compatibility with their

---

[104] Case C-260/11 *Edwards and Pallikaropoulos* [2013] ECLI:EU:C:2013:221.

[105] Findlay claims that: 'The purpose of the Aarhus Convention was not to limit cost recovery against defendants, only to limit cost exposure to those seeking to challenge relevant decisions etc. The inability to recover full costs is clearly relevant to the reality of access to environmental justice.' J Findlay, 'Protective Expenses Orders—a Settled Regime?' (2014) *Scottish Planning & Environmental Law* 53, 54.

[106] Opinion of Advocate General Kokkott in Case C-260/11 *Edwards and Pallikaropoulos* [2012] ECLI:EU:C:2012:645, para 44.

[107] See further on environmental judicial review costs: R Stech, 'A Carrot and Stick Approach? An Analysis of the UK Government's Proposals on Environmental Judicial Review' (2013) 15 (2) *Environmental Law Review* 139–51, 143–45.

[108] European Commission, 'Environment: Commission takes UK to court over excessive cost of challenging decisions' Brussels, 6 April 2011, IP/11/439.

Constitution.[109] As discussed, in a number of recent cases on Article 4 (2) TEU, the CJEU has stressed that national identity does not enjoy a higher status than, for instance, public policy interests do.[110] Instead, it is bound to be balanced by a rigid proportionality assessment against other legal interests relevant to the advancement of European integration. This is generally an accepted state of affairs in most Member States although certain national courts have protested that matters are not that simple. Almost as a counter-measure, they have abstained from making use of Article 4 (2) TEU as a channel to communicate to the CJEU what constitutes part of their identity (ie frame their identity claim in EU law terms). They have rather adopted an internal constitutional approach to the relationship between the national and EU legal order premised on the view that domestic constitutional provisions provide a different approach to national identity protection than that which is intended by the Treaty. This inwards approach to constitutional identity comprises various areas of national policy and necessitates specific in-depth study.[111]

Thus, even if the intention of the Treaty drafter was to bring national identity into the primary law toolkit and—in light of the ever expanding EU competences—recognise it expressly as a manifestation of national sovereignty, the result has been somewhat disappointing in enhancing communication between European and national courts about the latter's status of constitutional identity. As European and domestic case law advances we are witnessing a gradually widening schism between respect for national identity under Article 4 (2) TEU and the protection of national identity under the provisions of national Constitutions. As remarked earlier, against the CJEU's reasonings on Article 4 (2) TEU, the BVerfG, in its role as the protector of constitutionality against potential transgressions of powers by the EU institutions, relishes every opportunity to stress ominously that national identity may not be balanced against any other legal interests.

The abovementioned development is only indicative of a rising but still relatively small trend in some Member States which demonstrate (and perhaps justifiably so in some circumstances) different signs of 'unruliness to 'failing states' mentioned previously. They have (at least in theory) reserved the final say in cases of possible transgressions of EU competences, and thus have attributed themselves the role of 'halting' the EU institutions when acting undemocratically and against

---

[109] This idea has been entertained with regard to areas of hard conflict concerning fundamental rights, national constitutional peculiarities viz constitutional identity. The two have often been presented as one defence. See M Kumm, 'The Jurisprudence of Constitutional Conflict: Constitutional Supremacy in Europe before and after the Constitutional Treaty' (2005) 11 *European Law Journal* 262.
[110] Case C-208/09 *Sayn-Wittgenstein* [2010] ECR I-13693.
[111] B Gisbert, 'National Constitutional Identity in European Constitutionalism' in A Saiz Arnaiz and C Alcoberro Llivina (eds), *National Constitutional Identity and European Integration* (Cambridge, Intersentia, 2013); T Konstadinides, 'Constitutional Identity as a Shield and as a Sword: The European Legal Order within the Framework of National Constitutional Settlement' (2011) 13 *Cambridge Yearbook of European Legal Studies* 195.

the rule of law.[112] At first, their theoretical reaction to the primacy of EU law may be perceived as a sign of arrogance or disobedience, therefore, flirting with the idea of consciously breaching their membership obligations. It is questionable whether the rule of law in its disciplinarian function can be construed in such a way so as to include sanctions for such acts of disobedience. Conversely, the stream of potential ultra vires review by national courts can also be characterised as a par excellence example of whistle-blowing that the EU is defaulting in its own rule-of-law terms. In a marginal set of cases some national courts have entertained the possibility of resorting to 'counter-measures' (specifically, ultra vires or intra vires identity 'locks') in order to protect the state's constitutional order from transgressions of powers and EU arbitrariness.[113] Such 'locks', however, are last resort weapons that may pose the danger of ultimately 'constrain[ing] the institution imposing them, not just the institution that is the target of the constraint.'[114]

VI. CONCLUSION

This chapter looked broadly into how the EU can be held accountable under the rule of law. Incidentally, we also touched upon issues that raise Member State liability. We argued that in the absence of a rule-of-law targeted mechanism against EU acts inconsistent with the values of the EU, Article 263 TFEU constitutes the main feature and gatekeeper of the judicial review system of EU acts. Having said that, in practice judicial review through national courts comprises the main avenue to individual claims. Accordingly, if we take the view that national courts have become European courts for all purposes then EU-type cases (with the exception of challenges to the legality of the acts of EU Institutions) shall be settled before them. In cases where the legality of EU acts is put into question, national judges would have to resort to the preliminary reference procedure under Article 267 TFEU. We examined the most pertinent issues regarding the application of these provisions, selecting examples from the recent jurisprudence of the CJEU and, to a lesser degree, the ECtHR. With reference to direct challenges under Article 263 (4) TFEU there is a conceptual difference between the rhetoric on the existence of a system of remedies on the one hand and the actual right of access to court on the

---

[112] In practice things are different. Let us recall that the BVerfG declared in the OMT follow-up that: 'If interpreted in accordance with the Court of Justice's judgment, the OMT programme does not present a constitutionally relevant threat to the Bundestag's right to decide on the budget. Therefore, it can currently also not be established that implementation of the OMT programme would pose a threat to the overall budgetary responsibility.' See Press Release No 34/2016 of 21 June 2016, available from www.bundesverfassungsgericht.de/SharedDocs/Pressemitteilungen/EN/2016/bvg16-034.html.
[113] *R (on the application of HS2 Action Alliance Ltd) v Secretary of State for Transport* [2014] UKSC 3; [2014] 1 WLR 324; Case C-62/14 *Gauweiler v Deutscher Bundestag* [2015] EU:C:2015:400.
[114] P Craig and M Markakis, '*Gauweiler* and the Legality of Outright Monetary Transactions' 41(1) (2016) *European Law Review* 4.

other. The viability of the strategy of the CJEU to distinguish between rights and remedies therefore needs to be considered in light of the rule of law.

The argument made in this chapter is that although the maintenance of a system of remedies and access to justice comprise key features of what we generally refer to as effective judicial protection in EU law, at times the two seem to operate as mutually exclusive concepts. For instance while the right to effective judicial protection generates a picture where the CJEU is effectively responsible for securing a complete system of remedies, both old and new case law on standing rules under Article 263 TFEU reveals a different story with regard to the limited right to standing. It confirms that the procedural dimension of the rule of law does not constitute a *domain reservé* for the EU institutions. On the contrary, access to justice and the availability of remedies are largely dependent upon the will of national judges to provide individuals with the opportunity to challenge the acts of EU institutions (and by extension of their own governments) at home. The above is a welcome development from an integrationist perspective because it demonstrates synergy between the EU-28 national courts and the CJEU acting as a seamless judicial web in its own right. It hides, however, certain dangers that can impede individuals' rights to effective judicial protection, namely that not all national courts may be prepared or willing to grant individuals a platform to put EU acts into question. This development may lead to a comparable case to that under CFSP where since EU courts do not have jurisdiction in CFSP matters it is up to national courts to review the legality of the contested decisions and to hear the action for damages. As mentioned by the Advocate General in a case regarding an action for annulment directed against the Head of an EU mission established under CFSP:

> National procedures—with their own rules on standing, admissibility, legal representation, statute of limitation, evidence, confidentiality and so forth—might not be suitable for ruling on the validity of EU acts. Those are procedures conceived for other purposes and might not guarantee EU institutions and Member States procedural rights comparable to those that they enjoy before the CJEU.[115]

Notwithstanding this danger in non-CFSP cases, more often than not, individual claims challenging the legality of EU acts will be filtered by national judges who will then decide whether or not to refer the case at hand to the Luxembourg Court. In this regard, the torch of maintaining a complete system of remedies in EU law has been passed on to them which, according to the CJEU, are generally responsible for establishing a system of procedures and remedies in order to boost the right to effective judicial protection. Within this context, this chapter discussed the notion of effective judicial protection before national courts which operates under a decentralised model of access to justice. This indirect model of judicial review takes stock of the principle of subsidiarity, according to which national courts are significant players in safeguarding the rights of individuals. Yet, at the same time, shifting responsibility to national courts may not always provide individual

---

[115] Opinion of Advocate General Wahl in Case C-455/14 P *H v Council and Commission* [2016] ECLI:EU:C:2016:212, para 39, para 102.

applicants with a solution to their problem, therefore, undermining the imperative of judicial enforcement of rights in EU law and, by extension, the rule of law.

The litigation pertaining to the European Stability Mechanism (or ESM) is indicative of the above pitfalls.[116] National judges have faced insurmountable difficulties when hearing claims from investors and depositors viz establishing liability and attributing compensation for damages allegedly caused by the EU institutions. It is indeed difficult for claimants to find the EU law source of the bailouts / bail-in measures. The uncertainty as to whether the Memoranda of Understanding, outlining the program of reforms or fiscal consolidation, are to be classed as acts of the EU institutions has casted doubts viz the admissibility of referring questions to the CJEU relating to them for a preliminary reference.[117] It transpires that in both the EU 'Article 263 TFEU cases' and ESM challenges, a centralised and rather streamlined approach to stimulate progress or address fiscal problems has not been followed by a similarly centralised approach to judicial review. The modalities of direct challenges against the EU were discussed early in this chapter and do not merit any further explanation. As regards legal challenges to the bailout programmes of the ESM, however, we need to note that for some time there was a stark absence of judicial review by the CJEU, which coupled with obstacles to bring a case before the national courts, amounted to a de facto effective judicial protection deficit.

It is only recently that the CJEU attempted to partly mitigate for lack of effective judicial protection in the context of the financial crisis. It established that the actions of the Commission and the ECB under the ESM, and specifically when signing a Memorandum of Understanding, can be challenged in a private action for compensation based on their illegality under Articles 268 and 340 TFEU.[118] Having said that, the CJEU did not provide any tangible solution in the case at hand by awarding damages to the applicants. It rather dismissed the relevant action for annulment and compensation concerning the restructuring of the Cypriot banking sector. Despite the negative outcome of the case, however, the fact that the CJEU has assumed jurisdiction over cases regarding the depositors' right to property guaranteed by Article 17 (1) of the EU Charter of Fundamental

---

[116] The ESM has been criticised for comprising a transfer of fiscal competence from defaulting Member States to yet another international organisation which, contrary to the EU, has a very specific fiscal consolidation function and thus it is agnostic to fundamental rights, input legitimacy and rule of law protection. See G Beck, 'The Suspension of the Rule of Law in the Euro Zone and why Chancellor Merkel should not Place her Trust in Rules' *Eutopia law* (02.07.2012) available from http://eutopialaw.com/2012/07/02/the-suspension-of-the-rule-of-law-in-the-euro-zone-and-why-chancellor-merkel-should-not-place-her-trust-in-rules-part-1/.

[117] See for an overview of the background the ESM and the Memoranda of Understanding: F Fabbrini, 'The Euro-Crisis and the Courts: Judicial Review and the Political Process in Comparative Perspective' (2014) 32 (1) *Berkeley Journal of International Law* 64; C Kilpatrick, 'On the Rule of Law and Economic Emergency: The Degradation of Basic Legal Values in Europe's Bailouts' (2015) 35 (2) *Oxford Journal of Legal Studies* 325.

[118] Joined Cases C-8/15 P *Ledra Advertising v Commission*, 20 September 2016. See for comment: I Glinavos, 'CJEU Opens Door to Legal Challenges to Euro Rescue Measures in Key Decision', *VerfBlog*, 2016/9/21, available at http://verfassungsblog.de/cjeu-opens-door-to-legal-challenges-to-euro-rescue-measures-in-key-decision/.

Rights carries symbolic significance. For instance, it will potentially open the door to further actions which will clarify the position of the liability of the EU institutions and the relevant international bodies that carried out the relevant 'bailouts' pertaining to the Eurozone crisis. It also brings to the spotlight the liability of unaccountable actors in the Eurozone crisis such as the Eurogroup, which carries considerable political weight, and that the Member States feel bound by the agreements concluded within that forum.[119]

As discussed, the rule of law is a systemic feature of the EU as a legal system preserved and enforced through inter alia the availability of a complete system of remedies which is accessible for the individual to use in order to challenge the validity of the acts of the EU legislature. While this chapter has established that judicial review of EU acts is essential for the maintenance of the procedural aspects of the rule of law in the EU it has also identified that, being an ex post remedy, judicial review may only highlight problems in the application of EU legislation once the latter has produced effects in a case at hand unveiled before a national court. National courts, therefore, need to be apt to apply EU law on the facts of the case they have in front of them and provide timely and cost-effective procedures. After all, it is national legal and political institutions that determine how the rule of law operates within the Member States. This being the case, the efficiency, independence and quality of legal reasoning of national judiciaries are key for the disposition of the EU rule of law which cannot in all cases be preserved centrally by the EU legislature and the CJEU.

The contribution of national courts is therefore corrective and instrumental to the notion of the rule of law nourished at EU level. The constitutional function of national courts is increasingly important in the light of recent judgments which see national judges contributing to the rule of law as a polity building rationale, which takes into account national peculiarities, in particular, constitutional identity.[120] However, as remarked, when identity preservation turns into an insular approach from constitutional courts, resort to the preliminary reference procedure may become scarce. This is rather problematic not only because it creates a barrier to reviewing the compatibility of national acts with EU law but also (and most importantly for the purpose of this chapter) in the context of individual claimants challenging EU law indirectly via national courts. But still, following the ECtHR's jurisprudence there seems to be future potential for a safeguard to individuals who seek to compel national judges to engage with EU law more actively. Especially in those situations where there is a lack of knowledge of EU law amongst national judges, the ECtHR jurisprudence can offer a solution to individuals relying on EU law before national courts. As a result, national adjudicators may be stimulated to assess EU law carefully and to address more questions to European Courts.

---

[119] See Advocate General Wathelet's Opinion in Joined Cases C-105/15 P to C-109/15 P *Mallis and Others v European Commission and European Central Bank* [2016] ECLI:EU:C:2016:294.

[120] See T Konstadinides, 'Dealing with Parallel Universes: Antinomies of Sovereignty and the Protection of National Identity in European Judicial Discourse' (2015) 34 (1) *Yearbook of European Law* 127.

5

Holding Member States
to the Rule of Law

I. INTRODUCTION

S O FAR, WE have established that the rule of law constitutes a key organisational model of EU constitutional law. We have located both the express and
implied references to it within and outside the Treaty. We have also discussed
its scope and have interpreted the EU rule of law to generally represent access to
justice and judicial review of the acts of the EU administration by the Court of
Justice of the European Union (CJEU). To this purpose we have mentioned the
role of the principle of effectiveness in enforcement actions against the EU institutions where the EU's commitment to the rule of law has often been put into the
test. All this suggests a *juridification* of the rule of law based on the remedial system
of EU law—at least insofar as the EU institutions are held to the EU rule of law.
When it comes to the Member States' adherence to the rule of law, the role of the
courts is still of course crucial. This chapter will also add the gradual *politicisation*
of the rule of law as an additional component which has helped set out a new
EU Framework for the Rule of Law. This development implies a growing involvement of the EU political institutions in guaranteeing rule-of-law monitoring and
enforcement—thus, portraying the EU as less of a 'court-centric' legal system.

Holding the Member States to the rule of law still has a direct correlation with
the CJEU's pronouncement made with regard to judicial review of EU acts that
the EU is 'based on the rule of law in which its institutions are subject to judicial review of the compatibility of their acts with the Treaty and with the general
principles of law which include fundamental rights.'[1] The same standard of judicial review applies to national authorities. We shall be reminded however that, as
seen in the previous chapter with regard to EU liability, it is only in limited circumstances that the EU provides for direct routes to obtain judicial review of EU
acts. Thus, concludes the CJEU, 'it is for the Member States to establish a system
of legal remedies and procedures which ensure respect for the right to effective
judicial protection'.[2] Hence often the degree of judicial protection available to an

---

[1] Case C-50/00 P *UPA* [2002] ECR I-06677, paras 38, 39; Joined Cases C-402/05 P and C-415/05
P *Kadi* [2008] ECR I-06351, para 316.
[2] Case C-50/00 P *UPA* [2002] ECR I-6677, para 41; T-175/98, & T-177/98, *Salamander v European
Parliament and Council* [2000] ECR II-2487, para 74.

individual is made dependent on the ability of the national judge to provide such a remedy. Of course not all national judges may be prepared to grant individuals a platform to put EU acts into question—some courts may disregard EU law out of ignorance, rebellion, or plain failure to refer a case at hand to their counterpart court in Luxembourg.

The analysis will now turn to consider the political and legal authority of the EU in light of the responsibility of Member States to comply with their obligations under EU law and the authority of the CJEU and the EU political institutions (particularly the Commission) to hold them to the rule of law. Specifically, this chapter will focus on the mechanisms established by the Treaty which are capable of ensuring that the rule of law, as a constitutional asset of the EU legal order, is properly implemented at national level. Indeed, as has been argued elsewhere, the incremental harmonisation of national law has led to a 'strict' EU rule of law. The degree of harmonisation required by the EU often dictates the object of administrative acts to such an extent that the Member States' compliance with the expanding legislative *acquis* has significantly reduced the regulatory power exercised by national administrative agencies.[3]

In addition to the incremental development of EU competence, the Commission's power to oversee whether individual provisions of EU law are implemented and the CJEU's extension of the reach of Member State liability are evidence that the EU has taken a further constitutional step (related to the monitoring and enforcement of its norms). This time the EU constitutional vocabulary explicitly makes reference to the rule of law as a means of addressing the evolving issue of 'systemic deficiencies' in some Member States. Despite the inevitable symbolism viz an affirmation that the EU is a political union which respects common values, the EU's interference with the general commitment of the Member States to the rule of law carries significant ramifications for EU competence—blurring further the boundaries between European competences and domestic sovereignty. This is because the application of the new framework seems to go beyond checking whether individual provisions of EU law have or have not been implemented. This novelty in the enforcement of the rule of law would often require EU interference with matters that are effectively internal (eg the independence of national justice systems) and thus fall squarely outside EU competence.

Taking stock of the above, this chapter focuses on the increasing concern about some EU Member States' disregard for the rule of law. It discusses the utility of existing mechanisms to address those 'crises' and explores the advantages of the procedure to both prevent and address them. In the face of recent events that have revealed a lack of respect in some Member States for the fundamental values which the rule of law aims to protect, the EU institutions have responded with proposals

---

[3] T Konstadinides, 'The Competences of the European Union' in R Schütze and T Tridimas (eds), *The Oxford Principles of European Union Law, Vol 1: The European Union Legal Order* (Oxford, Oxford University Press, 2017).

for a 'framework' to strengthen the rule of law's consistency. Although both the European Parliament and the Member States have endorsed the quasi-judicial authority of the Commission as the guardian of the Treaties, some may find it hard to rationalise why a 'rule of law framework' is necessary. It is also difficult to see how such a framework will overlap with the Council's newly-launched 'rule-of-law dialogue' especially in delicate areas concerning how refugees and migrants are integrated into European societies (especially the discussion on hotspots and relocation).[4] Finally, it remains disputed how would the *politicisation* of the rule of law bridge the current enforcement 'gap' in EU law and resolve rule-of-law crises where the breach in question is entangled with internal practices in the Member States concerning the systemic organisation of state authority.

We will begin by, inter alia, providing some background on the term 'rule-of-law crises' and move outward from there in order to look into national legislation that risks infringing on EU fundamental values. Last but not least, we will provide an outline of the EU tools available to counter those risks.

II. COINING THE TERM 'RULE-OF-LAW CRISES'

In last five years or so, the rule of law has gained considerable impetus in EU political statements as one of the main values upon which the EU is founded. In his statement at the High Meeting on the Rule of Law on 24 September 2012 in New York,[5] the former EU Commission President Manuel Barrosso stated that the EU is a Union based on the rule of law as a principle at the heart of the EU capable of protecting every individual. Barrosso's statement pointed to a more determinate configuration of the rule of law. Earlier that year, in his annual State of the Union speech to the European Parliament delivered on 12 September 2012, Baroso highlighted the link between a political union and respect for the rule of law. Inter alia, he stressed the need for 'a better developed set of instruments—beyond the "soft power" of political persuasion and the "nuclear option" of Article 7 TEU' which lays down a procedure to ensure respect by the Member States of the values referred to in Article 3 Treaty on European Union (TEU).[6]

---

[4] In December 2014, the Council conclusions established an annual Rule of Law Dialogue based on the principles of objectivity, non-discrimination and equal treatment of all Member States. The first 'dialogue' took place during the Luxembourg Presidency on 17 November 2015. See more recently: 'Presidency non-paper for the Council (General Affairs) on 24 May 2016—Rule of law dialogue', Brussels, 13 May 2016, 8774/16. Available at http://data.consilium.europa.eu/doc/document/ST-8774-2016-INIT/en/pdf.

[5] JM Barroso, Statement at the High Level Meeting on the Rule of Law, 24 September 2012, Speech 12/637, available from http://europa.eu/rapid/press-release_SPEECH-12-637_en.htm?locale=en. Barosso made the following statement: 'The European Union is a Union of values and a community of law. Primary among these are the universal values: democracy, rule of law and respect for human rights … The rule of law is at the heart of our European Union … and it should assist and protect every person on this planet'.

[6] Available from http://ec.europa.eu/soteu2012/files/soeu_web.pdf.

Taking stock of the above political stimulus provided by Barosso, on 6 June 2013, the Justice and Home Affairs Council stated that 'respecting the rule of law is a prerequisite for the protection of fundamental rights' and called on the Commission to take forward the debate on shaping a collaborative and systematic method to tackle rule of law breaches. Indeed, on 4 September 2013 the then Vice-President of the European Commission and EU Justice Commissioner, Viviane Reding highlighted the role of the Commission as the guardian of the rule of law. This role chimed well with the European Parliament's earlier request that Member States be regularly assessed on their compliance with the requirement of democracy and the rule of law.[7]

The term 'rule-of-law crises' was thus officially coined by Viviane Reding. It was taken to include 'any deficiencies in the independence, efficiency or quality of the justice system in another Member State.'[8] Most importantly perhaps, apart from providing a working definition of rule-of-law crises, Reding's promotion of the rule of law as a principle with a defined structure suggested the construction of a systematic mechanism for handling rule-of-law crises within the EU.[9] From that point onwards, the possibility of a rule-of-law intervention mechanism generated considerable political debate and stimulus manifested in a Commission proposal for a common rule-of-law framework[10] and a number of European Council contributions concerning EU action to ensure respect for the rule of law.[11] Despite these concerted efforts, the institutional rhetoric about the formalisation of the rule of law soon became the subject matter of intense controversy, not the least due to doubts about the appropriateness of the Commission as the main EU institution to initiate ad hoc rule-of-law enquiries in the Member States.[12]

---

[7] See European Parliament, Committee on Civil Liberties, Justice and Home Affair, 'On the situation of fundamental rights: standards and practices in Hungary (pursuant to the European Parliament resolution of 16 February 2012)', 25 June 2013, (2012/2130(INI)). See also Report of 27 January 2014, (2013/2078(INI)); and Report on the evaluation of justice in relation to criminal justice and the rule of law, 17 February 2014, (2014/2006(INI)).

[8] V Reding, 'The EU and the Rule of Law—What next?', European Commission, SPEECH/13/677, CEPS, Brussels, 04.09.2013.

[9] ibid.

[10] Communication from the Commission to the European Parliament and the Council, 'A new EU Framework to strengthen the Rule of Law', Brussels, 19.3.2014 COM (2014) 158 final/2, available at http://ec.europa.eu/justice/effective-justice/files/com_2014_158_en.pdf.

[11] Council of the European Union, 'Ensuring respect for the rule of law in the European Union' 16862/14 COR 1, Brussels, 14 November 2014, available from: http://register.consilium.europa.eu/doc/srv?l=EN&f=ST%2015206%202014%20INIT. Conclusions of the Council of the European Union and the member states meeting within the Council on ensuring respect for the rule of law General Affairs Council meeting, Brussels, 16 December 2014, available from http://consilium.europa.eu/uedocs/cms_data/docs/pressdata/EN/genaff/146323.pdf.

[12] This argument has not found much support. Pech, for instance, argues that: 'As for the argument that the European Commission would allegedly overstep its mandate under the EU Treaties, this is a red herring. While it is true that according to an opinion of the Legal Service of the Council, the Commission's pre-Article 7 Framework would allegedly not be "compatible with the principle of conferral which governs the competences of the institutions of the Union", this opinion can be found both unpersuasive and ill reasoned.' Systemic Threat to the Rule of Law in Poland: What should the

But does rule-of-law enforcement only concern the question of who is best equipped to monitor and enforce it? Does it not include indicators about the kind of behaviour that we deem to be appropriate in order then to endeavour to sanction any deviations from it? The latter is problematic insofar as Member States agree to disagree on what should trigger the EU rule-of-law enforcement mechanism. For instance, what can be confidently described by the Commission as a 'rule-of-law crisis' may not be for some Member States so different from a breach of one of the common values already enshrined in the TEU or a deviation from a general principle of EU law which, as we know, is sanctioned differently. The argument is that since there are long-established enforcement mechanisms in place to discipline Member States for misbehaviour within the bounds of EU law, one may remain unconvinced about the added value of a new, and rather abstract in scope, enforcement mechanism.

Having said that, we may appreciate the counter-argument about the rationale of an independent rule-of-law monitoring mechanism. Under Article 49 TEU, respect for the rule of law forms a precondition for EU membership. Yet, the EU seems to lack a specific rule-of-law monitoring mechanism following a Member State's accession to the EU. For instance, the EU does not possess a specific instrument to assess whether the rule of law and the independence of judges still command respect post-accession.[13] Ironically, perhaps, such matters appear to fall outside EU competence once a candidate state becomes a full member of the EU. As it is standard practice, the EU does not have *Kompetenz Kompetenz*—ie the power to establish a rule-of-law mechanism outside the areas where the EU has no explicit competence to act.[14] This is perhaps why, instead of devising a new system, Reding relied on the existing option of Article 7 TEU (introduced with the Amsterdam Treaty, as a precursor to the EU's enlargement). This is as a prevention mechanism also allowing for remedial action by the EU against a Member State that poses a clear risk or a serious and persistent breach of one of the common values that the EU is founded upon.

Despite the somewhat past failed attempts to activate Article 7 TEU,[15] the time seemed ripe for entertaining the possibility of a rule-of-law mechanism whether

Commission do next?, EUI Constitutionalism and Politics Blog, 1 November 2016, available from: https://blogs.eui.eu/constitutionalism-politics-working-group/2016/11/01/systemic-threat-rule-law-poland-commission-next/.

[13] See European Parliament Plenary debate on the political situation in Romania, 12 September 2012, available at www.europarl.europa.eu/sides/getDoc.do?pubRef=-//EP//TEXT+CRE+20120912+ITEM-011+DOC+XML+V0//EN.

[14] See on EU considerable transgressions of competences the BVerfG's *Honeywell Decision* BVerfGE 126. See also A Dyevre, 'European Integration and National Courts: Defending Sovereignty under Institutional Constraints?' (2013) 9 (1) *European Constitutional Review* 139.

[15] See G Budó, 'EU Common Values at Stake: Is Article 7 TEU an Effective Protection Mechanism', Barcelona Institute for International Affairs, Documents CIDOB, May 2014, available from www.cidob.org/ … /1/file/DOCUMENTS%20CIDOB_01_EUROPA.pdf. Budó provides a brief analysis of the past resort of Art 7 TEU in the 'Haider case' in Austria, the Constitutional Reform in Hungary, the Roma expulsions in France, and the political struggle between President Basescu and Prime Minister Ponta in Romania.

under a new system or by strengthening the existing mechanism under Article 7 TEU to protect EU values. The year 2013–14 was marked by the remnants of the financial crisis, the enforcement of various memoranda in the Member States and increasing support for extremist Eurosceptic parties both in the European Parliament elections and at the domestic level. These developments generated uncertainty and provided the pretext (or even the justification) for potential transformation of the EU rule of law from a declaratory and programmatic value towards a more concrete and justiciable principle against defaulting Member States. At the same time, however, the legal constraints (related to the lack of legal basis) pertaining to the establishment of a new supervision mechanism on top of Article 7 TEU were not overcome. More specifically, there was no discussion about setting up a new mechanism between Member States at least within the framework of the existing Treaties. An incentive to have a new rule-of-law 'surveillance' mechanism established outside the framework of the Treaties was, therefore, gradually developed.

Developments in Europe created the necessary momentum for a rule-of-law monitoring mechanism. A number of threats to the legal and democratic fabric in some Member States tested the resilience of the EU's constitutional arsenal and institutional capability to respond effectively to rule-of-law challenges using the established mechanisms in place. Three cases indicative of 'rule-of-law crises' were mentioned by Viviane Reding covering the period between 2010 and 2012. These were the Roma repatriation crisis in France in 2010, the constitutional crisis in Hungary in 2011 and the political crisis in Romania in 2012. What these crises had in common was the claim of illegality of national decrees with constitutional practice viz limits to the powers of the Constitutional Court. In view of these constitutional crises, it was argued, that despite the EU institutions' capacity to act in situations of EU law violations by using the Treaty's set of tools, there was a noticeable void between the Commission's infringement role and the Article 7 TEU mechanism. The question was who is going to fill it and how. The Commission, therefore, turned the above deficiency into an opportunity to push for a new collaborative and systematic general framework based on monitoring and warning. Apart from its rule-of-law focus, the Commission's proposal aimed to establish a means to resolve the uncertainty shadowing the effective enforcement of EU common values in the Member States.[16]

Following Reding's proposal, the Italian Presidency presented a paper, titled 'Ensuring respect for the Rule of law in the European Union', which analysed the state of play in terms of instruments for respecting the rule of law in the EU.[17] The paper established that the rule of law is one of the founding principles stemming

---

[16] Communication from the Commission to the European Parliament and the Council, 'A new EU framework to strengthen the rule of law' COM (2014) 158 final.

[17] Council of the EU, Presidency, 'Ensuring respect for the rule of law in the European Union, Brussels', 14 November 2014, available from http://register.consilium.europa.eu/doc/srv?l=EN&f=ST%2015206%202014%20INIT.

from the common constitutional traditions of all the Member States of the EU and one of the key values on which the EU is founded. It acknowledged the central role of the European Council in the effort to build a common understanding on compliance with the rule of law in accordance with the Treaties. Furthermore, the Italian Presidency emphasised the role of external institutions outside the EU classic configuration such as the Council of Europe; the Venice Commission; the UN; and the Organization for Security and Co-operation in Europe (OSCE) in the development and implementation of rule-of-law standards. It further contended that the European Council should relish the opportunity to apply the procedure under Article 7 TEU, inclusive of the *ultima ratio* remedy under paragraph 3 of suspension of certain rights deriving from the application of the Treaties to the Member State in question.

As a result of the above reflection from the Italian Presidency, there was an agreement for the Council to play a central role in discussions with Member States on the respect for the rule of law within the EU. Specifically, EU ministers adopted the decision that a rule of law 'dialogue' will take place once a year in the Council in its General Affairs configuration, and be prepared by the Committee of the Permanent Representatives of the Governments of the Member States to the European Union (COREPER).[18] Then the Council would decide, as needed, to launch debates on thematic subject matters. Accordingly, the experience of resorting to Article 7 TEU was to be evaluated by the end of 2016. In the meantime, the Commission issued in 2014 a brief Communication for a new Framework to strengthen the rule of law.[19] It stressed that the current EU legal framework is ill-designed in addressing internal, systemic threats to the rule of law. Thus, the idea was that the Commission would still rely on the infringement procedure under Articles 258–260 Treaty on the Functioning of the European Union (TFEU) in the event Article 7 TEU falls short of ensuring an effective and timely response to threats to the rule of law. Still, however, the possibility for a rule-of-law mechanism set up outside the framework of the existing Treaties remains thin despite new challenges, discussed later in this chapter, such as the reforms introduced by the Polish Government under Beata Szydło concerning the replacement of top intelligence officials, a reform of the public media and the disempowerment of the Constitutional Court.[20]

---

[18] Conclusions of the Council of the European Union and the Member States meeting within the Council on Ensuring Respect for the Rule of Law, General Affairs Council meeting, Brussels, 16.12.2014, available from www.consilium.europa.eu/en/meetings/gac/2014/12/16/.

[19] Communication from the Commission to the European Parliament and the Council 'A new EU Framework to strengthen the Rule of Law' COM/2014/0158 final.

[20] 'EU takes unprecedented step against Poland over rule of law', *EurActiv*, 04.01.2016, available from www.euractiv.com/sections/eu-priorities-2020/eu-takes-unprecedented-step-against-poland-over-rule-law-320634.

III. THREE RULE-OF-LAW CRISES

A. The Conflation of the Rule of Law with Security

The conflation of the rule of law with security and law and order has become commonplace in recent years, especially in relation to the Member States' plans to secure their borders, reform immigration and restore the 'rule of law'. In particular, public interest considerations are particularly important in immigration and deportation cases. For instance, in his 2015 letter to the President of the European Council, Donald Tusk, former UK Prime Minister, David Cameron mentioned that:

> We also need to crack down on the abuse of free movement ... This includes tougher and longer re-entry bans for fraudsters and people who collude in sham marriages. It means addressing the fact that it is easier for an EU citizen to bring a non-EU spouse to Britain than it is for a British citizen to do the same. It means stronger power to deport criminals and stop them coming back, as well as preventing entry in the first place.[21]

One can see how the rule of law conflates with law and order. It has been argued, however, that 'although law and order is often conflated with the rule of law, the two concepts are asymmetrically opposed.'[22] This appears to be increasingly the case in immigration exclusion proceedings with regard to 'undesired' individuals, including EU citizens who exercise their right to free movement and entitlement to social care. As David Cameron submitted in his above-mentioned letter to Donald Tusk, 'we can reduce the flow of people coming from within the EU by reducing the draw that our welfare system can exert across Europe.'[23] One can also see here how the rule of law conflates with the imperative or overriding requirements in the public or general interest viz precluding recourse to social security benefits.

   A rule-of-law compatible approach normally mandates that when national security is at stake, Member States put measures in place which, subject to the rule of law, provide for the possibility of adversarial proceedings before an independent body which possesses power to review the government's reasons for the expulsion decision.[24] Member States have, however, often interpreted national security rather strictly depriving individuals from such a review and, therefore, undermining basic fundamental rights. In those cases, the alleged maintenance of national security has generated what Reding described as rule-of-law crises based on human rights violations. A good example of the divide between the rule of law as enshrined in the EU legal order and a rule by law that breaches fundamental

---

[21] D Cameron, 'A New Settlement for the UK in a Reformed European Union', 10 November 2015, 5, available at.www.gov.uk/government/uploads/system/uploads/attachment_data/file/475679/Donald_Tusk_letter.pdf.
[22] N Cheesman, 'Law and Order as Asymmetrical Opposite to the Rule of Law' (2014) 6 (1) *Hague Journal on the Rule of Law* 96.
[23] See above (n 21) at 5.
[24] See *IR and GT v UK*, ECtHR, App Nos 14876/12 and 63339/12.

rights and legitimises state authority is the 'Roma repatriation crisis' that took place in France in 2010. The 'Roma crisis' commonly refers to the then President Sarkozy's 'voluntary' repatriation programme aimed at decreasing the Roma population in France.[25] Indeed, such a trend, evident in a less systematic form in other Member States, blurred the line between what is perceived to be a voluntary and gradual return and what can be criticised as a practice of mass deportation and ethnic cleansing.

The rights enjoyed by the Romani population under the Treaty's EU citizenship provisions as well as the EU Citizenship Directive (2004/38) and the Race Equality Directive (2000/43) have been traditionally breached by two national practices. First, there is a general policy of exclusion and inequality against the Romani within the Member States in which they reside. Second, since such policy often pushes them to migrate to another Member State, in most cases there is a general failure by the country of destination to cope with Romani migrants seeking residence in its territory. The above ongoing problems strike at the epicentre of the EU's human rights and rule-of-law protection because in the absence of commonly agreed standards they encourage arbitrary practices by the host states. Hence, Roma discrimination has deepened in recent years through lack of EU involvement, and most recently, it has escalated with collective expulsions undertaken against them justified on the grounds of public security, a legitimate ground for derogation of EU law free movement provisions. National aggressive campaigns to expel the Romani have raised considerable concern in the Council of Europe institutions and non-governmental organisations (NGOs) who have produced reports to expose the problem.[26]

It is salient to observe the European Committee of Social Rights' (ECSR) decision in *Centre on Housing Rights and Evictions (COHRE) v France*[27] on whether France's decision to close down 300 illegal Roma sites from their dwellings and their expulsions from France in the summer of 2010 violated Articles 16 (right of the family to social, legal and economic protection), 31 (right to housing) and 19 (8) (guarantees concerning deportation) of the Revised Charter and (Article E) discrimination in the enjoyment of the above-mentioned rights.[28] The French Government contended that Roma migrants in France are often illegal by virtue of both EU law and national law because they do not possess sufficient resources to avoid becoming 'a burden' on the state according to Directive 2004/38/EC. France was justified in deporting them as illegal migrants so as to safeguard

---

[25] CT Gunther, 'France's Repatriation of Roma: Violation of Fundamental Freedoms?' (2012) 45 *Cornell International Law Journal* 205.

[26] See indicatively: Commissioner for Human Rights, 'Human Rights of Roma and Travellers in Europe', Council of Europe Publications, 2012, available fromwww.coe.int/t/commissioner/source/prems/prems79611_GBR_CouvHumanRightsOfRoma_WEB.pdf.

[27] Complaint No 63/2010. See also *Centre on Housing Rights and Evictions (COHRE) v Italy*, decision on the merits, 25 June 2010.

[28] H O'Nions, 'Roma Expulsions and Discrimination: The Elephant in Brussels' (2011) 13 (4) *European Journal of Migration and Law* 361.

internal security. By contrast, the ECSR stressed that returning Romanian and Bulgarian Roma to their countries of origin was based on discriminatory provisions that directly targeted them as a group and, therefore, amounted to collective expulsions.

The aforementioned developments aside, no public enforcement action was taken against France by the Commission. Such an enforcement inertia contradicts the jurisprudence of the CJEU which provides that national authorities must always disclose the essence of the grounds for an expulsion order of an EU citizen and that this is 'a minimum requirement which cannot yield to the demands of national security' notwithstanding that the related evidence 'may be withheld from disclosure for reasons of national security.'[29] Not only that, but by remaining idle, the EU institutions seem to almost go against the spirit of Article 47 of the EU Charter of Fundamental Rights which provides for the right to an effective remedy. This right, read in light of Article 52 of the Charter, guarantees an equivalent right to access to a court under Article 6 ECHR.

Against the above background, a general policy of exclusion against certain individuals seems to have passed the high threshold of the CJEU for incurring liability. The most recent manifestation of tolerance from the part of the CJEU was in the case of *Dano* where the CJEU dealt with Germany's refusal to grant basic income support (*Grundsicherung*) to EU citizens who move to a Member State, other than that of their nationality, solely in order to obtain social benefits.[30] The CJEU held that Germany may refuse, on the basis of a general criterion that demonstrates the absence of a genuine link with the host Member State, nationals of other Member States social security benefits for jobseekers who are in need of assistance. Contrary to the French Roma expulsions discussed above, the legitimate objective pursued by the exclusion of 'benefit tourists' in *Dano* was to prevent unreasonable recourse to national social security benefits rather than to maintain national security. It was also concerned with an application for access to social benefits, not expulsion from Germany. As such, we can claim that the *Dano* decision gave the green light for 'unequal' treatment only in respect of the granting of social assistance benefits between nationals of a host Member State and other EU citizens. The CJEU also emphasised that when the Member States lay down the conditions for the grant of social benefits they are not implementing EU law. As such, the EU Charter of Fundamental Rights may not be applicable in such cases.[31]

---

[29] Case C-300/11 *ZZ v Secretary of State for Home Department*; See also the follow up at the Court of Appeal [2014] EWCA Civ 7.

[30] Case C-333/13 *Dano* [2014] ECLI:EU:C:2014:2358.

[31] See discussion above on Case C-67/14 *Alimanovic* [2015] ECLI:EU:C:2015:597 and Case C-308/14 *European Commission v UK* [2016] EU:C:2016:436. See also A Tryfonidou, 'The Notions of "Restriction" and "Discrimination" in the Context of the Free Movement of Persons Provisions: From a Relationship of Interdependence to One of (Almost Complete) Independence' (2014) *Yearbook of European Law* 33.

B. Crackdown on Judicial Independence and the Rule of Law

Judicial independence is traditionally deemed to ensure individuals about the impartiality of adjudication. The EU's commitment to judicial independence is fairly recent and has become key in the enforcement of the EU rule of law. The independence, competence and transparency of the judiciary in the Member States has been recently questioned in a number of EU Member States. In particular, recent changes to the Polish constitutional court fuelled protests and opposition complaints that they threatened judicial independence.[32] These changes also attracted direct criticism from EU officials that Poland's rule of law is under systematic threat.[33] The allegation against the Polish Government under Beata Szydło pertained the appointment of judges to the Constitutional Tribunal; recent legislation amending the law on the Constitutional Tribunal and the relevant judgments of this Court relating to this new law; as well as the effectiveness of the constitutional review of new legislation which has been effective since 2016.

While the Commission was aware that some of these reforms were in the pipeline since the end of 2015, its initial response was delayed and mainly consisted of a dialogue between Brussels and Warsaw with a view to enhance mutual understanding and 'clarify the facts in an objective way'.[34] No fast-track sanctions were imposed by the EU institutions against the Polish Government—evidence of the fact that the EU institutions were acutely aware of the broader political issues (sensibilities) surrounding the enforcement of the rule of law in the Member States. We shall also note that under current rules, the decision to impose sanctions against defaulting Member States has to be unanimous. The unanimity rule adds a layer of difficulty to the process of establishing rule-of-law liability as some Member States may naturally disagree to punish their counterparts (not the least because they may incur liability of their own in the future for their own rule-of-law violations).

The procedure concerning the rule of law in Poland is still underway but, at the time of writing, EU demands have not been fulfilled.[35] Furthermore, the Venice Commission has published a critical Opinion about the situation in Poland— therefore amplifying the EU's claim that the amendments to the Constitutional

---

[32] See European Commission Press Release, 'Rule of Law: Commission discusses latest developments and issues complementary Recommendation to Poland', 21 December 2016, available from http://europa.eu/rapid/press-release_IP-16-4476_en.htm.

[33] This appears to still be the case viz. the composition and the judgments of the constitutional of the tribunal, despite some concessions from the part of Poland. See: 'EU's Timmermans says rule of law row with Poland not resolved', *Reuters*, 13.09.2016, available from http://in.reuters.com/article/poland-politics-court-eu-idINKCN11J28B.

[34] 'Brussels launches unprecedented EU inquiry into rule of law in Poland' *The Guardian* (13.01.2016) available from www.theguardian.com/world/2016/jan/13/ec-to-investigate-polish-governments-controversial-new-laws. The article stresses that the Commission's assessment is likely to be concluded in March 2016, following a separate report by the Council of Europe's Venice Commission.

[35] Żurek comments characteristically that 'We haven't been in such a situation since the overthrow of communism in 1989'. See W Żurek, 'The National Council of the Judiciary is under Attack in Different Ways', *VerfBlog*, 11 October 2016, available from: http://verfassungsblog.de/the-national-council-of-the-judiciary-is-under-attack-in-different-ways/.

Tribunal Act of December 2015 have been detrimental for the independence of the judges of the Tribunal and the separation of powers viz the position of the constitutional court as the final arbiter in constitutional issues.[36] Yet, despite some improvements made to the Act by the Polish authorities (viz the reduction of the majority vote for a judgment from two-thirds to a simple majority, and disciplinary proceedings against judges by the Polish President and Justice Minister), not all of the Venice Commission's recommendations have been acted upon.[37]

The same concerns the proposals that emerged from the initial phase of the Commission's rule-of-law monitoring which consisted of an assessment, recommendation and follow-up to the recommendation prior to resorting to the Article 7 TEU procedure. Following a six-month dialogue with the relevant authorities, the Commission's assessment was formalised through a rule-of-law Opinion adopted on 1 June 2016.[38] The Opinion set out the concerns of the Commission and served to focus the ongoing dialogue. The Commission then adopted on 27 July 2016 a rule of law 'recommendation' on the situation.[39] It highlighted that important issues of concern regarding the rule of law in Poland remain and set out recommendations to the relevant authorities on how to address them. Given the lack of reform in Poland (especially in relation to the system of proposing candidates for the president of the Tribunal to the Polish president and the Prime Minister's refusal to publish judgments, despite the statutory obligation to do so) the Commission's conviction that there is a systemic threat to the rule of law in Poland remains unchanged. Whether or not the imposition of sanctions (such as suspension of voting rights) under the Article 7 TEU procedure is now a real possibility is very much an area in development and one which is 'touch-and-go' for the EU institutions given that the Polish situation constitutes the first rule-of-law enforcement shot against a Member State since the so-called 'Haider incident' in Austria.[40]

Of course, the crackdown on judicial independence is a symptom of a broader constitutional crisis within the EU which is currently manifesting itself in the form of smaller systemic rule-of-law crises spread in some Member States. We shall remind the reader that prior to the events in Poland, the EU had rejected a proposal to use Article 7 TEU against Hungary. Other Member States like Romania also raised rule-of-law concerns in the past but no sanctions were imposed, inter

---

[36] Venice Commission, 'Opinion on amendments to the Act of 25 June 2015 on the Constitutional Tribunal of Poland, 106th Plenary Session, Venice, 11-12 March 2016, CDL-AD(2016)001-e.

[37] See more recent assessment of the situation: Venice Commission, 'New Polish law on constitutional tribunal gives excessive power to parliament and the executive over the judiciary', 14 October 2016, Press release—DC162(2016).

[38] European Commission—Press release, 'Commission adopts Rule of Law Opinion on the situation in Poland', 1 June 2016, available from http://europa.eu/rapid/press-release_IP-16-2015_en.htm.

[39] European Commission—Press release, 'Rule of Law: Commission issues recommendation to Poland', 27 July 2016, available from http://europa.eu/rapid/press-release_IP-16-2643_en.htm.

[40] Resort to the Art 7 TEU procedure was first contemplated in the case of Austria, in response to the arrival in government of the far-right Freedom Party (FPÖ) of Jörg Haider, who in 1999 received 27% of the vote in national elections as its leader. In the end, instead of resorting on Art 7 TEU, bilateral sanctions were imposed on Austria by the other 14 Member States, outside the EU framework.

alia, primarily due to the lack of a threshold for a national measure to classify as serious breach. Hence, there is a good reason why it can be contended that this is also a crisis of 'self' (ie the EU and its legal system)—not merely a crisis of 'other' (ie certain 'unruly' Member States). In this climate, rule-of-law enforcement is important to our understanding of the EU rule-of-law concept and the EU's involvement in 'national affairs'.

Yet, the problem that still remains even in the scenario where EU sanctions against backsliding Member States are imposed, is their little chance of being implemented by their respective governments. We cannot also dismiss the possibility that sanctions against Member States where the EU's popularity has declined may ignite nationalism, therefore legitimising governmental actions that contradicted the rule of law in the first place. After all, the governments of the otherwise rule-of-law defaulting Member States may have a strong public mandate to carry out what may be perceived by the EU as 'undemocratic reforms'. Last, the EU institutions need to emerge with a clear narrative as regards their 'rule-of-law intervention' competence over what may seemingly be national affairs. For instance, the Polish government has stressed that neither the restructuring of the Constitutional Tribunal nor the EU's concerns over freedom and pluralism of the media following new legislation in Poland breached any EU law obligations. It is unlikely that a solution outside the Treaties would be reached in the near future. But even in the event the above issues are to be resolved by a new international agreement signed between Member States which will set up a rule-of-law mechanism or merely an inter-institutional agreement without any further legal basis,[41] such a mechanism shall not compromise the possibility for the EU to use the powers provided for in Article 7 TEU and Articles 258–260 TFEU.[42]

C. Conduct of External Relations in Breach of Fundamental Rights

Since the book focuses on the internal dimension of the rule of law, we shall mention briefly a rule-of-law concern which relates to the Member States' external conduct but yet involves deficiencies related to their democratic accountability mechanisms at home. It pertains to the blocking of public scrutiny in the Member States viz the rendition, torture and ill-treatment of detainees abroad.[43] While we would like to think that the so-called 'state of exception' is more akin to post-9/11

---

[41] See P Bard et al, 'An EU Mechanism on Democracy, the Rule of Law and Fundamental Rights', CEPS Paper in Liberty and Security in Europe, No 91/ April 2016, 91.

[42] Council of the EU, Opinion of the Legal Service, 'Commission's Communication on a new EU Framework to strengthen the Rule of Law: compatibility with the Treaties', 27 May 2014, Doc 10296/14.

[43] Redress, 'Investigating Lithuania's complicity in the USA's CIA Rendition, Detention and Interrogation Programme', Submission to the United Nations Committee Against Torture for consideration of Lithuania's 3rd State Party Report, 11 April 2014, available at www.redress.org/downloads/publications/lithuania-submission-to-cat-hrmi-redress-repreive-ai-interights.pdf.

US detention policy and, therefore, far from our European doorstep, there is evidence against certain Member States whose intelligence services were involved in US rendition and torture programmes as part of the 'War on Terror'.[44] Poland, Romania and Lithuania were named by a European Parliament Resolution as Member States that need to conduct a thorough investigation regarding the establishment of CIA secret detention centres on their territory that existed entirely outside the law. Likewise, the UK was compelled to conclude its investigations into the rendition of foreign nationals overseas.[45] In the follow up to its Resolution, the European Parliament announced that outside one cross-party fact-finding mission to Romania conducted in 2015, fact-finding missions were yet to be organised in those Member States which were complicit in the CIA rendition and secret detention programmes led by US administration.[46]

Such events demonstrate that it is not sufficient that the rule of law and respect to fundamental rights is only respected as an admission requirement— ie when a country applies to become an EU Member State. For instance, signing the European Convention on Human Rights (ECHR) is one thing for a Member State and providing for the full and prompt execution of European Court of Human Rights (ECtHR) judgments against it is another.[47] The latter should be as important as the former in order for a state to retain its EU membership rights and privileges. Last, the EU rule of law must also be actively promoted by all Member States in their external relations, especially with regard to their firm adherence and loyalty to EU law provisions on asylum and judicial cooperation. Last, given that there is political consensus at the EU level, we could assume a broad rule-of-law obligation beyond the scope of substantive EU powers. We could even reconsider the relevant EU Treaty provisions as encompassing a broad EU monitoring power regarding the EU rule of law. To this effect, we could claim that such a power would be similar to economic coordination and the EU institutions could hold coordination and monitoring powers beyond substantive ones. This is important not only for the EU's self-preservation but also for the discussion of the rule of law in the international arena. In other words, failure of all EU actors to take up the above mandate will undermine the

---

[44] S Douglas-Scott, *The Law After Modernity* (Oxford, Hart Publishing, 2013) 234. See also 'Detention, Interrogation and Security: Oversight and Accountability', Bingham Centre Conference Report, 5 March 2015, available from www.biicl.org/documents/527_bingham_centre_event_detention_report_-_final.pdf?showdocument=1. It is telling that neither a judicial inquiry on the matter was initiated in the UK nor did the EU sanction the UK for undermining the objectives listed in Art 2 TEU.

[45] See European Parliament resolution of 11 February 2015 on the US Senate report on the use of torture by the CIA, 11 February 2015 - Strasbourg (2014/2997(RSP)). See also S Raphael et al, 'Tracking Rendition Aircraft as a Way to Understand CIA Secret Detention and Torture in Europe' (2015) 20 (1) *The International Journal of Human Rights* 78.

[46] European Parliament resolution of 8 June 2016 on follow-up to the European Parliament resolution of 11 February 2015 on the US Senate report on the use of torture by the CIA (2016/2573(RSP)).

[47] *Abu Zubaydah v Lithuania* no 46454/11, ECtHR, 10 May 2013; *Al Nashiri v Romania* no 33234/12, ECtHR, 29 June 2016; *Al Nashiri v Poland* no 28761/11, ECtHR, 24 July 2014; *Abu Zubaydah v Poland* no 7511/13, 24 July 2014; *Nasr and Ghali v Italy* no 44883/09 ECtHR, 23 February 2016.

commitment of states and individuals to international organisations as platforms for, inter alia, strengthening the rule of law. This is especially the case since, by contrast to the EU, most international organisations lack binding governance and a court with uniform jurisdiction. As such, the role of the EU as a rule-of-law trendsetter is important.

IV. RULE-OF-LAW ENFORCEMENT MECHANISMS IN THE TREATY

This section will examine whether there are sufficient legal bases for the EU to reinforce oversight of the Member States' rule-of-law performance. In light of the above-mentioned disputes, there has been concern about the protection of the rule of law within the EU. As mentioned, the EU institutions can generally sanction infringements of EU law via the Commission or Member States bringing infringement proceedings pursuant to Articles 258–260 TFEU and can punish a Member State for serious and continuing breaches of EU values, including the rule of law via Articles 2 and 7 TEU.

The first sub-section will commence by examining the likelihood of liability under Article 2 TEU. It will then move on to consider the public enforcement procedure as an instrument that addresses certain rule-of-law concerns related to breaches of specific provisions of EU law. It will acknowledge the limitations located in the very nature of Articles 258–260 TFEU which were drafted with the purpose of covering situations which strictly fall within the scope of EU law and are therefore considered as prima facie breaches of obligations under the Treaties. The second sub-section aims to look into the broadly construed political sanction mechanism of Article 7 TEU. It will look into its legal foundations and the means by which the EU institutions can exert influence upon defaulting Member States where non-compliance is rooted in a dispute over the application of the EU's democratic values inherent in Article 2 TEU. It will critique the character of Article 7 TEU as an alternative mechanism to the general EU infringement procedure under Articles 258–260 TFEU in order to systematise Member State compliance with the rule of law.

A. Exploring the Possibility of Member State Liability Under Article 2 TEU

The sequence of rule-of-law crises illustrated by Reding in 2013 and unveiled recently in a number of Member States has not merely demonstrated sensitivity from the part of the EU to deal with large-scale democratic defects occurring in the Member States. It has also legitimised a form of constitutional troubleshooting which is indicative of the maturity of the European constitutional project that places the individual at its centre and protects her from state arbitrariness. Hence, beyond functionality it can be argued that the EU seeks to qualify as a manifestation of the rule of law through its bold statement in Article 2 TEU.

The rule-of-law enforcement efforts from the part of the EU institutions—especially fundamental rights as a frame of reference for the rule of law—correspond with Weiler's claim that 'a legal regime not validated in democratic practices and not respecting human rights would not qualify as a manifestation of the "rule of law".'[48] Such a substantive take on the rule of law has recently been manifest in decisions such as *Pál Aranyosi and Robert Căldăraru* where the CJEU held that, against the preamble of the Framework Decision on the European Arrest Warrant (EAW),[49] the execution of a EAW must be deferred if there is a serious risk of inhuman treatment viz the prison conditions of the suspect in the issuing Member State.[50] Accordingly the respective national authorities responsible for the execution of a EAW must assess that risk, inclusive of receiving reassurances concerning the prison conditions from the requesting state, before deciding on the surrender of an individual.

The EU's subscription to the substantive dimension of the rule of law is not explicit in Article 2 TEU. Likewise, the approach of the judges in Luxembourg has not always been led by substantive considerations. There are examples where the CJEU has regressed to a more formalist approach so as to be receptive of the respective political climate in the Member States viz arguments about the need to maintain the financial equilibrium of the national social security systems. As it has transpired, in *Dano* and *Alimanovic* the CJEU backtracked somewhat from its previous, more liberal case law.[51] In *Dano*, the CJEU held that Member States may exclude from entitlement to social assistance EU citizens who arrive in their territory without intending to find a job. In *Alimanovic*, the CJEU held that EU citizens who travel to a Member State of which they are not nationals in order to seek employment may be excluded from entitlement to certain social benefits.[52] This apparent trend is in sync with most national governments' current view on the matter of free movement as regards access to social benefits. It has also

---

[48] JHH Weiler, 'Europe in Crisis—On "Political Messianism", "Legitimacy" and the "Rule of Law"' (2012) *Singapore Journal of Legal Studies* 248, 261.

[49] 'This Framework Decision respects fundamental rights and observes the principles recognised by Article 6 of the Treaty on European Union and reflected in the Charter of Fundamental Rights of the European Union, in particular Chapter VI thereof. Nothing in this Framework Decision may be interpreted as prohibiting refusal to surrender a person for whom a European arrest warrant has been issued when there are reasons to believe, on the basis of objective elements, that the said arrest warrant has been issued for the purpose of prosecuting or punishing a person on the grounds of his or her sex, race, religion, ethnic origin, nationality, language, political opinions or sexual orientation, or that that person's position may be prejudiced for any of these reasons.'

[50] Joined Cases C-404/15 and C-659/15 PPU *Pál Aranyosi and Robert Căldăraru* (2016) ECLI:EU: C:2016:198. It has been argued that 'the European Court of Justice tried to make the best of it and provided procedural safeguards to protect the system of the Framework Decision from total collapse in relation to member states convicted by the European Court of Human Rights.' See Editorial (2016) 12 (2) *European Constitutional Law* Review 213, 220.

[51] Case C-333/13 *Dano* [2014] ECLI:EU:C:2014:2358; Case C-67/14 *Alimanovic* [2015] ECLI:EU: C:2015:597.

[52] See further: A Iliopoulou-Penot, 'Deconstructing the Former Edifice of Union Citizenship? The *Alimanovic* Judgment' (2016) 53(4) *Common Market Law Review* 1007.

been embraced by more recent CJEU case law. For instance, the CJEU appeared accommodating with the UK's discriminatory tendencies over its 'right to reside test' which prevents any EU national who does not meet the criteria in Article 7, Directive 2004/38 from receiving Child Benefit or Child Tax Credit.[53]

Notwithstanding the abovementioned developments in the CJEU's case law, Weiler's narrative about the transformation of the EU from an organisation based on a polity of values laid on substantive foundations was echoed in Reding's rhetoric. For the largest part, her proposals placed emphasis upon the repercussions of abuses of political power upon individual citizens. Such problems go beyond individual fundamental rights abuses or one-off systemic deficiencies that can be remedied over a short period of time. They rather concern systematic breaches where self-healing is usually out of the question for the Member State concerned. Hence intervention from outside is considered well-suited, almost as a gesture of solidarity, to resolve domestic problems of fundamental nature and restore the rule of law promptly.

Linking the restoration of the rule of law with the principle of solidarity would be an interesting development, especially since the Treaty of Lisbon has placed a lot of emphasis on solidarity to tackle immigration flow issues, financial crises and threats to civil protection.[54] Yet, in practice, as it has been rightly remarked by recent reflections on the migration crisis, 'far from embracing the European principles of solidarity and the rule of law, several member states appear, paradoxically, to reject those European principles in the face of a perceived threat to their own construction of European identity.'[55] How long it will take to question the rule-of-law compliance of those Member States remains open to speculation as Article 2 TEU generates no particular commitments in this direction.

One of the main problems with rule-of-law enforcement under Article 2 TEU appears to be the absence of guidelines as to what constitutes a rule-of-law breach according to EU law. In an attempt to provide some direction, Closa et al argue that problems of fundamental nature are characterised by: i) unconstitutional constitutionalism ('or a constitutional coup d'Etat: a profound reschuffling and abuse of power through perfectly legal means'); ii) dismantlement of the liberal democratic state and; iii) systemic corruption.[56] Without doubt, all these state

---

[53] See for instance: Case C-308/14 *European Commission v UK* [2016] EU:C:2016:436. Here the CJEU approved UK legislation requiring claimants for child benefit and child tax credit to have a right to reside.

[54] See on solidarity in the context of the EU rule of law: 'Presidency non-paper for the Council (General Affairs) on 24 May 2016—Rule of law dialogue', Brussels, 13 May 2016, 8774/16, available at http://data.consilium.europa.eu/doc/document/ST-8774-2016-INIT/en/pdf. See on the principle of solidarity in general: A Biondi, E Dagilyte and E Kucuk, *Solidarity in EU Law: Legal Principle in the Making* (Cheltenham, Edward Elgar, 2016).

[55] J Borg-Barthet and C Lyons, 'The European Union Migration Crisis' (2016) 20(2) *Edinburgh Law Review* 230, 233.

[56] C Closa, D Kochenov and JHH Weiler, 'Reinforcing Rule of Law Oversight in the European Union' EUI Working Paper RSCAS 2014/25, 5, available at www.eui.eu/RSCAS/Publications/; see on the above quote on 'unconstitutional constitutionalism': G Palombella, 'Beyond Legality—Before Democracy' in C Closa and D Kochenov (eds), *Reinforcing Rule of Law Oversight in the European Union* (Cambridge, Cambridge University Press, 2016) 49.

malfunctions undermine the common values enshrined in Article 2 TEU but they can be interpreted very broadly and they also do not necessarily relate to identifiable substantive breaches of EU law. As stressed by the German Federal Foreign Office:

> [T]he decision on whether to launch procedures to protect the fundamental values enshrined in Article 2 TEU cannot be made on the basis of individual criteria (a 'scoreboard'), but requires an overall assessment of all relevant circumstances and prognoses regarding further developments in the Member State in question. An assessment could also be made of the extent to which the so-called 'pilot proceedings' introduced by the Commission and the Member States in the area of treaty infringements could provide some guidance in this respect.[57]

The question therefore turns to whether Article 2 TEU can generate liability against Member States in the absence of a specific type of behaviour concerning a violation of EU law *stricto sensu*. The answer seems to be in the positive because a Member State's breach of the values protected in Article 2 TEU can jeopardise the legitimacy of EU law as a whole. Hillion mentions two rationales to explain why the Treaties make EU membership rights contingent upon adherence to EU common values:

> First, a Member State contravening such values would endanger the legitimacy of EU decision-making as a whole, and possibly impede the lawfulness of subsequent EU decisions. Second, rule of law deficiencies potentially disrupt the very functioning of the Union legal order, based as it is on mutually legal interdependence and mutual trust among its members.[58]

Despite the above convincing argument, it has also been claimed that Article 2 TEU cannot be a cause of judicial action due to its open-endedness.[59] Still, however, habitual reference to 'deficiencies' has become central in the discussion regarding EU rule-of-law monitoring and compliance. Von Bogdandy and Ioannidis were some of the first commentators to introduce the concept of 'systemic deficiency', which is an umbrella term encompassing any national practice that may be threatening one or more of the values of Article 2 TEU.[60] Despite the readiness of some national governments to monitor the rule of law in the EU as a means of addressing 'systemic deficiencies', we need to be explicit that Article 2 TEU cannot be enforced against Member States in the abstract. Unfettered EU intervention in domestic affairs may jeopardise the principles of conferral, subsidiarity and proportionality enshrined in Article 5 TEU.

---

[57] Position Paper of the German Federal Government, 'The Future Development of the JHA Area' 2014, 16, available from www.statewatch.org/news/2014/jan/eu-council-new-jha-prog-germany.pdf.
[58] C Hillion, 'Overseeing the Rule of Law in the European Union Legal Mandate and Means', Swedish Institute for European Policy Studies (SIEPS), European Policy Analysis, Issue 2016:1epa, 2.
[59] D Kochenov and L Pech, 'Monitoring and Enforcement of the Rule of Law in the EU: Rhetoric and Reality' (2015) 11(3) *European Constitutional Law Review* 512, 520.
[60] A Von Bogdandy and M Ioannidis, 'Systemic Deficiency in the Rule of Law: What it is, What has been done, What can be done' (2014) 51 *Common Market Law Review* 59.

The above sentiment aside, there is still an argument in favour of EU law involvement in national affairs despite the absence of specific breaches of EU law provisions. It is predicated on two grounds: first, in the universality of the values underpinned in Article 2 TEU and second, in the negative impact of a Member State's violation of EU common values upon the application of substantive rights in the EU as a whole. For instance, it can be argued that if one or more Member States arbitrarily decide to suddenly lower their standards regarding the rule of law such a decision will inevitably undermine the unity of EU law and its application to migrant EU citizens. As such, the decision to render the values inherent in Article 2 TEU justiciable before the CJEU implies remedying situations, which although at first sight do not appear to concern a breach of EU law, may, nonetheless, create certain discomfort vis-à-vis the uniform application of rights guaranteed by EU law in the Member States.

Hence a national breach that may at first appear to be unrelated to EU law can, nonetheless, affect the democratic profile and constitutional integrity of EU law. In other words, what initially appears to be a domestic problem confined with the boundaries of a Member State is capable of having a knock-on effect on the operation of EU law and, ultimately, become an EU problem. This is especially the case with reference to the harmonious function of the principle of mutual recognition beyond the internal market context—a domain about which the ECtHR has recently expressed serious reservations.[61] Having said that, the Commission has stressed that 'mutual trust among EU Member States and their respective legal systems is the foundation of the Union. The way the rule of law is implemented at national level plays a key role in this respect.'[62]

One should consider the Commission's choice of words (mutual trust) as opposed to the enormous constitutional relevance that the Treaty has placed upon the principle of mutual recognition, especially in matters of criminal justice under the TFEU. As it has been argued elsewhere, mutual recognition does not imply mutual trust or confidence.[63] For instance, although mutual legal assistance in criminal matters is implicit in the Treaty, Member States will show a certain reticence to cooperate with a Member State they do not trust. To give an example, a Member State would be reticent to cooperate with one of its counterparts if the latter violates within its domestic procedures the common objectives upon which the EU is built, including the right to fair trial. Such reticence will be present regardless of whether or not a Member State's defaulting counterpart has generally acknowledged mutual recognition in the Treaty on substantive matters. The Commission

---

[61] In *Avotiņš v Latvia*, App No 17502/07, ECtHR, 23 May 2016 the ECtHR for the first time applied the '*Bosphorus* presumption' to a case concerning obligations of mutual recognition under EU law.
[62] Communication from the Commission to the European Parliament and the Council, 'A new EU framework to strengthen the rule of law' COM (2014) 158 final.
[63] T Konstadinides, 'The Europeanisation of Extradition: How Many Light Years Away to Mutual Confidence?' in C Eckes and T Konstadinides (eds), *Crime within the Area of Freedom Security and Justice: A European Public Order* (Cambridge, Cambridge University Press, 2011) Ch 7.

is, therefore, right in using the word 'trust' instead of 'recognition' which connotes a lighter commitment between Member States viz mutual cooperation.

Moving on, we shall remind the reader that the confidence of EU citizens and national authorities in the functioning of the rule of law in the EU has to be counterbalanced against the formal attribution of EU competences by the Treaty. For instance, as already pointed out, it is uncertain whether Article 2 TEU is applicable where the facts of a case are strictly confined within the territory of a Member State. It is equally unclear whether, even where there is a cross-border element present, an alleged breach of the rule of law in a Member State may automatically expand the jurisdiction of the CJEU to hear cases on Article 2 TEU. The fuzziness that serious and persistent Article 2 TEU breaches may generate to the application of EU law provide some justification for the development of the new EU rule-of-law mechanism granting the Commission interventionist powers. Equally, there is a valid argument why a Member State that has resorted to a rule-of-law breach shall borrow help from an external actor—a democratic 'bail-out' of sorts deriving from actors independent from the state authorities that may themselves act undemocratically. Yet, as mentioned, under the current dispensation, such an approach may be on the margins of the principle of conferral and, therefore, challenged by the 'defaulting' government as ultra vires. Even a theoretical discussion of the possibility of a democratic 'bail-out' may provoke criticism even in non-defaulting Member States that are worried about their sovereignty. Such Member States may criticise the EU institutions for using the rule of law as a Trojan horse to bring just about every national practice within the scope of EU law scrutiny.

The above is all the more crucial since it is generally accepted that the Constitutions and judicial systems of the Member States are well designed to protect citizens against any threat to the rule of law. We may recall, for instance, Lord Hope in the controversial case of *Jackson* concerning the legal validity of the British Fox Hunting Act 2004. He emphasised that 'the rule of law enforced by the courts is the ultimate controlling factor on which our constitution is based.'[64] British courts have adopted a similar approach with regard to obligations flowing from the UK's participation in other international organisations such as the implementation of UN Security Council Resolutions regarding terrorist asset freezing. In *Ahmed et al v HM Treasury*, for instance, the Supreme Court held that any restrictions upon the right of access to justice, a fundamental component of the rule of law, could only be amended by Parliament's express consent.[65]

In light of the analysis provided in this section, although we can see why EU intervention may be desirable when Member States deviate from commonly adhered norms, the EU is yet to make a strong case for justifying its competence to sanction Member States' internal deliberations by virtue of Article 2 TEU. After all, the EU is bound by the Treaty to act, inter alia, in a spirit of loyalty and

---

[64] *Jackson v Attorney General* [2005] UKHL 56, para 107.
[65] *HM Treasury v Ahmed* [2010] UKSC 2. See also A Johnston and E Nanopoulos, 'The New UK Supreme Court, the Separation of Powers and Anti-terrorism Measures' (2010) 69 *Cambridge Law Review* 21.

conformity with the principle of subsidiarity and respect for the national identities of the Member States—a claim of selfhood, which as discussed, is often construed rather broadly by some Member States, albeit without concrete results.[66] Judging from recent developments regarding the Commission's Article 7 TEU warning shots against Poland, it appears that any act of the administration that can be characterised by the EU institutions as a violation of Article 2 TEU makes the cut as a condition to trigger action under Article 7 TEU. Interpreted in this way, the scope of Article 7 TFEU becomes indefinite—reaching beyond situations where it can be demonstrated that the alleged breach falls squarely within the EU's field of action. It would be naïve to claim that the EU institutions are unaware of the dangers looming when crossing the line. Still, however, while the EU institutions may appreciate that there is a strong correlation between the EU competence to legislate and EU competence to sanction, they seem to have surrendered to the political drive over the EU's jurisdiction to sanction what have become known as systemic deficiencies in the Member States. The irony is that such deficiencies in the democratic fabric of the Member States have so far been manifest in fields traditionally reserved by domestic law.

One may, of course, find it difficult to disagree with the political imperative of building an EU that provides more security and justice. At the same time, however, there is an impending legal / constitutional danger that by adopting a laissez-faire attitude towards policing the rule of law, the Commission may be perceived to be pushing for more EU interference in national affairs (and perhaps new future legal competences through the back door). Such a development would surely be against the wishes of the Member States concerned and, most importantly, the spirit of the Treaty (both in terms of the legal situation that would emerge after the EU has transcended its competence limitations but also in terms of undermining constitutional principles such as legal certainty and consistency which are akin to the rule of law).

B. The Public Enforcement 'Infringement' Procedure

Although the Treaty does not provide the EU institutions with specific means to sanction an identified category of rule of law breaches, it is generally accepted that the Commission's role as the guardian of the Treaties, inclusive of EU values under Article 2 TEU, is key in holding the Member States to the rule of law. The study of the Commission's role in supervising national compliance with EU law under Articles 258–260 TFEU is key to securing the enforcement of the rule of law. Public enforcement of EU law through what are often referred to as 'direct actions' against Member States constitutes perhaps the most pragmatic procedure

---

[66] See generally Arts 4 (2) and 5 (3) TEU. See also n 95, p 51. See more recently the case of the Belgian constitutional court of 28 April 2016, decision n° 62/2016 (http://www.const-court.be/cgi/judgments_popup.php?lang=en&ArrestID=4097). This is a case on the ESM where the Belgian court adopts the constitutional identity discourse in an obiter dictum that has no bearing on the decision. The reference to identity here appears to be a mere repetition of Article 4 (2) TEU but read on the basis of the Constitution.

employed to remedy national infringements of EU law and correcting any rule-of-law deviation.

To provide an example of the corrective function of Article 258 TFEU, the infamous case of *Commission v* France can be labelled as one where the root of the problem was, by today's standards, a rule-of-law deficiency. The case concerned French farmers who having suffered economic losses from competition with Spanish producers launched a barrage of attacks against imports and importers over a period of 10 years.[67] During this period, French officials (and particularly the French Police) did little or nothing to stop French farmers from destroying agricultural goods from other Member States. As Davies commented:

> Whether or not one thinks the farmers had a point, it is difficult to imagine a more direct and deliberate attack on the internal market and a more conscious rejection of its basic principles, or a more vivid realisation of the idea of an 'obstacle to free movement' ... Unsurprisingly, carriers, importers, foreign producers, and other member state governments were incensed. They regarded France as little more than a lawless bandit state, in which the government and the delinquent and criminal farmers were in league against foreigners, free trade, honesty and the rule of law.[68]

As it is well-documented, in the end the CJEU held that France had failed to adopt all necessary and proportionate measures in order to prevent the free movement of goods from being obstructed by actions by the farmers. Hence, France had breached Article 34 TFEU, in conjunction with the principle of loyalty under Article 4 (3) TEU.

The public enforcement procedure under Articles 258–260 TFEU constitutes a 'dialectical exercise in which the Commission and the Court of Justice help refine and flesh out EU law.'[69] Truly, the procedure is cooperative in that it recognises the Member States' margin of discretion when implementing EU law and requires the Commission to engage in dialogue. At the same time, public enforcement also secures a high degree of compliance of Member States to EU norms. What is more, the pre-litigation phase of Article 258 TFEU is testament of the joint problem-solving capacity of the Commission and the Member States. It is perhaps the most effective means of obtaining a declaration that the conduct of a Member State is in breach of EU law and that it will be terminated.

On the other hand, the punitive function of Article 260 TFEU concerning failure to comply with judgments of the CJEU according to Article 258 TFEU renders sanctions more functional compared to those applicable in most organisations operating under the norms of public international law. Having said that, it is ultimately the Member States' responsibility to comply with their EU law obligations, inclusive of the transposition of secondary legislation into domestic law. As such

---

[67] Case C-265/95 *Commission v France* [1995] ECR I-4443.
[68] G Davies, *European Union Internal Market* (London, Routledge, 2003) 182.
[69] S Andersen, *The Enforcement of EU Law: The Role of the European Commission* (Oxford, Oxford University Press, 2012) 3.

even in cases where Article 260 TFEU sanctions are imposed, the Commission and the CJEU cannot prescribe how a Member State should comply with its obligations. Such an approach by the CJEU would contradict Article 102 of its rules of procedure.[70] Since the EU infringement procedure has received much attention in scholarship, it will only be considered briefly in this chapter.[71]

At this point we should note that the Commission does not pursue all cases—it rather has enforcement priorities which, according to the Commission's White Paper on Governance going back as far as 2001, also include 'infringements that undermine the foundations of the rule of law'.[72] Alternatively, the Commission has encouraged the improvement of enforcement procedures at national level, through national courts. Such an expectation derives from the CJEU's development of a set of principles which can be utilised by national courts. Indeed, through the principles of direct effect, primacy and state liability the CJEU has advanced a constitutional framework in which individuals have been enabled to monitor Member State compliance with EU law at home. Yet, as it has been reported, state liability has in recent years been trumped by the difficulty of individuals proving sufficiently serious breach (which is problematic for the development of the EU rule of law).[73]

C. The Political Sanction Mechanism Under Article 7 TEU

We have mentioned Article 7 TEU several times so far in this book. As discussed, this rule-of-law framework which is complementary (but much broader) to the classic infringement procedure under Article 258–260 TFEU was designed primarily in order to curb abuses against EU values in the Member States. Indeed, Article 7 TEU provides the EU institutions with a mechanism for ensuring that Member States observe the fundamental values specified in Article 2 TEU, including the protection of fundamental and minority rights. In essence, a breach of Article 2 TEU can give rise to an Article 7 TEU investigation against a Member State and may, in exceptional circumstances, lead to suspension of its voting rights in the Council. As discussed, the new EU rule-of-law framework lays down a procedure which begins once the Commission determines that there is a situation of systemic threat to the rule of law. It is only if there is an unsatisfactory follow-up to the recommendations made to the backsliding Member State that the Commission will look into the possibility of activating one of the mechanisms set out in Article 7 TEU—and not automatically resort into sanctions.

---

[70] See also Case 503/04 *Commission v Germany* [2007] ECR I-6153.
[71] ibid 6.
[72] Commission Communication, 'European Governance' COM 2001/428.
[73] See for instance: Case C-420/11 *Leth* [2013] ECLI:EU:C:2013:166 and T Lock, 'Is Private Enforcement of EU law through State Liability a Myth? An Assessment 20 years after *Francovich*' (2012) *Common Market Law Review* 1675–702.

As regards its ultimate penalty, Article 7 TEU is using equivalent language to Article 8 of the Statute of the Council of Europe which provides that any serious violations of the ECHR by a member of the Council of Europe will result in suspension of its rights of representation. Article 8 of the Statute of the Council of Europe also highlights that, inter alia, every signatory state must accept the principle of the rule of law and shall collaborate sincerely and effectively. This reference raises parallels to the EU law principles of sincere cooperation and effectiveness that we discussed previously. On a similar note, Article 6 of the UN Charter provides for sanctions against states that act in violation of the principles underpinning the Charter. By contrast to Article 7 TEU, however, the UN Charter is stricter in that it foresees the possibility of defaulting states getting expelled from the UN by the General Assembly upon the recommendation of the UN Security Council.

When it comes to its operation, the mechanism under Article 7 TEU has three stages. In the first stage, the Commission will collect information, including from the Council of Europe and the EU Fundamental Rights Agency. There is no reference to what may trigger such an initial investigation. If the Commission believes that there is a systemic threat to the rule of law, it will send a 'rule-of-law opinion' to the Member State concerned, setting out its concerns and asking its authorities to respond. This will happen following meetings with the Member State. Pursuant to Article 4 (3) TEU, the Member State in question would be under an obligation to cooperate with the Commission.

It is interesting that while the Commission's assessment and opinion will be public, the content of the discussions will not. If there is no satisfactory settlement, the Commission will move to the second phase which entails a 'rule-of-law recommendation' providing objective evidence of a systemic threat which the Member State under investigation has failed to address. The recommendation would indicate the reasons for the concerns and the steps to be taken, including specific action points which that Member State should adopt. The recommendation would be public. The third phase consists of a follow-up to the recommendation, examining whether problems continue to recur. In the event this assessment is unsatisfactory, the Commission may trigger Article 7 TEU. As it will be illustrated below, this process is cumbersome. Alternatively the Commission could hand the process over to the CJEU, but such a rule-of-law jurisdiction cannot be conferred to the Luxembourg Court. It would first require Treaty amendment.

As it has been discussed, the Article 7 TEU 'nuclear option' has not been used to its full extent. There are various reasons why it remains idle. First, Article 7 TEU has only been reserved for extreme situations. The current investigation into Poland's ruling Law and Justice Party constitutional reforms are the closest the EU institutions have got in terms of utilising Article 7 TEU. Second, the Treaty's rule-of-law mechanism is relatively new. It is only since the Treaty of Amsterdam 1999 established through Article F (1) TEU that any Member State violating EU common values in a serious and persistent way may lose its rights under the Treaty. What is more, it was soon after the 'Haider incident' that the scope of Article 7 TEU was expanded to cover situations where a Member State puts EU values at risk. A new paragraph was, therefore, inserted into the Treaty of Nice in 2000 which added a preventative aspect to the already reactive character of the political sanction mechanism.

Third, the procedure for activating the political sanction mechanism is rather cumbersome. The proposal for making a determination of rule-of-law infringement is put forward under Article 7 TEU either by the Commission or one-third of the Member States acting together. Then, the Council, after acting unanimously, save the Member State in question, has the right to determine the existence of a serious breach of the fundamental principles included in Article 2 TEU. By way of sanction, the Council may decide the suspension of certain rights derived from the Treaty against the defaulting Member State. These rights include voting rights of the representative of the national executive in the Council. Accordingly, Article 354 TFEU provides for the voting rules with reference to the suspension of rights viz that the sanctioned Member State cannot vote and that a Member State's abstention will not count.

The above procedure aside, we shall note that once the Council has determined the seriousness and persistence of the alleged breach, it may choose not to penalise the non-compliant Member State. As the Polish situation demonstrates, there is ample room for reaching a diplomatic solution to the situation following identification of a serious and persistent breach of EU common values. The diplomacy feature inherent in Article 7 TEU indicates the political nature of the rule-of-law mechanism. This is even manifest at the early stage of the process where the Council warns a Member State that there is a 'clear risk' of its conduct breaching EU common values. Such action requires four-fifths of the Member States. What is more, the threshold to punish a Member State pursuant to Article 7 TEU is very high, requiring the unanimity of all Member States. As noted, this makes the prospects of its deployment rather minimal.

But is there an added value to be gained as a result of Article 7 TEU? The resolution of this question turns out to have a practical point viz what the EU rule of law is supposed to protect in the context of a Member State contravening hard-earned EU values. Respect for these values is explicit in Article 49 TEU as a *sine qua* condition of membership of the EU. Furthermore, Articles 7, 269, and 354 TFEU provide the EU institutions with the means of ensuring that all Member States comply with EU values. Hence, according to the Commission's Communication on respect for and promotion of EU values the risk or breach identified must go beyond specific situations and concern a more systematic problem.[74] To provide an example, Article 7 TEU could be an important legal provision for tackling 'breaches (or the risk of breaches) of the rights of minorities in the Member States' utilised, for instance, in cases relating to 'imminent risks of ethnic cleansing'.[75]

[74] Communication from the Commission to the Council and the European Parliament on Article 7 of the Treaty on European Union: Respect for and promotion of values on which the Union is based 15.10.2003 COM (2003) final.
[75] T Ahmed, 'The Treaty of Lisbon and beyond: The Evolution of European Union Minority Protection' (2013) 38 (1) *European Law Review* 30, 35.

Others have claimed that 'It would only be in the most egregious circumstances of human rights violations that any intervention was likely, which would leave the vast rump of abuses subject only to the domestic judiciary's willingness to challenge government policy and legislation.'[76] We shall once again highlight, however, that Article 7 TEU is not intended to substitute the other EU mechanisms in place in the Treaty which aim to ensure compliance with fundamental rights. It is rather complementary to the enforcement of Member States' obligations to respect fundamental rights under public enforcement proceedings or preliminary rulings.[77]

As already discussed, the issue of EU competence is deemed to become a big part of EU rule-of-law enforcement against the Member States, especially since it has been argued by the Council Legal Service (and not merely a defaulting Member State's government) that the Commission's rule-of-law framework has no legal base and 'is not compatible with the principle of conferral which governs the competences of the institutions of the EU.'[78] At the same time, we shall bear in mind that the general presumption is that the rule of law entails specific virtues which were attained at a certain stage by candidate states in order to move from association to full membership. As such, it has been rightly argued that 'the priority in values-promotion has traditionally been confined to the pre-accession/external relations context, leaving the internal Rule of Law issues to Member States themselves.'[79]

In the post accession context we could, therefore, envisage Article 7 TEU as a broad rule-of-law obligation beyond the scope of substantive EU powers. In order to do so, however, we would have to reframe it as encompassing a broad EU monitoring power regarding compliance with the EU rule of law. Yet, when it comes to employing such a monitoring competence against an alleged rule-of-law violation, the EU institutions would need to identify pointers as to what exactly constitutes a clear risk of a serious breach of the rule of law.[80] Besides, their power to monitor defaulting Member States with respect to Article 2 TEU can be linked to the powers of the Council and the right of initiative of the Parliament, Commission and Member States with respect to Article 7 TEU. Given the political nature of Article 7 TEU, the CJEU is still not in a position to provide an inventory of possible scenarios

---

[76] A Williams, 'The European Convention on Human Rights, the EU and the UK: Confronting a Heresy' (2013) 24 (4) *European Journal of International Law* 1157.

[77] Case 5/88 *Wachauf* [1989] ECR 2609; Case C-260/89 *ERT* [1991] ECR I-2925.

[78] Council Legal Service, 'Commision's Communicationon a new EU Framework to strengthen the Rule of Law—compatibility with the Treaties', 27 May 2014. 10296/14, available fromhttp://data.consilium.europa.eu/doc/document/ST-10296-2014-INIT/en/pdf, para 28.

[79] C Closa and D Kochenov, 'Reinforcement of the Rule of Law Oversight in the EU: Key Options' in W Schroeder (ed), *Strengthening the Rule of Law in Europe: From a Common Concept to Mechanisms for Implementation* (Oxford, Hart Publishing, 2016) 173.

[80] See M Steinbeis, 'Is the EU Commission's Rule of Law Fight about Poland already lost?' *VerfBlog*, 2016/10/17, available from http://verfassungsblog.de/is-the-eu-commissions-rule-of-law-fight-about-poland-already-lost/.

that could trigger it, especially with reference to what amounts to sufficient grounds for it to be activated.

The issue of competence also remains important with reference to the scope of application of Article 7 TEU which can potentially cover fundamental rights situations which go beyond the strict implementation of EU law. In theory, anything that poses a threat to the values underpinned by Article 2 TEU may fall under the realm of the Treaties. At the same time, however, Article 2 TEU does not confer any competence upon the EU but similar to the EU Charter of Fundamental Rights it only provides for a number of values that need to be adhered to by the EU institutions and the Member States when they act within the limits of their powers as conferred to them by the Treaty. This express limitation may not be fully reassuring given recent experience from the CJEU Charter jurisprudence which is often characterised by lack of clarity regarding the rubric of implementing EU law and an incremental human rights culture developed within the CJEU which has expanded the types of questions falling within its jurisdictional boundaries. One may therefore wonder whether Article 7 TEU can potentially create claims which are similar to *Kompetenz-Kompetenz* in the sense that EU institutions have moved towards determining conclusively the limits of their powers to sanction Member States. The Council Legal Service fuels such criticism by providing, for instance, that:

> Respect of the rule of law by the Member States cannot be, under the Treaties, the subject matter of an action by the institutions of the Union irrespective of the existence of a specific material competence to frame this action, with the sole exception of the procedure described at Article 7 TEU. Only this legal basis provides for a Union competence to supervise the application of the rule of law, as a value of the Union, in a context that is not related to a specific material competence or that exceeds its scope.[81]

We have to be reminded, however, that the past reaction to EU *Kompetenz-Kompetenz* concerned a judicial response of the BVerfG towards the CJEU's teleological interpretation of EU legislative powers. By contrast, when it comes to Article 7 TEU, the obligation in question would not be enforced by the CJEU but by the Council. Likewise, it is the Council which would determine the existence of a serious and persistent breach by a Member State of the values referred to in Article 2 TEU and shall hear the Member State in question. The CJEU shall only, at the request of the defaulting Member State, have jurisdiction, according to Article 269 TFEU, to decide on the legality of the suspension of Member States' rights by the Council. In case the Council has decided to suspend membership rights, the CJEU would only be able to verify if the procedure has been followed. It has no competence to verify the grounds because Article 7 TEU constitutes a political weapon.

---

[81] Council of the EU,' Commision's Communicationon a new EU Framework to strengthen the Rule of Law—compatibility with the Treaties', 27 May 2014. 10296/14, available from http://data.consilium. europa.eu/doc/document/ST-10296-2014-INIT/en/pdf. See in particular para 17.

V. CONCLUSION

As discussed, the legal possibility to take action whenever a Member State acts in contravention of the rule of law involves a lot more EU institutional actors than merely the CJEU (as it is the case for instance when the EU is held to the rule of law). EU primary law provides a constitutional basis in Article 7 TEU for EU engagement to ensure compliance with the values of Article 2 TEU—the rule of law inclusive. Still, however, many of the problems that the EU is facing at the moment (the renewed Greek government-debt crisis; Europe's migration crisis; EU's dependence on Russian gas imports and the prolonged crisis in Ukraine;[82] and calls for the secession of territories from existing Member States)[83] are not directly related to Member States' non-compliance with EU law or even a wide rule-of-law deficit. They often concern a multitude of politico-socio-legal factors which often owe to the passive stance of national executives to act in a spirit of solidarity and push daring regulatory proposals into the EU legislative process. Still, when the Member States (through the EU institutions) are finally putting forward proposals that demand action outside the strict purview of EU law, these compromises fuel scepticism about the EU institutions' democratic mandate and legitimacy to push the envelope. The new issue that has emerged with the potential resort to Article 7 TEU is firmly related to national authorities becoming comfortable with EU intervention outside the strict bounds of EU law for the sake of preserving the effectiveness of EU law (broadly construed).

We shall note that besides the existing political sanction mechanisms in the Treaty put in place to ensure national compliance with EU law, Vivianne Reding's rule-of-law initiative included a less discussed proposal: that is an extension of the jurisdiction of the CJEU to Article 2 TEU, allowing, therefore, the CJEU to hear cases on inter alia rule-of-law breaches. If we take the rule of law as the starting point of all substantive laws and procedural requirements then there is no reason why the CJEU should be excluded from having jurisdiction over the application of Article 2 TEU.[84] Yet, one may legitimately question how we can measure a violation of Article 2 TEU in court. Since the notion of the rule of law may not be justiciable in its own right, it is debatable whether, for instance, a serious breach of the ECHR (eg a systematic practice of expulsion of aliens contrary to Article 4 of Protocol 4 to the ECHR) by a Member State's law enforcement authorities in the context of Police and Judicial Co-operation in Criminal Matters (PJCCM) could give rise to a claim in EU law under Article 2 TEU. The same can be argued about

---

[82] See T Dyson and T Konstadinides, 'Enhancing Energy Security in the European Union: Pathways to Reduce Europe's Dependence on Russian Gas Imports' (2016) 41 (4) *European Law Review* 535.

[83] See C Closa, 'Secession from a Member State and EU Memberships: the View from the Union' (2016) 12 (2) *European Constitutional Law Review* 240.

[84] See C Hillion, 'Overseeing the Rule of Law in the EU: Legal Mandate and Means' in Closa and Kochenov (n 56).

utilising Article 7 TEU, given the difficulty of establishing a serious and persistent breach even in cases which fall prima facie within the scope of EU law.

The above example is all the more important in light of provisions like Article 276 TFEU which provides a justification for defaulting Member States by expressly excluding the CJEU from having any jurisdiction to review the validity or proportionality of operations carried out by national police or law enforcement authorities. Article 276 TFEU further curtails EU involvement vis-à-vis 'the exercise of the responsibilities incumbent upon Member States with regard to the maintenance of law and order and the safeguarding of internal security.' Such jurisdictional limitation is a lot more restrictive than that in provisions such as Article 275 TFEU, which excludes the CJEU from adjudicating over Common Foreign and Security Policy (CFSP) provisions save where the rights of individuals have been restricted by EU legislation. Schütze criticises Articles 275 and 276 TFEU provisions claiming that 'these two "holes" in the judicial competences of the Court are deeply regrettable, for they both replace the "rule of law" with the rule of the [national] executive.'[85] Having said that, however, one needs to take into account the current broader landscape in which the CJEU operates, as a guardian of the rule of law for instance, which demonstrate that the Luxembourg judges are not as powerless as one may think at first encounter.[86]

Also, despite the CJEU's jurisdictional limitations, the current rule-of-law enforcement dispensation under Article 7 TEU may still be functional in competence borderline cases if, for instance, it is complemented by reports of impartial outside observers such as the Venice Commission or the Council of Europe. In this setting, the EU rule of law could hypothetically avoid facing a hostile domestic institutional environment, at least in the rest of the Member States which would be called to vote against their counterpart. The confirmation of an international body outside the EU institutional structure that a Member State has acted against the rule of law may be perceived both de facto and de jure as if this Member State is breaching commonly acknowledged sources of international law. In the long run, a new quasi-judicial mediation body could be set up, avoiding both criticism of politicisation (as it may be the case with the CJEU) and, therefore, the risk of non-enforcement of its judgments. Such a body could present a defaulting Member State with objective, reliable and comparable information on the functioning of the justice systems of its law-abiding counterparts with a view to encourage and support effective systemic reforms. Still, however, as mentioned, the adoption of any new rule-of-law mechanism in the Treaty would require a time-consuming and cumbersome Treaty revision.

---

[85] R Schütze, *European Constitutional Law* (Cambridge, Cambridge University Press, 2012) 261.
[86] See C Hillion, 'A Powerless Court? The European Court of Justice and the Common Foreign and Security Policy' in M Cremona and A Thies (eds), *The European Court of Justice and External Relations Law* (Oxford, Hart Publishing, 2014). See also C Eckes, 'Common Foreign and Security Policy: The Consequences of the Court's Extended Jurisdiction' (2016) 22 (4) *European Law Journal* 492.

To sum up, Article 7 TEU is here to stay. As stressed, there is no legal basis in the Treaty which gives the EU institutions the power to either amend, change or supplement Article 7 TEU or build a new rule-of-law supervision mechanism on top of it.[87] Still, the old adage 'where there is a will there is a way' holds true in the case of the EU legislature. For instance, the *petite révision* clause of Article 352 TFEU traditionally employed by the EU institutions in order to legislate in areas not yet covered by express legal provisions to meet the implied objectives of the Treaty, could be employed towards this end. Hence a body equivalent to the EU Agency for Fundamental Rights (FRAl). Scientific Committee could be set up by virtue of Article 352 TFEU to carry out periodic rule-of-law assessments in the Member States.[88] But still, the Treaty's flexibility clause is not there to undermine, but rather to reaffirm the fact that the EU legal system is built upon the principle of conferral.[89] By virtue of the principle of conferral, resort to the residual power of Article 352 TFEU is constrained by the application of the rule of thumb that a specific legal basis available in the Treaty takes precedence over a general one (*lex specialis derogat legi generali*). Having said that, in rare cases, Article 352 TFEU has been used to create new rights, superimposed on national rights, through the creation of new legal forms governed by EU law.[90] As such, the revolving door of Article 352 TFEU could arguably be employed in the future to initiate discussion on a new EU framework (inclusive of a supervisory authority) for the observance of the rule of law. Until then, the EU can insist on a broad interpretation of Article 2 TEU as part of its principles promotion mandate, including obligations of conduct for the Member States, in order to ensure rule-of-law compliance.[91]

---

[87]   For example, Art 70 TFEU, Art 241 TFEU or Art 337 TFEU do not offer sufficient legal bases for new rule-of-law frameworks outside Art 7 TEU.

[88]   Bard et al (n 41) 92.

[89]   See on the particulars of Art 352 TFEU: T Konstadinides, 'Drawing the Line between Circumvention and Gap-Filling: An Exploration of the Conceptual Limits of the Treaty's Flexibility Clause' (2012) 31 (1) *Yearbook of European Law* 227.

[90]   See Case C-436/03 *European Parliament v Council* [2006] ECR I-03733, para 46; Case C-377/98 *Netherlands v Parliament and Council* [2001] ECR I-7079, para 24.

[91]   See again Hillion (n 84).

Conclusion

THIS WAS A book about the rule of law as an entrenched value of the EU legal system: one that is overarching in the conduct of the main actors in European integration (primarily the EU institutions and the Member States' authorities) and enforceable when they overstep the limits of their powers. The centrality of the rule of law to the evolution and scope of the EU constitutional project is undisputed. Indeed, the EU is based on the rule of law, perhaps to a far greater extent than any other international organisation. Respect for the rule of law, as enshrined in Article 2 Treaty on European Union (TEU) of the Lisbon Treaty, is an endogenous feature of the EU and constitutes part of a bundle of fundamental values highlighted in the same provision.

As discussed, the declaratory nature of Article 2 TEU prompts us to treat the concept of the EU rule of law with considerable caution, being mindful of the argument that it means different things to different people (and Member States) and applies variably in different contexts. Against this stereotypical backdrop, the book took the view that the EU rule-of-law model is closely linked with national expressions of the rule of law.[1] It is based on shared characteristics that define the narrative of liberal democratic Constitutions and give them credibility. At the same time, however, there are distinctive properties, often of intimate constitutional nature, that have been firmly attached to the conception of the rule of law as it has developed over the years in the Member States. The same has occurred within the EU legal order which, although much younger, has also grown fond of certain principles that are now unique to its 'Constitution'. The tension often identified in this book emanates from the occasional conflict between the domestic and EU 'constitutional properties' that may erroneously give the impression that the EU institutions are only concerned with the latter, therefore establishing and perpetuating their own power. Accordingly, conceptual problems may emerge if we start reading too much into this 'conflict'—ie perceive it to be a fundamental clash between two rule of law versions: the EU rule of law and the national one—both seeking primacy over one another or at least endeavouring not to be displaced by one another.

---

[1] See P Birkinshaw and K Kombos, 'The UK Approach to the Emergence of European Constitutionalism Repositioning the Debate: Departure from Constitutional Ontology and the Introduction of the Typological Discussion', *Report to the XVIIth International Congress of Comparative Law, July 2006,* (2006) 10 (3) *Electronic Journal of Comparative Law* 1, 17, available from www.ejcl.org. The authors also argue at 3 that 'the attention should turn beyond ontology and towards typology that is defined as the systematic study of types of constitutions that share functional characteristics.'

The book located the EU rule of law against the background of established and evolving law, politics and judicial practice. With regard to evolving law, we acknowledged that the Lisbon Treaty introduced a number of rule-of-law enhancing provisions on, inter alia, the binding nature of the Charter of Fundamental Rights and the new test introduced by Article 263 (4) Treaty on the Functioning of the European Union (TFEU) on *locus standi* viz reviewing the legality of acts of the EU institutions. Indeed, these provisions have somewhat contributed to the EU's rule-of-law claim and by implication the Treaties' 'self referential body of constitutional law'.[2] At the same time, however, we need to anticipate that the EU rule of law relates to multiple projects running in parallel due to the EU's simultaneous pursuit of numerous agendas and objectives. These agendas and objectives do not always cohere with each other. As observed, the substantive orientation of the EU rule of law has occasionally been undermined by the integrative spirit of the Treaty and the EU's 'emergency' responses aimed to address the multiple crises in Europe that we mentioned in this book. For instance, EU post-crisis measures may be criticised for substituting obedience to the rule of law with that of necessity as the key driver for the adoption of supranational measures. Hence, one could argue that sometimes key tenets of the rule of law, such as fundamental rights protection, remain inconclusive in the EU legal order.

As far as the political dimension of the rule of law is concerned, the EU institutions have been emphatic about the protection of the rule of law at all costs. Much of the criticism levelled against the EU and the Member States is in the context of the handling of the European debt or migration crisis but also goes beyond it to highlight endemic issues related to the large diversity and levels of trust within the EU. For instance, the adoption of the EU's *acquis* by the Member States does not automatically imply respect of EU rules and procedures. Additionally, there are Member States which have challenged the way the EU pursues its objectives and exercises its powers. The fact that no sanctions have been imposed so far under Article 7 TEU may imply, at least to the critical eye, that the rule of law only serves as a 'poster principle'. Accordingly, it is part of the EU's integrative rhetoric and only manifests itself in 'state of the Union speeches' or equivalent EU political statements. If we adopt this argument, then the rule of law consists of a rhetoric— a by-word for political ideals used by the EU institutions in order to legitimise the legal order that the they represent and serve—and, by extension, their actions. We would like to express a more optimistic view in this book—for instance, the responses to the Hungarian developments can be useful: not least because they demonstrate that Article 7 TEU is not the only weapon to rule-of-law liability of the Member States.[3] After all, 'generally, Member States comply with the Court's

---

[2] ibid 11.

[3] The EU has also resorted to other 'softer' means in order to issue a warning to Hungary to comply with EU fundamental values. The Commission recently registered a European Citizens Initiative entitled 'Wake Up Europe' whose sole purpose is to call on the European Commission to trigger Art 7 of TEU and bring the Hungarian issue to the Council. Hungary challenged this decision on 3 November 2016

rulings even if occasionally with some long delays.'[4] What is more, it is perhaps early to rule out the potential Article 7 TEU mechanism since the procedure has only just started and is still underway.

Despite the lack of a sound political narrative as to what lies beneath the EU's soaring attention to the rule of law, two uses of the principle stood out and were observed in this book. Both are disciplinary in character and, judging by their result, they are not without their flaws. First the rule of law is promoted as a way to effectively review the acts of the EU administration (and limit arbitrariness) and second, it is put forward as a means to discipline Member States who undermine EU common values and act contrary to their obligations under the Treaty. It was argued in this book that in both cases the content and orientation of the EU rule of law is highly political (integration driven) and may not always be mindful of the Member States' subsidiarity concerns or indeed the individual's rights-oriented point of view. Hence, the question remains: what does the EU expect to get out of its rule-of-law preoccupation? This is an important question following the legacy of the multi-crises in the continent that have rendered the rule of law weaker than what the EU institutions give it credit for. As it was discussed, the crises in Europe are indicative of crises of 'self' (ie the EU and its legal system) rather than merely crises of the 'other' (ie certain 'unruly' Member States). As such, developing resilience against rule-of-law crises has been perceived as a vehicle towards restoring as much the well-being of the Member States and their citizens as the internal coherence of the EU legal order.

With reference to its legal dimension, we observed how the rule of law has morphed into a legal compliance tool within the developing jurisprudence of the Court of Justice of the European Union (CJEU). Indeed, Luxembourg judges have taken an important lead in ensuring that EU law is observed in all cases. Yet, the meaning of the EU rule of law in relation to judicial review matters exposes fundamental tensions within EU administrative arrangements. These tensions are rooted in the limited scope of judicial review at the EU level—both in terms of its availability and function. They also bring to the fore the perennial question about which EU institution can best claim to represent the 'European interest' and what that interest entails. The lack of a rule-of-law yardstick is crucial in the present discussion not only a symptom of the EU legal order. For instance, as Richard Gordon QC stressed in relation to a similar tension emerging from the meaning of the rule of law in the UK as it relates to judicial review:

> If you don't have a rule for what the rule of law means, some kind of broad yardstick for what it means, you are going to get the judges possibly being able to hold, in some shape,

---

in the pending Case T-50/16 *Hungary v Commission* 2016/C 145/36. On the European Citizens Initiative see: A Karatzia, 'The European Citizens' Initiative in Practice: Legal Admissibility Concerns' (2015) 40 (4) *European Law Review* 509.

[4] L Prete and B Smulders, 'The Coming of age of Infringement Proceedings' (2010) 47 *Common Market Law Review* 9, 12.

size or form, that the rule of law is not being upheld in certain contexts and that paves the way for tension.[5]

But does the EU respect, uphold and safeguard the rule of law adequately or has it grown unassertive as its legacy and its constitutional order has grown? Does the EU disseminate the rule-of-law constituent elements well to third parties? Who is responsible and therefore liable when there is a lapse of the rule of law and justice is denied at the EU level? Do different standards of liability apply between the various actors in European integration, therefore jeopardising or corrupting ideals considered to be at the heart of the EU Constitution? Do standards of liability also differ from one policy area to another? Is the EU rule of law merely aspirational in nature or is it rather aimed to be a device for reinforcing discipline? These are questions often asked but seldom answered to satisfaction. They are questions that pose political, legal and social challenges (which are subject to change from time to time) and cannot, therefore, be fully resolved within the margins of a single EU rule-of-law framework.

Still, one may ask why the above considerations are important and why it is pertinent for a book on the rule of law to address them. A short answer would be because the rule of law, however slippery and problematic a notion it may be, is overarching. It constitutes a precondition for the observance of the totality of rights and obligations contained in EU law (both primary and secondary). Despite its defects, when confronted with the question 'shall we do without it?' we seem to answer in the negative. This is perhaps because in our conscience the rule of law protects us from anomy and chaos. It ensures that all public powers are constrained by law, in accordance with the values of democracy and fundamental rights, and under the control of independent and impartial courts with expanded membership and responsibilities.[6] Hence its observance and enforcement are vital for more than constitutional euphony at the EU level. Compliance with the rule of law at all levels of governance can eradicate arbitrariness and improve the quality of life of individuals in their capacity as students, migrant workers, service recipients, asylum-seekers or convicts. To this purpose, it matters that the EU takes positive steps to counter what it views as systemic threats to the rule of law both within its institutions and its Member States. This is a rather unique function which has no real comparator at the international level.[7]

This book also attempted to offer, in so far as it is possible, coherent instructions about the contents and function of the EU rule of law. We discussed the meaning

---

[5] House of Commons Select Committee, Political and Constitutional Reform—Fourteenth Report,'Constitutional role of the judiciary if there were a codified constitution—Political and Constitutional Reform', 8 May 2014. at para 51, available from www.publications.parliament.uk/pa/cm201314/cmselect/cmpolcon/802/80202.htm.

[6] 'European Court of Justice doubles number of judges' *Financial Times* (12.04.2015) available from www.ft.com/cms/s/0/562d0236-df97-11e4-a6c4-00144feab7de.html#axzz3wx4EdDxT.

[7] There are similarities that can be raised with the Member States. For instance in federal systems, local government may engage in an activity only if it is specifically sanctioned by the state government. The federal government can take corrective steps and legal sanctions for non-compliance.

and located the rule of law within the primary sources of EU law as well as examined its capacity to be enforced by and against the EU institutions, the Member States and, to a lesser extent, the individual. We also demonstrated that the principle of the rule of law has progressively become increasingly relevant to instil confidence into the organisational model of EU public law. As recently noted by Advocate General Bot:

> [C]onfidence is based on the fundamental premise that each Member State shares with all the other Member States, and recognises that they share with it, a set of common values on which the Union is founded, such as respect for human dignity, freedom, democracy, equality, the rule of law and respect for human rights, as stated in Article 2 TEU. Accordingly, all the Member States showed, when they created the European Communities or acceded to them, that they were States governed by the rule of law which respected fundamental rights.[8]

The above remark emphasises how important it is that along with common policies the EU ensures a common basis in European norms and standards. Yet, as it has been contended, assimilating policies is not the same as assimilating norms. The EU has made considerable efforts tiptoeing between what Timmermans, a former CJEU judge, calls 'natural convergence', and 'imposed uniformity'.[9] As we have observed, when the EU is tilting towards the latter there is a risk of loss of face from the part of the EU institutions and an open rift among Member States—hence some caution is necessary especially in using the rule of law as a 'stick' to ensure domestic adherence with the fundamental values underpinned by the Treaty.

While uniformity in the application of the rule of law at EU level is legally desirable in order to ensure consistency and effectiveness in the application of EU law, there are differences and gaps (sometimes fundamental) in the way the Member States, the EU institutions and the individual perceive or are indeed held to the rule of law. For instance, as witnessed, the CJEU's standards of review for tempering arbitrariness often appear to be higher for the Member States as compared to the EU institutions. What is more, (although we only examined the internal dimension of the rule of law in this book), the rule of law applies differently in EU internal policies as opposed to EU foreign policy.[10] Last, the specific mechanisms which are meant to ensure compliance with the rule of law in the Member States are yet to be fully tested. At the same time, there are no official mechanisms in place equivalent to Article 7 TEU to ensure adherence to the rule of law by the EU institutions. Hence, other than the Treaty's judicial review provisions that can be utilised to challenge EU legislation, the arbitrariness of EU institutions can

---

[8] Advocate General Bot Opinion in Case C-659/15 PPU *Căldăraru*, 03/03/2016, ECLI:EU:C:2016:140.

[9] C Timmermans, 'Developing Administrative Law in Europe: Natural Convergence or imposed Uniformity?', Association of the Councils of State and Supreme Administrative Jurisdictions of the EU, 29 November 2013, available at www.aca-europe.eu/.

[10] See L Pech, 'Rule of Law as a Guiding Principle of the European Union's External Action' (2012) 3 CLEER Working Papers.

be minimised by national 'constitutional identity checks' and 'sovereignty locks' imposed unilaterally by a minority of national courts which, as it is the case with Article 7 TEU, they have not yet been put fully into function. In order to address national concerns of the Member States over sovereignty, the CJEU could move beyond providing guarantees over, for instance, the robust protection of fundamental rights and the rule of law in the EU. It could also acknowledge more explicitly in its future case law the attention that constitutional courts place in the special bond between the individual and the state as against, for instance, the logic of mutual recognition.[11]

Whether or not it is a work in progress, the EU's commitment to the rule of law has an immense impact upon the official activities of governments and the individual. It also affects the relationship between the EU and international rule of law. Not only does this relationship involve compliance from the part of EU institutions to international law but it also includes the possibility of individuals resorting to international law norms in order to defend their interests against the undesirable effect of EU legislation in certain areas. As has been stressed by commentators examining the tension between EU and international law, whilst the invocation of international law by private parties appears relatively unproblematic, the smooth adherence of EU law to international law seems to find resistance before the CJEU.[12] Indeed, the CJEU has made noble efforts in the past to insulate the EU legal order from the distorting effect of international legal norms in cases of judicial review of EU legislation. More recently, however, as the EU is enlarging and 'European' values become more attractive its obligation of reception of international law has become one of gradual contribution to its norms.[13] Such contribution can take place naturally or through force. It is telling, for instance, that the CJEU is relying on European Court of Human Rights (ECtHR) case law not only in order to emphasise the consistency between the two courts but also to put pressure on the ECtHR 'to hold the line' in similar cases appearing in Strasbourg.[14] This is an area for future research where the EU rule of law is also currently unsettled and likely to develop in the years to come.

[11]   See V Mitsilegas, *EU Criminal Law* (Oxford, Hart Publishing, 2011) 141–42.

[12]   RA Wessel and S Blockmans (eds), *Between Autonomy and Dependence: The EU Legal Order Under the Influence of International Organisations* (The Hague, Asser Press, 2013).

[13]   See RA Wessel, 'Flipping the Question: The Reception of EU Law in the International Legal Order' (2016) 35 (1) *Yearbook of European Law*.

[14]   L Woods, 'Data Retention and National Law: the ECJ Ruling in Joined Cases C-203/15 and C-698/15 *Tele2 and Watson* (Grand Chamber)' *EU Law Analysis* (21.12.2016) available from http://eulawanalysis.blogspot.co.uk/2016/12/data-retention-and-national-law-ecj.html.

Index